John Wesley's View and Use of Scripture

John Wesley's View and Use of Scripture

Mark L. Weeter

Wipf & Stock
PUBLISHERS
Eugene, Oregon

JOHN WESLEY'S VIEW AND USE OF SCRIPTURE

Copyright © 2007 Mark L. Weeter. All rights reserved. Except for brief quotations in critical publications or reviews, no part of this book may be reproduced in any manner without prior written permission from the publisher. Write: Permissions, Wipf & Stock, 199 W. 8th Ave., Eugene, OR 97401.

ISBN: 1-59752-876-5
ISBN 13: 978-1-59752-876-4

Manufactured in the U.S.A.

Contents

Abbreviations / viii

Introduction / 1

SECTION I
JOHN WESLEY'S VIEW OF SCRIPTURAL INSTRUCTION

1 The Formation of Wesley's Views on Scripture—Part 1 / 5
   The Influence of John Wesley's Family / 6
   The Oxford Influence / 8
   The Anglican Influence / 20

2 The Formation of Wesley's Views on Scripture—Part 2 / 37
   The Influence of Patristic Writings / 37
   The Influence of the Missionary Trip to Georgia / 56
   The Mystic Influence / 58
   The Influence of Aldersgate / 60

3 John Wesley's View on Scriptural Authority—Part 1 / 65
   A Summary of Wesley's View on Scriptural Authority / 66
   Wesley's View of Scripture and the Reformers / 69

4 John Wesley's View on Scriptural Authority—Part 2 / 93
   Wesley's View of Scripture and Eighteenth Century Protestantism / 93
   Wesley's Faith in the Bible / 101
   The Bible as the Source of All Doctrine
      and the Ground of All Judgement / 105
   The Sources of Scriptural Authority / 115

5 John Wesley and Biblical Instruction / 118
   Wesley's Use of the Bible in Preaching / 118
   Wesley's Use of the Bible in Instruction / 125
   Wesley's Use of the Bible in His Letters / 131
   Wesley's Use of the Bible in His Hymns / 132
   Wesley and the Greek New Testament / 136
   Wesley and His Explanatory Notes / 137
   Wesley and Bibliomancy / 152
   Wesley: A Man of One Thousand and One Books / 154

Section II
John Wesley's View of Inspiration and Infallibility

6 John Wesley and the Inspiration of Scripture / 159
   Proofs of Inspiration for Wesley / 162
   Wesley's View of Divine Inspiration / 164

7 John Wesley and the Infallibility of Scripture / 170
   Wesley's Views upon Infallibility / 171
   Interpreting Wesley's Views on Infallibility / 173

Section III
John Wesley's View of Scriptural Interpretation

8 John Wesley's Rules of Scriptural Interpretation—Part 1 / 189
   Interpretation Requires Inspiration / 192
   Scripture Should Be Interpreted Literally / 194
   Scripture Should Be Interpreted according to Context / 198
   Interpret Scripture according to Scripture / 201
   Interpretation Is Linked to Application / 205

9 John Wesley's Rules of Scriptural Interpretation—Part 2 / 208
   The Use of Reason in Interpreting Scripture / 210
   The Use of Experience in Interpreting Scripture / 214
   The Use of Tradition in Interpreting Scripture / 222
   Was Wesley a Critical Scholar? / 227

10 Closing Thoughts / 233
   Wesley's Advice for Bible Study / 233
   Final Thoughts on Wesley's Views of Scripture / 238

   Bibliography / 245

Abbreviations

Calvin	*A Compend of the Institutes of the Christian Religion.* John Calvin. Philadelphia, Pa.: Presbyterian Board of Christian Education, 1939.
Journals	*The Journals of the Rev. John Wesley A.M. 8 vols.* Nehemiah Curnock. London, England: Charles Kelly, nd.
Letters	*The Letters of the Rev. John Wesley A.M. 8 vols.* John Telford. London, England: Epworth Press, 1931.
Luther	*Luther's Works.* Jaroslav Pelikan. Philadelphia, Penn.: Fortress Press.
Sermons	*The Standard Sermons of John Wesley 2 vols.* E. H. Sugden. London, England: Epworth Press, 1961.
Works	*The Works of the Rev. John Wesley A.M. 13 vols.* Thomas Jackson. London, England: John Mason, 1829.

Introduction

IN LIGHT of John Wesley's own declaration that, "In 1730 I began to be *homo unius libri*, to study (comparatively) no book but the Bible,"[1] it may seem presumptuous to ask the question, what was John Wesley's view of the Scripture? A reader of Wesley's works, familiar with his constant use of Scripture in all aspects of his life and ministry might maintain that his attitude toward Scripture is nothing if not obvious. And yet, a survey of Wesleyana discovers there are areas of controversy concerning Wesley's view of Scripture, particularly concerning elements such as inspiration, authority and infallibility. These areas of debate are, in all likelihood, merely reflections of the larger disagreements over scriptural authority within the twenty-first century church.

The debate over scriptural authority has become a critical and often divisive issue. The arguments transcend squabbles between so called "liberal" and "conservative" denominations. In fact differing views of biblical authority have become argumentative and divisive issues between evangelical groups within what would be considered evangelical denominations with a traditionally high view of the inspiration, authority, and even the infallibility of Scripture.

In light of the present controversy over the Scripture, surely it would be valuable as stated by Daryl McCarthy, "to demonstrate in clear terms and with close reference to his own writings, what actually was Wesley's view of the Scripture."[2] Since those in the Wesleyan tradition are "unavoidably drawn into this debate,"[3] it would certainly behoove us to take a long, hard look at our historic roots when it comes to the issue of biblical authority and inspiration.

---

[1] *Letters* 4:299.

[2] Daryl McCarthy, "Early Wesleyan Views of Scripture," *Wesleyan Theological Society 16* (1981) 95.

[3] Daryl Climenahge, "Interpreting the Scripture," *Brethren In Christ History and Life* (1987) 202.

Introduction

Without question the Methodist Church and all other "Wesleyan" movements over the last two centuries have been greatly influenced by all of Wesley's teachings and doctrines. Recognizing our indebtedness to Wesley in turn leads to many questions which should be asked. How crucial to his ministry, and to the Wesleyan heritage, was Wesley's view of Scripture? Even taking into account the variable of eighteenth-century culture and religion, as well as the personal peculiarities of John Wesley and the circumstances under which he lived, to what extent was Wesley's view of Scripture the force that was the key to his great success? What was the position of Scripture in the Wesleyan Quadrilateral of reason, experience, Scripture and tradition? Was the Bible one source of authority, or the central focus around which the others revolved?[4] What were Wesley's views on inspiration and infallibility, and how would his principles of interpretation line up against modern, critical scholarship? These are only a few of the questions which should be considered.

My primary purposes therefore are to explore the formative influences on Wesley's view of Scripture, determine his views of scriptural authority, inspiration, and infallibility, consider his practical uses of Scripture, and study his hermeneutical principles. This will be accomplished by reviewing secondary sources, but will concentrate on Wesley's own writings to allow Wesley to speak for himself. In attempting to discern Wesley's views no attempt will be made to claim infallibility for Wesley, or to ignore the learning and progress of the last two centuries. However, every effort will be made to understand Wesley's writings in light of his own culture and context without reading in twenty-first century presuppositions. One must not expect uniformity of vocabulary or expressions, but I will attempt to understand his beliefs and intentions as reflected in his *Journal*, sermons, letters, and essays. My primary desire, is to understand what Wesley thought and said about Scripture, not what others have to say about his views.

---

[4] Wilber Dayton, "The Bible in the Wesleyan Tradition," *Asbury Theological Journal* 40 (1983) 22.

Section I

John Wesley's View of Scriptural Instruction

John Wesley's View on
Scriptural Inspiration

1

The Formation of Wesley's Views on Scripture

Part 1

THE TIME would come, when Wesley would state that he was "a man of one book"[1] and a "Yea, I am a Bible bigot. I follow it in all things, both great and small."[2] His views however, did not spring up overnight or develop in a vacuum. As Stephen Gunter states, "Wesley's Aldersgate experience on May 1738 is without question pivotal, but his subsequent concentration of emphasis on *sola fide* had a rather lengthy period of incubation. Wesley's theology was not something newly discovered."[3]

In later chapters I show how totally immersed John Wesley was in the Bible, in all aspects of his life and ministry. Before we launch out into an in-depth study of Wesley's scriptural views, we must trace the influences that developed within Wesley such a love and familiarity with the Bible. The sources of Wesley's subsequent views of Scripture are evident when one explores the influences upon Wesley of his family, his Oxford experiences, his Anglican background, his interest in Patristics, his Georgia mission; mystical influences, and the influence of Aldersgate. These influences furnished the matrix underlying Wesley's views. According to Richard Heitzenrater, "A grasp of Wesley's relationship to his sources is necessary to the development of an adequate hermeneutic for understanding Wesley's own writings."[4]

---

[1] *Letters* 4:299.

[2] Richard Heitzenrater and Reginald Ward. *The Works of John Wesley. Vol. 22.* (Nashville, Tenn.: Abingdon Press, 1993) 42.

[3] Stephen Gunter. *The Limits of Divine Love.* (Nashville, Tenn.: Abingdon Press, 1989) 68.

[4] Richard Heitzenrater. *The Elusive Mr. Wesley-John Wesley as His Own Biographer.* (Nashville, Tenn.: Abingdon Press, 1984) 2:211.

The Influence of John Wesley's Family

John Wesley was born in Epworth, Lincolnshire in June 1703. His father Samuel was the rector at Epworth, while his mother Susannah was both matriarch and saint presiding over the large and impoverished family.[5] John Wesley was born into a home where the Bible was not only a moral guide of life, but also the primer out of which the children learned the alphabet and to read.[6]

John Wesley states clearly the powerful influence of his family when he writes in his "Farther Thoughts on Separation from the Church" (1789):

> From a child I was taught to love and reverence the Scripture, the oracles of God, and next to these to esteem the primitive Fathers, the writers of the first three centuries. Next after the primitive Church I esteemed our own, the Church of England, as the most scriptural national church in the world.[7]

Quite often the influence of Susannah upon her son is stressed, and I will not neglect her, but we must not forget the influence of Samuel upon his son. Samuel Wesley had a great personal commitment to the Word of God, and he wrote a number of scholarly works on the Bible, such as his commentary on Job. Samuel urged John not to enter into holy orders unprepared, and a large portion of this preparation was to include a personal study of the Bible based upon a knowledge of the original languages. Consider the following letter to John in 1724 while he was attending Oxford :

> The knowledge of the languages is a very considerable help in this matter, which, I thank God, all my three sons have to a very laudable degree, though God knows I had ne'er more than a smattering of any of 'em. But then this must be prosecuted to the thorough understanding of the original text of the Scriptures, by constant and long conversing with them. You ask me, which is the best commentary on the Bible, I answer the Bible.[8]

Wesley's views were even more greatly influenced by the training of his mother Susannah. Bible study was a habit formed in childhood and a daily,

---

[5] Duncan Ferguson, "John Wesley on the Scripture: The Hermeneutics of Pietism," *Methodist History* (1984) 235.

[6] William Pellowe, "John Wesley's Use of the Bible," *Methodist Review* (1923) 355.

[7] Rupert Davies. *The Work of John Wesley. Vol. 9.* (Nashville, Tenn.: Abingdon Press, 1989) 538.

[8] Frank Baker. *The Works of John Wesley. Vol. 25* (Oxford, England: Oxford University Press, 1980) 158.

and almost hourly occupation to the end of his life. It was the basis of all his work in teaching and preaching.[9] The foundation of this discipline and view of the highest authority was certainly mediated through the parental discipline of Susannah.

From the moment of birth the Wesley children were focused into a disciplined method of both worship and Bible study. Susannah, in a letter at John's request in 1732, described her principles for educating children:

> The children of this family were taught, as soon as they could speak, the Lord's Prayer, which they were made to say at rising, and bed time constantly; to which, as they grew bigger, were added a short prayer for their parents, and some collects; a short catechism, and some portions of Scripture, as their memories could bear.[10]

Clearly, the Bible became an important part of the lives of the Wesley children even before they could read.

The Bible also played a prominent part, not only in church worship and family prayers, but in the education at Susannah's knee. To amplify on an earlier thought, the Bible was the primer out of which the Wesley children learned.[11] The children were taught their alphabet on their fifth birthday by Mrs. Wesley, and the Bible was their first reader. They began in the first chapter of Genesis spelling out each verse, then reading it over and over until they could read it without hesitation. Thus, the earliest impressions of John Wesley were bound up in the Bible. Susannah kept the children at their home schooling for six hours a day, and soon they knew many passages of the Bible intimately.[12]

The Bible remained the central study. Each morning the children would read a psalm and a chapter in the Old Testament. Every evening they would read a psalm and a chapter from the New Testament. The prayers were prescribed in the Calendar of the *Book of Common Prayer*, which became almost as familiar to them as the Bible itself. Such daily reading Wesley maintained throughout his life.[13]

This daily practice not only helped develop John Wesley's own rigorous and disciplined approach to Bible study and the whole practice of his

---

[9] W. E. Sangster. *The Path to Perfection*. (Nashville, Tenn.: Abingdon Press, 1943) 33.

[10] Reginald Ward and Richard Heitzenrater. *The Works of John Wesley. Vol. 19*. (Nashville, Tenn.: Abingdon Press, 1990) 288.

[11] William Arnett, "John Wesley—The Man of One Book" (Ph.D. diss, Drew University, 1954).

[12] Frank Baker. *John Wesley and the Church of England*. (London, England: Epworth Press, 1970) 8.

[13] Ibid., 9.

religious life, but it also influenced his whole concept of divine revelation and biblical authority. In the process of his religious training Wesley was encouraged by his parents to discuss religious doubts and was taught that although God's being and nature were made known mainly through divine revelation in the Bible, His will for humanity could be discovered through human reason supplemented by revelation, and when discovered it must be obeyed implicitly. This approach to religion through faith and reason was sincerely practiced by both parents.[14] As Henry Carter states, "No need to wonder that when their evangelical conversion had thrust forth John and Charles Wesley to be apostles of Christ to England, their teaching was Bible centered."[15]

The child is the father of the man and by the time ten year old John Wesley left Epworth for the Charterhouse School in 1714, the guiding principles of his life had already been formulated. The carefully instilled habits of religious discipline played their part so effectively that when removed from parental oversight he continued faithfully to say his prayers, read his Bible morning and night and remained outwardly diligent and respectfully and inwardly devout.[16]

While at Charterhouse, Wesley studied Hebrew, Latin, and Greek. By the age of 14 he had gained recognition for his proficiency in the Hebrew language. The foundation laid by his father, and more especially his mother, was built upon by the clergymen who taught him at Charterhouse, and even more one suspects, by his brother Samuel who was the junior master at nearby Westminster School and with whom he spent Sundays and holidays.[17]

The Oxford Influence

Oxford University in the early eighteenth century reflected many of the problems that characterized English society as a whole. C. E. Vulliamy in his book *John Wesley,* describes this period well as a time marked by the awkwardness and horrors of transition seeking refuge in formulas. There was a shell of tawdry elegance, but the age was course, dark, and brutal. Philosophic doubt born from freedom of thought forced orthodoxy into rigid and extravagant forms. Churchmen were discouraged and the minis-

---

[14] Ibid., 8.

[15] William Arnett. "John Wesley—A Man of One Book," (Ph.D. diss., Drew University, 1954).

[16] Frank Baker. *John Wesley and the Church of England.* (London, England: Epworth Press, 1970) 10.

[17] Ibid., 11.

try was near a state of demoralization. Here and there was a dim religion, under a mantel of gloom, putting out a little despondent poetry about graveyards.[18]

According to V. H. H. Green, in his book *The Young Mr. Wesley*, Oxford University in the first half of the eighteenth century was suffering from the lassitude, which in the history of institutions, so often follows a period of energy and action. In pages 13–40, he describes the impact of religion and politics upon Oxford during this period. To summarize his views, Green states that by identifying itself with the religious and political orthodoxy, the University gave opportunity to a growing number of dissidents in religion and politics to question its effectiveness as a home of learning and morality.[19] In his book *Religion at Oxford and Cambridge*, Green describes religious life at Oxford as being, "associated with ideas and teachings that were rapidly going out of fashion, and were heartily disliked by the established order in the Church and State after 1714; Whig in politics, latitudinarianism and neo-Erastian in religion." Green goes on to describe Oxford churchmanship as neo-Jacobite and neo-Laudian with Oxford theologians discarding Puritan tradition, finding in Caroline piety the simple ingredients of loyalty to Church and King. Their theology was primarily patristic and orthodox with Grabe, Potter, and Beveridge being their guides. For their devotional lives they nourished themselves in the works the poems of George Herbert, the writings of his later successor John Norris and the works of the neo-Catholic mystics like Castaniza. There also remained a fundamental respect for the Crown which became, after Hanoverian succession, an indiscreet, preference for the Jacobites.[20]

By the time of Wesley, much of the public associated Oxford with good, if coarse mannered living, neglect of scholarship, and reactionary principles. It is true that many of the University critics were men with their own axe to grind. Critics such as Humphrey Prideaux, John Toland and Nicholas Amherst wished to discredit the University to insure it followed a subservient political line and to undermine its championship of Anglicanism.[21]

The consensus of many later historians on the conditions at Oxford concludes that in the 18th century, Oxford was a world of drab ideals, a small society where disillusioned Jacobites and half-hearted Hanoverians

---

[18] C. E. Vulliamy. *John Wesley*. (Westover, N.J.: Barbour and Company Inc., 1985) 16.

[19] V. H. H. Green. *The Young Mr. Wesley*. (New York, N.Y.: St. Martin's Press, 1961) 13–40.

[20] V. H. H. Green. *Religion at Oxford and Cambridge*. (London, England: SCM Press Ltd., 1964) 179.

[21] V. H. H. Green. *The Young Mr. Wesley*. (New York, N.Y.: St. Martin's Press, 1961) 13–16.

contended with each other, where scholars disinclined to study encountered teachers as indifferent as themselves, where dreamers found enthusiasm discouraged, education deadened, endowments ill-applied.

Recent scholarship has softened some of the harsher judgments. For example V. H. H. Green states, "The religious life of Oxford at the beginning of the eighteenth century was by no means the spent force that some have suggested."[22] Richard Heitzenrater continues this theme when he remarks in his book *Diary of an Oxford Methodist*,[23] that Oxford University in the first half of the eighteenth century was the object of a great deal of criticism. Most of the criticism came from outside the university and was often agitated by political concerns. Most of the attacks centered on the poor state of the spiritual and intellectual climate in the university. There certainly seems to have been cause for concern, though at times it may have been exaggerated. Some of the negative views have been off set by examples of diligence and devotion by certain tutors, and by explaining the circumstances under which the university operated. Henry Rack maintains that Gibbon, and others, misjudged Oxford, if it was to be compared to Scottish or European universities as a center of scholarship, energetic teaching and modern thought. Instead, many English contemporaries felt the university was to be a conservative, not innovative, institution. Rack refers to L. G. Mitchell who states the role of the university was believed to be to prove a body of traditional learning on which religious orthodoxy, political and social order was thought to depend. There were few who would have imagined the university should be concerned with pure research or disinterested scholarship.[24]

While recognizing that some of the criticism might be mitigated by a better understanding of the university function, it is probably correct to state that religiously, morally, and educationally Oxford University was at low ebb during Wesley's period of study. The problems that confronted England in general, confronted John Wesley at Oxford, in his relationship with the University and the condition of the city and surrounding area.[25]

In the summer of 1720 Wesley left Charterhouse School and was elected to Christ Church College at Oxford, the largest, and some say, most distinguished college in the university. Wesley's period at Christ Church, as well as his years as a Fellow at Lincoln College, were a tremendously

---

[22] Henry Rack. *Reasonable Enthusiast*. (Nashville, Tenn.: Abingdon Press, 1993) 179.

[23] Richard Heitzenrater. *Diary of an Oxford Methodist*. (Durham, N.C.: 1985) 39.

[24] Henry Rack. *Reasonable Enthusiast*. (Nashville, Tenn.: Abingdon Press, 1993) 62.

[25] Richard Heitzenrater. *Wesley and the People Called Methodists*. (Nashville, Tenn.: Abingdon Press, 1995) 31.

important period in both his personal spiritual development, and the development of his view of the authority and interpretation of Scripture. At Oxford, Wesley received training that would greatly influence his understanding of the Bible. This interpretive method, which will be considered in detail in a later chapter, may seem somewhat out of date, but it made him a careful, painstaking, student of the Word. He became a scholar who was not easily caught up by fanaticism and who spurned superficial interpretation.[26]

The religious life at Oxford was conventional, and in many ways, arid and free of enthusiasm, but the University stood theologically for a strong conception of the church, its offices, and sacraments. Its teaching on the great questions of revelation, reason, dogma, miracles, and the Trinity were conventionally orthodox.[27] There was compulsory attendance at chapel, lectures on the Greek New Testament, which Wesley performed at Lincoln, and instruction in divinity for undergraduates.[28] Emphasis was placed upon the Book of Common Prayer with morning and evening prayers said in the chapels. The Holy Communion was regularly, if infrequently, celebrated. There were no hymns, and except in the bigger colleges, no organs. At Christ Church the cathedral choir sang anthems. There was a university sermon every Sunday at St. Mary's Church, which seems to have been well attended.[29]

The University was an Anglican institution, and still a chief training ground for the ministry of the church, and open only to its members. All who sought membership at the University had to accept the Thirty-Nine Articles, though Gibbon insisted the Thirty-Nine Articles were "signed by more than read, and read by more than believe them."[30] The majority of scholars at Oxford were preparing for positions in government, medicine, law or the church. The tutors and fellows of the different colleges, responsible for implementing the curriculum, were almost all men of the cloth.[31]

When all these factors are considered, it would seem that Oxford should have been a center of the Christian faith in England. Unfortunately, it appears that the letter had contrived to stifle the spirit. As Green points

---

[26] William Pellowe, "John Wesley's Use of the Bible," *Methodist Review* (1923) 357.

[27] V. H. H. Green. *The Young Mr. Wesley.* (New York, N.Y.: St. Martin's Press, 1961) 28–29.

[28] Henry Rack. *Reasonable Enthusiast.* (Nashville, Tenn.: Abingdon Press, 1993) 67.

[29] V. H. H. Green. *Religion at Oxford and Cambridge.* (London, England: SCM Press Ltd., 1964) 179.

[30] Henry Rack. *Reasonable Enthusiast.* (Nashville, Tenn.: Abingdon Press, 1993) 62.

[31] Richard Heitzenrater. *Wesley and the People Called Methodists.* (Nashville, Tenn.: Abingdon Press, 1995) 34.

out in his book *Religion at Oxford,* many of the Dons were devout men, but there were others who were mainly interested in a college fellowship, and who lived on the edge, if not over the edge, of propriety. There was little or no concern with fostering spiritual life among junior members by establishing religious societies. The religious life of the university was stale, formal, and conventional.[32] This statement, that there were no religious societies, seems overdone when one remembers Wesley himself became a member of a "Holy Club." This "club," seems to have consisted of several small groups in separate colleges, varying in the closeness of their association with Wesley.[33]

There is ample evidence of gambling, heavy drinking, and moral looseness among the students and tutors. Students seemed more concerned with amusing themselves with billiards, partying in the town of Merton Garden, boating on the River Isis, or racing their horses at Port Meadow. Vulliamy writes, "Coffee Houses were opened, and amiable young men clanked their pint pots."[34] Richard Graves, in 1732, spoke of some young men at Pembroke who were:

> 'Jolly, sprightly, young fellows. who drank ale, smoked tobacco, and sang bacchanalian catches the whole evening,' as well as 'flying squadrons of plain, sensible men,' who had 'come to the university on the way to the Temple, or to get a slight smattering of the sciences before they settled in the country.' But his own 'set' was 'a very sober little group who amused themselves in the evening reading Greek and drinking water.'[35]

However, though scandal certainly existed at Oxford, it should not be assumed that self-indulgence and loose living were typical of all or even the majority of the senior members of the University. Again, according to Green, "It is unlikely that the morals of the undergraduates in the first half of the eighteenth century were noticeably worse than they were at an earlier or later date."[36]

What is clear however, is that the religious atmosphere at Oxford lacked one of the principal ingredients of the Epworth rectory; a deep sense of religious purpose, of moral earnestness, of divine providence, and of vo-

---

[32] V. H. H. Green. *Religion at Oxford and Cambridge.* (London, England: SCM Press Ltd., 1964) 179.

[33] Henry Rack. *Reasonable Enthusiast.* (Nashville, Tenn.: Abingdon Press, 1993) 87.

[34] C. E. Vulliamy. *John Wesley.* (Westover, N.J.: Barbour and Company Inc., 1985) 21.

[35] V. H. H. Green. *Religion at Oxford and Cambridge.* (London, England: SCM Press Ltd., 1964) 115.

[36] V. H. H. Green. *The Young Mr. Wesley.* (New York, N.Y.: St. Martin's Press, 1961) 30–31.

cation. John and Charles found the spiritual climate of the place too cold and conventional, and too open to the cold winds of deism.[37]

Another serious, and perhaps even more substantiated charge, was the sad state of scholarship at Oxford during the early part of the eighteenth century. There is evidence to indicate that as a center of scholarship the University was in decline. As far as junior members were concerned there was no incentive to do research. The examination system did not challenge the student to study and the tutors had little pressure to teach.[38]

According to Hearnes in 1729, "Learning is at so low an ebb at present, that hardly anything of that kind is sought after, except it be English, Scottish, or Irish History."[39]

There were statutes imposed to force regular attendance at lecture courses. These, however, had little effect. In reality the professors often forgot to deliver the lectures. Edward Gibbon says of the time he spent at Oxford:

> I spent fourteen months at Magdalen College: they proved the fourteen most idle and unprofitable of my whole life. The 'public professors' have these many years given up altogether even the pretence of teaching.[40]

Gibbon went on to say of his second tutor that, "he well remembered that he had a salary to receive and only forgot that he had a duty to perform."[41]

Whenever the professors did appear, they usually found the audience to consist of two or three young people, and the reason for their presence was to avoid asking permission for absence from the dean of the faculty, as the rule required. It was easier to put in an appearance at least at some lectures.[42] In practice the only real qualification for a degree was money and residence.[43]

It could not be claimed that a long stay at Oxford would be distinguished by a brilliant course of study. Wesley musing in his *Journal,* wrote in 1747:

---

[37] Ibid., 180–81.

[38] Ibid., 34.

[39] Henry Rack. *Reasonable Enthusiast.* (Nashville, Tenn.: Abingdon Press, 1993) 61.

[40] Ibid., 61.

[41] Ibid., 62.

[42] Maximin Piette. *John Wesley in the Evolution of Protestantism.* (London, England: Sheed and Ward, 1937) 238.

[43] C. E. Vulliamy. *John Wesley.* (Westover, N.J.: Barbour and Company Inc., 1985) 238.

> March 4, being Ash Wednesday, I spent some hours in reading the exhortations of Ephraem Syrus. Surely never did any man, since David, give us such a picture of a broken and contrite heart.
>
> This week I read over with some young man a compendium of rhetoric, and a system of ethics. I see not why a man of tolerable understanding may not learn in six months time more of solid philosophy than is commonly learned at Oxford in four (perhaps seven) years.[44]

However, it should be noted, that in spite of the evidence of intellectual decline, not all professors failed to lecture. Also, research did continue, and even if dimly, the University did contribute to the intellectual life of the church and nation.[45] Fortunately, there were tutors attached to each college which helped make up for the short comings of the professors. Tutors gave lessons in their rooms to students assigned to them. Not all felt this system of instruction an asset however. Again Edward Gibbon comments:

> The silence of the Oxford professors, which deprives the youth of public instruction, is imperfectly supplied by the tutors, as they were styled, of the several colleges.[46]

While it is probably accurate that some college tutors were inefficient and slack, there were certainly some conscientious men, like Wesley himself, who took their duties seriously and tried their best to educate the men under their supervision. Later Wesley wrote, in 1776, of this period in his life, "and I should have thought myself little better than a highwayman if I had not lectured them everyday in the year but Sundays."[47]

The curriculum at Oxford, according to Henry Rack in his book *Reasonable Enthusiast,* was basically a carry over from the Middle Ages based on a limited number of classical authors and Aristotelian science. The students had a mixture of lectures, scholastic disputations and oral exams. The exams apparently were often repeated exactly and the answers easily learned. The strength of the system were certain college tutors who made an effort not only to instruct their students, but also discipline them in conduct and religion. Rules for tutors suggested by Prideaux in 1715 and the statutes at Hertford College in 1739 suggests changes were needed.

---

[44] Reginald Ward and Richard Heitzenrater. *The Works of John Wesley. Vol. 20.* (Nashville, Tenn.: Abingdon Press, 1991) 162.

[45] V. H. H. Green. *The Young Mr. Wesley.* (New York, NY.: St. Martin's Press, 1961) 36–48.

[46] Ibid., 35.

[47] Reginald Ward and Richard Heitzenrater. *The Works of John Wesley. Vol. 23.* (Nashville, Tenn.: Abingdon Press, 1995) 19.

However, there is evidence some tutors lived up to the ideal.[48] There is little information concerning Wesley's training at Oxford, because it was prior to the beginning of his *Journal*. However, there is more general information available concerning ministerial training in the Church of England during this time period.

In the Church of England, after the attainment of a Bachelor of Arts degree, an examination was held under the authority of the bishop, prior to ordination as a deacon. After two years in a probationary status, which included continued academic studies toward an M.A., another examination was held under the bishop resulting in ordination as a presbyter or priest. It should be understood, that while the academic and ecclesiastical processes were parallel, they were still separate. According to Richard Heitzenrater, the Bachelor of Divinity was not an expectation, or a pre-requisite, for parish ministry, but it was a requirement for most fellows of colleges within seven years of receiving their degree.[49]

For Wesley it was five years after his arrival at Oxford before he awakened to the serious purpose of his life. Religion had become inflexible and spiritless, and the undergraduate life, gay and dissolute. He later accused himself of being sinful, but the habits of home, of praying and Bible reading stayed with him and probably restrained him from flagrant vice.[50] He describes this period in his *Journal* in 1738 and emphasizes his dedication to Bible study even though religion was not yet the business of his life. Wesley remarks:

> Being removed to the university for five years, I still said my prayers both public and private, and read with the Scriptures several other books of religion, especially on the New Testament. Yet I had not all the while so much as a notion of inward holiness; nay, went on habitually and (for the most part) very contentedly, in some or the other known sin. I cannot well tell what I hoped to be saved by now, when I was continually sinning against the little light I had, unless by those transient fits of what many divines taught me to call 'repentance.'[51]

---

[48] Henry Rack. *Reasonable Enthusiast*. (Nashville, Tenn.: Abingdon Press, 1993) 64–65.

[49] Richard Heitzenrater. *Wesley and the People Called Methodists*. (Nashville, Tenn.: Abingdon Press, 1995) 34–35.

[50] By a Methodist Preacher. *John Wesley the Methodist*. (New York, N.Y.: Methodist Book Concern, 1903) 57.

[51] Reginald Ward and Richard Heitzenrater. *The Works of John Wesley. Vol.18*. (Nashville, Tenn.: Abingdon Press, 1988) 243.

In 1725, at the age of 22, Wesley faced the question of his future work. He wrote home in regard to entering the ministry. There were a number of significant influences upon Wesley at this time, including his rich heritage from home, the stimulation of the university environment, and the introduction to the mystic writers, such as Thomas A Kempis' *Imitation of Christ*, Jeremy Taylor's *Holy Living*, and William Law's *A Serious Call to a Devout and Holy Life*, and *Christian Perfection*.[52]

Wesley began to prepare for the ministry and was ordained a deacon on September 19, 1725 and a priest September 27, 1728. Also, in March 1726, he was elected a Fellow of Lincoln College and in 1727 received his Master's degree.[53]

As a Fellow at Lincoln College, Wesley shared in the common revenues of the college, receiving a computed share whether he was in residence or not. Though not wealthy, a fellow had an adequate income, and good surroundings, as long as he did not marry.[54]

The demands made upon the fellow's time were relatively small, but as mentioned earlier, he did engage in private instruction. Another responsibility included presiding over disputations. These public disputations formed a large part of university training in those days. The moderator was the chairman and arbitrator over the discussions. At Lincoln College, these exercises were held everyday, so that the junior fellows gained a thorough grasp of logic, which Wesley gratefully acknowledged in 1766:

> For several years I was Moderator in the disputations which were held six times a week at Lincoln College, in Oxford. I could not avoid acquiring hereby some degree of expertness in arguing, and especially in discerning and pointing out well-covered and plausible fallacies. I have since found abundant reason to praise God for giving me this honest art. By this, when men have hedged me in by what they called demonstration, I have been many times able to dash them to pieces; in spite of all its covers, to touch the very point where the fallacy lay; and it flew open in a moment.[55]

Though we lack specific details of Wesley's training, there were several men who had a great influence on Wesley's view of biblical authority and preaching. One was, Dr. George Wigan, Wesley's first tutor. Wigan was

---

[52] Duncan Ferguson, "John Wesley on the Scripture: The Hermeneutics of Pietism," *Methodist History* (1984) 235.

[53] By a Methodist. *John Wesley the Methodist*. (New York, N.Y.: Methodist Book Concern, 1903) 60–61.

[54] V. H. H. Green. *The Young Mr. Wesley*. (New York, N.Y.: St. Martin's Press, 1961) 86–87.

[55] *Works* 10:353.

described by Thomas Hearne as "a great and a very good tutor. a disciplinarian and a sober, studious, regular, and learned man."[56]

It may be that the foundation for Wesley's expository preaching was laid by Dr. Wigan. According to Martin Schmidt, Dr. Wigan was a biblical linguist following in the steps of the notable German scholar Johann Ernst Grabe.[57]

Perhaps it is partially from Dr. Wigan, that Wesley derived the meticulous care in his treatment of the scriptural text marked in his sermons, and even more explicitly in his *Notes* on both the Old and New Testaments.[58]

Wigan was succeeded after three years by Henry Sherman. Wesley was also strongly influenced by the Christ Church Precentor, Jonathan Colley. They were both High Churchmen who influenced Wesley to accept the Anglican position, that the primary source for discovering God's supreme law was the Bible, and where one scriptural passage was obscure or ambiguous, others should be considered to resolve difficulties. Always read Scripture in the plainest most obvious sense. These men helped develop Wesley's view of the authority and interpretation of the Bible in the light of the general Anglican position. This position, so important to Wesley, will be more fully discussed in the next section. Even without details of all of Wesley's studies, it is clear by 1727, at the age of 24, Wesley spent several hours a day in the reading of Scripture in the original tongues.[59] He laid down a plan of study of Scripture and carefully followed it. At Oxford, John and Charles said daily devotions in Greek. Later he was able to say he had examined every word in the Greek New Testament. It was said he could correct wrong quotations from the New Testament by quoting from memory the Greek.[60]

In 1726 brother Charles came to Christ Church, a lively young fellow. Later he began to change and adopt discipline, certain rules for right living, and appointed times for study and religious duties. Other companions joined and when John returned from serving as his father's curate at Epworth, he became the leader of the small group. Wesley spoke of their

---

[56] V. H. H. Green. *The Young Mr. Wesley.* (New York, N.Y.: St. Martin's Press, 1961) 61.

[57] Martin Schmidt. *John Wesley a Theological Biography Vol. 2., Part 1.* (Nashville, Tenn.: Abingdon Press, 1972) 72.

[58] A. Skevington Wood. *The Burning Heart.* (Grand Rapids, Mich.: Wm B Eerdmanns Pub. Co., 1967) 34.

[59] Luke Tyerman. *The Life and Times of the Reverend John Wesley Vol. 1* (New York, N.Y.: Harper Bros., 1870) 52.

[60] George Turner. *Inspiration and Interpretation.* (Grand Rapids, Mich.: Wm. B. Erdmanns Pub. Co., 1957) 164.

obtaining the name Methodists and also pointed out the importance of the Bible to the group in his "Short History of Methodism" (1765):

> 5. The exact regularity of their lives, as well as studies, occasioned a young gentleman of Christ Church to say, 'Here is a new set of Methodists sprung up,'—alluding to some ancient physicians who were so called. The name was new and quaint, so it took immediately, and the Methodists were known all over the university.
>
> 6. They were all zealous members of the Church of England, not only tenacious of all her doctrines, so far as they knew them, but of all her discipline, to the minutest circumstances. They were all likewise zealous observers of all university statutes, and that for conscience sake. But they observed neither these nor anything else any further than they conceived it was bound upon them by their one book, the Bible, it being their one desire and design to be downright Bible Christians-taking the Bible, as interpreted by the primitive Church and our own, for their whole and sole rule.[61]

The first work of the Methodists, or Holy Club, was the study of the Bible. The members were concerned about their own spiritual conditions and humanitarian activities, but their first concern was the searching of Scripture. Again Wesley describes it best in his sermon "On God's Vineyard" (1787):

> From the very beginning, from the time four young men united together, each of them was *Homo Unius Libri*- a man of one book. God taught them all to make His Word 'a lantern unto their feet and a light in all their paths' (Ps.119:105). They had one and only one rule of judgment with regard to all their tempers, words, and actions, namely, the oracles of God. They were one and all determined to be 'Bible Christians.' They were continually reproached for this very thing; some terming them in derision 'Bible bigots;' others as Bible moths—feeding, they said, upon the Bible as moths do upon cloth. And indeed unto this day it is their constant endeavour to think and speak as the oracles of God.[62]

In his *Plain Account of Christian Perfection* Wesley mentions this period of his biblical development:

> In the year 1729 I began not only to read, but to study the Bible as the one, the only standard of truth, and the only model of pure religion. Hence I saw, in a clearer and clearer light, the indispensable

---

[61] Rupert Davies. *The Works of John Wesley.* Vol. 9. (Nashville, Tenn.: Abingdon Press, 1989) 368.

[62] Albert Outler. *The Works of John Wesley.* Vol. 3 (Nashville, Tenn.: Abingdon Press, 1986) 504.

necessity of having the 'mind which was in Christ,' 'and of walking as Christ also walked.'[63]

The Holy Club spent six evenings a week from six until nine o'clock partly in reading and considering the Greek New Testament, and partly in close conversation.[64] This study of the Bible was not merely devotional, but the Bible was viewed as an authoritative handbook upon every aspect of life both social and personal, both theological and moral. Since they were Englishmen, their Bible study was practical. Since they were pietists, their Bible study was for devotion. Unlike many pietists however, they used the Bible also as their authoritative rule of doctrine.[65]

John Gambold outlined clearly Wesley's desire for himself and the other members of the Holy Club in the article, *The Character of Mr. John Wesley*, in the Methodist Magazine in 1798 published posthumously after Gambold's death:

> It was his earnest care to introduce them to the treasures of wisdom and hope in the Holy Scriptures; to teach them not only to endure that book (for which, I fear, all before their conversion, especially scholars, have not a particular relish, but a particular loathing), but to form themselves by it, and to fly to it as the great antidote against the darkness of the world. For some years past he and his friends read the New Testament together at evening. After every portion of it, having heard the conjectures the rest had to offer, he made his observations on the phrase, design, and difficult places; one or two wrote these down from his mouth.[66]

Such an important place did the Scriptures play in his life from this period onward, even the practice of bibliomancy, the random opening of the Bible to find a word of God upon an issue which would not yield to reason or prayer, was practiced. This appears to have begun at Oxford, rather than later in Georgia.[67] I will discuss Wesley and bibliomancy in chapter five.

---

[63] John Wesley. *A Plain Account of Christian Perfection*. (Kansas City, Mo.: Beacon Hill Press, 1971) 11.

[64] Luke Tyerman. *The Life and Times of the Reverend John Wesley 2 Vols*. (New York, N.Y.: Harper Bros., 1870) 83.

[65] George Allen Turner. *Inspiration and Interpretation*. (Grand Rapids, Mich.: Wm B. Eerdmanns Pub. Co., 1957) 164.

[66] Richard Heitzenrater. *The Elusive Mr. Wesley—John Wesley as Seen by Contemporaries and Biographers*. (Nashville, Tenn.: Abingdon Press, 1984) 42.

[67] Frank Baker. *John Wesley and the Church of England*. (London, England: Epworth Press, 1970) 30.

The Anglican Influence

It would be difficult to overestimate the influence of the Anglican Church on the development of John Wesley's view of the Scripture. Both of his parents were from dissenting families, but had returned to the Church of England. Samuel Wesley was a zealous churchman who emphasized the rules and disciplines of the church and had the highest regard for its liturgy and worship. This home atmosphere instilled within Wesley a great respect and love for the church.[68]

> From a child I was taught to love and reverence the Scripture, the oracles of God and next to these to esteem the primitive Fathers, the writers of the first three centuries. Next after the primitive Church I esteemed our own, the Church of England, as the most scriptural national church in the world. 2. In this judgment and with this spirit I went to America, strongly attached to the Bible, the primitive church, and the Church of England, from which I would not vary one jot or tittle on any account whatever.[69]

At Oxford, and in Georgia, Wesley was most certainly a High Churchman. Wesley described the Holy Club in his own words when he said "They were all zealous members of the Church of England, not only tenacious to all her doctrines so far as they knew them, but of all her disciplines to the minutest circumstance."[70]

In fact, Wesley's love and esteem for the church led him early to an almost prejudiced view towards it, "In my youth I was not only a member of the Church of England, but a bigot to it, believing none but the members of it to be in a state of salvation."[71]

In Wesley's earlier years there was perhaps no one more exact and scrupulous in his obedience to all the customs and rubrics of the Church of England. Consider the following quotation from Dr. Riggs concerning Wesley's early practices as found in John Telford's *The Life of John Wesley*:

> The resemblance of his practice to that of modern High Anglicanism is, in the most points, exceedingly striking. He had early, and also forenoon service everyday; he divided the morning service, taking the litany as a separate service; he inculcated fasting and confession and weekly communion; he restricted the Lord's Supper to all who had been baptized by a minister episcopally ordained; he insisted on

---

[68] William Arnett, "John Wesley—A Man of One Book," (Ph.D. diss., Drew University, 1954).
[69] Rupert Davies. *The Works of John Wesley. Vol. 9.* (Nashville, Tenn.: Abingdon Press, 1989) 538.
[70] Ibid., 368.
[71] *Works* 13:238.

baptism by immersion; he baptized the children of dissenters; and he refused to bury all who had not received episcopal baptism.[72]

Wesley was certainly unlike John Newman, who said he would not forsake the Church of Rome and return to his ancestral church because, "The thought of the Anglican service makes me shudder, and the thought of the Thirty-Nine Articles makes me shudder."[73]

Wesley certainly did not shudder at the thought of the Anglican service or the Thirty-Nine Articles. Instead a faithful reading of Wesley's writings show how totally attached he was to the doctrines of the Church of England.

There is, of course, contention among scholars concerning how loyal a churchman Wesley truly was, in light of the eventual schism between Methodism and the Church of England. After interpreting Wesley's role, some, like the afore-mentioned Dr. Riggs, in his book *The Churchmanship of John Wesley and His High Anglicanism*, state that Wesley was a "schismatic and no other than a dissenter, whatever else he might fancy himself."[74] Dr. Hugh Price in an open letter in 1899 stated:

> Until you learn to distinguish between what Wesley said in sentimental moments, and what he did at the great crises of his public life, his career can only mystify you. Whatever the saintly and illustrious Wesley said out of love to the Anglican Church, he deliberately paved the way for everything that has happened since.[75]

There are others, of course, who feel Wesley was faithful to his promise made to the Archbishop of Canterbury in 1739, that both he and Charles would remain in the church as long as she did not abandon her Articles and homilies. The Archbishop assured them that he had no knowledge of the likelihood of any such changes.[76] As late as 1788 Wesley attempted to show his continued commitment to the Church of England in describing the activities at conference:

> One of the most important things considered at this Conference was that of leaving the church. The sum of the long conversation was,

---

[72] John Telford. *The Life of John Wesley.* (London, England: Robert Culley Publisher, 1910) 303.

[73] David Baines-Griffith. *Wesley the Anglican.* (London, England: McMillan and Co. Ltd., 1919) 107.

[74] William Harrison, "Wesley the Anglican," *Methodist Review 102* (1919) 910.

[75] Ibid., 911

[76] Maxamin Piette. *John Wesley and the Evolution of Protestantism.* (London, England: Sheed and Ward., 1937) 433.

(1) That, in a course of fifty years, we had neither premeditatively nor willingly varied from it in one article either of doctrine or discipline;

(2) That we were not yet conscious of varying from it in any point of doctrine.[77]

I am sure it was statements such as these which led Dr. Finch in *The Christian Walk* (1919) to make statements like:

> It will be a surprise to many to find how loyal an Anglican Wesley was to the end: how he considered himself a High Churchman, how he always looked with some little scorn upon dissenters, and how he resisted the attempts to separate the Methodist societies from the Anglican Church. The severance from the Church of the Methodist Societies was, in Wesley's eyes, a despicable thing.[78]

It is not my desire to debate how responsible Wesley was for the split between Methodism and the Church of England. I am concerned, however, with the accuracy of Wesley's statement that he never strayed from the Church "in one article, either of doctrine or discipline."[79] How true an Anglican Churchman was Wesley in submission to the Thirty-nine Articles of Religion, particularly to Article Six, which we shall see directly relates to the place of Scripture in the Church? Was John Telford speaking accurately when he said, "Throughout life Wesley was faithful to all the doctrines of the Reformation and the English Church?"[80]

The question of scriptural authority would be more specifically raised for Wesley at the time of his ordination. For Wesley to receive holy orders in the Church of England it required acceptance of the Thirty-nine Articles of Religion. After much consideration and a careful study of John Ellis' *A Defense of the 39 Articles of the Church of England* Wesley was able to commit himself to the Articles.[81]

Wesley's true commitment to the Thirty-nine Articles of Religion might well be questioned when it is noted that he abridged the Articles for what later became the Methodist Episcopal Church in America. In 1775 John Fletcher called for Wesley to make an abridgment. His Twenty-four Article abridgment was included in the "Sunday Service for Methodists in

---

[77] *Journals* 7:422.

[78] William Harrison, "Wesley the Anglican," *Methodist Review 102* (1919) 909.

[79] *Journals* 7:422.

[80] John Telford. *The Life of John Wesley.* (London, England: Robert Culley Publisher, 1910) 112.

[81] Allen Coppedge. *John Wesley in Theological Debate.* (Wilmore, Ky.: Wesley Heritage Press, 1987) 63.

the United States of America" which he sent to America by Thomas Coke in 1784 (Blankenship, 1964, 36). One article was added at the Conference, "Of the Rulers of the United States of America." These Twenty-five Articles of Religion were published in the *Disciplines* in 1788.[82]

In working on his abridgment, Wesley gives no indication why he made particular changes. He seems to have done with the Prayer Book, as he did with other volumes he abridged. He struck out sentences, paragraphs, pages, and entire sections he felt could be discarded. His desire seems to have been to leave out anything he considered unnecessary. He entirely omitted several complete Articles: (3) Descent into Hell; (8) Of the Creeds; (13) Works Before Justification; (15) Christ Alone Without Sin; (17) Predestination and Election; (18) Eternal Salvation only by the Name of Christ; (20) Authority of the Church; (21) Authority of General Councils; (23) Ministering in the Congregation; (24) Unworthiness of Ministers; (29) Of the Wicked which Eat not the Body of Christ in the use of the Lord's supper; (33) Excommunication; (35) Homilies; (36) Consecration of Bishops and Ministers. As Nolan Harmon states, "serving no useful purpose, will account for many of his omissions."[83]

Paul Blankenship, in his article entitled "The Significance of John Wesley's Abridgment of the 39 Articles as Seen From His Deletions," draws some overall conclusions. Blankenship suggests deletions were made in order to help the brethren in the new nation follow the Scripture and the Primitive Church, to reflect possible doctrinal differences, and to provide clarity. He finishes with seven conclusions, three of which directly apply here:

> (1) Wesley's Twenty-four Articles (made Twenty-five by the Christmas Conference), are an abridgment, rather than a revision.
>
> (2) Wesley evidently did not consider the Twenty-four Articles the only standard of doctrine for American Methodism.
>
> (3) Most of Wesley's deletions are in line with his emphasis that all doctrine should be based on Scripture.[84]

The exclusion of Article III "Descent into Hell," may have been ascribed to a lack of clear Scriptural support. In a few instances, he deleted

---

[82] Thomas Oden. *Doctrinal Standards in the Wesleyan Tradition*. (Grand Rapids, Mich.: Zondervan Publishing House, 1988) 105.

[83] Nolan Harmon and John Bardsley, "John Wesley and the Articles of Religion," *Religion in Life 22, No. 2*(1953) 280–91.

[84] Paul Blankenship, "The Significance of John Wesley's Abridgement of the Thirty-Nine Articles As Seen From His Deletions," *Methodist History* (1964) 38–44.

Articles which he believed to be scriptural, but only when their retention would give rise to more confusion than their deletion. The omission of Article VIII "Of the Creeds," may have been in line with Wesley's announced intent to leave American Methodism free, "simply to follow the Scripture, and the Primitive Church."[85] Edwin Lewis perhaps provides the best analysis of these omissions when he states:

> Wesley accepted for himself both the Nicene and Athanasian Symbols, so far as their intent was concerned, but he objected to their non-biblical terms especially 'Persons' and 'Trinity,' and he disapproved of the damnatory clauses. The Apostles' Creed he certainly accepted, and it was included in the Order of Public Worship of the Methodist Episcopal Church (the Conference of 1786 omitting the clause on the Descent into Hades).[86] Besides, each of these scriptural articles were still valid for Wesley and his followers, simply because they were scriptural.[87]

The last point speaks most to my concerns. Wesley seemed to feel at liberty to delete certain of the Articles, but not if they were firmly proven in Scripture. How did this affect Wesley's use of Article VI? An examination reveals Wesley's abridgment made only minor grammatical changes, and excluded the apocryphal books. Article VI in the *Book of Common Prayer* (868–69) states:

VI. Of the Sufficiency of the Holy Scriptures for Salvation

> Holy Scripture containeth all things necessary to salvation: so that whatsoever is not read therein, nor may be proved thereby, is not to be required of any man, that it should be believed as an article of the faith, or be thought requisite or necessary to salvation. In the name of the Holy Scripture we do understand those canonical Books of the Old and New Testament, of whose authority was never any doubt in the Church.

---

[85] *Works 13:218-19*.

[86] Thomas Oden. *Doctrinal Standards in the Wesleyan Tradition*. (Grand Rapids, Mich.: Zondervan Publishing House, 1988) 3–4.

[87] Paul Blankenship, "The Significance of John Wesley's Abridgement of the Thirty-Nine Articles As Seen From His Deletions," *Methodist History* (1964) 44–45.

The Formation of Wesley's Views on Scripture: Part 1

Of the Names and Number of the Canonical Books.

Genesis	The First Book of Samuel, The Book of Esther
Exodus	The Second Book of Samuel, The Book of Job
Leviticus	The First Book of Kings, The Psalms
Numbers	The Second Book of Kings, The Proverbs
Deuteronomy	The First Book of Chronicles, Ecclesiastes or Preacher
Joshua	The Second Book of Chronicles, Cantica, or Songs of Solomon
Judges	The First Book of Esdras, Four Prophets the greater
Ruth	The Second Book of Esdras Twelve Prophets the less

And the other Books (as Hierome saith) the Church doth read for example of life and instruction of manners; but yet doth it not apply them to establish and doctrine; such are these following:

Genesis	The First Book of Samuel, The Book of Esther
The Third Book of Esdras	The rest of the Book of Esther
The Fourth Book of Esdras	The Book of Wisdom
The Book of Tobias	Jesus the Son of Sirach
The Book of Judith	Baruch the Prophet
The Song of the Three Children	The Prayer of Manasses
The Story of Susannah	The First Book of Maccabees
Of Bel and the Dragon	The Second Book of Maccabees

All the Books of the New Testament, as they are commonly received, we do receive, and account them Canonical.

We see the Article makes a distinction between the canonical books, whose authority was never in doubt in the church, and the apocryphal books, the latter being read by the church for examples of life and instruction of manner, but were not applied to doctrine. By this, the Church of England aligned itself with classical Protestantism in commitment to "sola scriptura."[88]

In considering Wesley's abridgment, we find he removed the phrase "and Number," in the title of the second section. He changed the names of the First and Second Book of Esdras to, the Book of Ezra and the Book of Nehemiah. Finally, he omitted the section dealing with the apocryphal books.

In recognizing Wesley's almost total acceptance of Article VI, the question then becomes how does this article reflect the total views of the Church of England toward Scripture prior to and during Wesley's era? Also, how did the views of the Church of England influence the development of Wesley's views, and is the view Wesley actually espouses consistent with the views of the Anglican Church in his day?

The fact that the Church of England recognized the Scripture as the final authority in all matters of doctrine was not lost on the conscientious young Wesley. For Wesley, ordination in the Church of England carried with it an intellectual commitment to the church's official position on the primary authority of Scripture and of the Articles of Religion as the essential core of biblical doctrine. The Article on Scripture makes it quite clear that no doctrine is to be accepted as an article of faith unless it may be read in the Bible. By this declaration the Holy Scriptures were established as the final authority in the church and clearly distinguished from tradition.[89] Anglican theology was attempting to steer a middle course between the extremes of Roman Catholicism and radical Protestantism. The Counter-Reformation had opted for the inerrant tradition of the present church, while the Reformation had chosen Scripture as the self-declaring authority and criterion. The Bible, not the church, contains "in all sufficiency and abundance the pure water of life and whatever is necessary to make God's people wise unto salvation," yet the church was recognized to have a subordinate role, to guide, preserve, and direct the right understanding of Scripture. The Bible, though offered as the only standard of faith, was never quite free from the church in the true Protestant sense.[90]

The Church of England, as we shall see, continued to maintain the centrality of Scripture, but at the same time eighteenth century Anglicanism

---

[88] Allen Coppedge. *John Wesley in Theological Debate.* (Wilmore, Ky.: Wesley Heritage Press, 1987) 63.

[89] Ibid., 29.

[90] William Cannon. *The Theology of John Wesley.* (Nashville, Tenn.: Abingdon Press, 1946) 32.

saw no solution to the problem of authority which did not admit the mutually illuminating relationship of Scripture, antiquity, and reason. It refused any solution which did not include the testimony of history and the free action of reason.[91]

Bishop H. R. McAdoo demonstrated how during the seventeenth century Anglican theologians agreed in the basic approach to the question of final authority. He used as his example a portion of Richard Hooker's *Laws of Ecclesiastical Polity*.[92] Here Hooker dealt with the basic issue of ecclesiastical authority and thought. Hooker's solution, which became the model for the Church of England, was three-fold:

> 1. Scripture—(but not used as the Puritans) provides the main source of truth, and the basic test of Christian veracity, but was not to be used in the manner of the Puritan understanding of sola scriptura. Scripture was not a handbook that provided specific answers to all questions, to be followed to the letter; doing all the things spelled out there, omitting all things not found there. Hooker suggested that the Scriptures, as the primary source, should be seen as a whole and could provide guidelines for thought and actions in many areas.
>
> 2. Tradition—(but not as used by the Roman Catholics) provides a view of life and thought from the earliest centuries of Christianity, closest to the purity of the apostolic witness and most liable to be (in its consensus) an authentic reflection and explication of the biblical testimony-certainly not to be venerated equally with Scripture (as the Council of Trent had decreed) and by all means limited to the first few centuries of the church, excluding the innovations of the medieval church. Hooker saw the value of tradition as an early authoritative explanation of scriptural truths.
>
> 3. Reason—(but not as used by the Platonists) furnishes the means by which Scripture and tradition can be scrutinized and understood by thoughtful persons. Revealed truth may at times be above reason, but can never be contrary to reason. Hooker was willing to discern connections between revelation and reason as sources and measures of truth in order to develop doctrines that were cogent and credible.[93]

---

[91] Henry McAdoo. *The Spirit of Anglicanism.* (New York, N.Y.: Charles Scribner's Sons, 1965) 410.

[92] Frank Baker. *John Wesley and the Church of England.* (London, England: Epworth Press, 1970) 14.

[93] Richard Heitzenrater. *Wesley and the People Called Methodists.* (Nashville, Tenn.: Abingdon Press, 1995) 10.

Dean Paget in his introduction to the fifth book of Hooker's *Laws of Ecclesiastical Polity* demonstrates the influence of Hooker's views stating that Hooker's appeal for guidance in all things spiritual to a three fold count of authority based upon reason, Scripture, and tradition all coming from God, who is the one true source of all light, and each in certain areas being primary sources, but in all areas blending together and cooperating, as Hooker's most abiding work. Equal loyalty to reason, Scripture and tradition was the distinctive strength of the English Church.[94]

That this approach was unique is not claimed. That it was distinctive of eighteenth century Anglicanism can be proven. McAdoo worked his way through the writings of forty writers in this period beginning with Hooker, and showed there were no essential differences in their views. Each employed the same theological method in seeking final truth by means of Scripture, reason, and tradition.[95] By the eighteenth century Hooker was a standard authority. Samuel Wesley's "Advice to Young Clergymen" (1735), assumed that any aspiring cleric would be well grounded in Hooker.[96] This was also the climate that Wesley absorbed, first at Epworth and later in his readings and academic relationships at Oxford.

When one considers Wesley's views on Scriptural authority, as will be done in chapter four, the influence of seventeenth and eighteenth century Anglican thought is obvious and pervasive. Allow me to outline these views by explaining somewhat more completely the Anglican triad of Scripture, reason and tradition supplemented by quotations from Anglican authors from this period. These views will be more fully explored when Wesley's views are considered. At this point I will simply attempt to show the underpinnings of Wesley's views on scriptural authority, as it relates to seventeenth and eighteenth century Anglican theology.

First, it should be recognized that in the seventeenth century, Hooker and others made a clear distinction between the fundamentals that were necessary for salvation, and the non-essentials. These essentials were summed up in the creeds, particularly the Apostles' Creed. Behind the creeds, guaranteeing their truth and correcting them when they went astray, was the sacred canon. William Chillingworth, while allowing the importance of tradition, still spoke of the Bible as the sole religion of the Protestants:

---

[94] Richard Baker. *John Wesley and the Church of England.* (London, England: Epworth Press, 1970) 14.

[95] Ibid., 15.

[96] Richard Heitzenrater. *Wesley and the People Called Methodists.* (Nashville, Tenn.: Abingdon Press, 1995) 10.

> I am fully convinced that God does not, and therefore that man ought not, to require any more of any man than this, to believe Scripture to be God's Word, to endeavour to find the true sense of it, and to live according to it.[97]

Chillingworth further expresses the primacy of Scripture in his book *The Religion of Protestants* (1719):

> The (Bible), I say, the Bible is the Religion of the Protestants. In a word there is no sufficient certainty but Scripture only, for any considering man to build upon. Propose me anything out of the Book, and require whether I believe it or no, and seem it never so incomprehensible to human reason, I will subscribe to it with hand and heart, as knowing no demonstration can be stronger than this: 'God hath said so,' so, therefore, it is true.[98]

Compare these comments with Wesley's in his sermon "On Faith" (1788):

> 8. The faith of the Protestants, in general, embraces only those truths as necessary to salvation which are clearly revealed in the oracles of God. Whatever is plainly declared in the Old and New Testament is the object of their faith. They believe neither more nor less than what is manifestly contained in, and provable by, the Holy Scriptures.[99]

Jeremy Taylor, whose book, *The Rules and Exercises of Holy Living*, had such an influence on Wesley, commented on Scripture as the ultimate authority in 1667 when he wrote:

> That the Scripture is a full, sufficient rule to Christians in faith and manners, a full and perfect declaration of the Will of God, is therefore certain, because we have no other. For, if we consider the grounds upon which all Christians believe the Scriptures to be the Word of God, the same grounds prove that nothing else is.[100]

William Beveridge espouses a similar viewpoint when he states, "I know the Scripture is the rule of faith, and the supreme judge of all controversies whatsoever, so that there is no controversy of faith that ought to be determined, but from Scripture."[101]

---

[97] Paul More and Frank Cross. *Anglicanism*. (London, England: SPCK Press, 1957) XXV.
[98] Ibid., 104.
[99] Albert Outler. *The Works of John Wesley. Vol. 3*. (Nashville, Tenn.: Abingdon Press, 1986) 496.
[100] Paul More and Frank Cross. *Anglicanism*. (London, England: SPCK Press, 1957) 89.
[101] Ibid., 95.

Again, for the purpose of comparison, let me introduce a few quotations from Wesley, that illustrate similarities. In his Sermon "The Witness of Our Own Spirit" (1746), "But the Christian rule of right and wrong, is the Word of God, the writings of the Old and New Testament."[102]

From "A Roman Catechism with a Reply Thereto":

> The Scripture, therefore, is a rule sufficient in itself, and was by men divinely inspired, at once delivered to the world; and so neither needs nor is capable of any further addition. For as all faith is founded upon divine authority, so there is now no divine authority but the Scriptures; and therefore no one can make that to be of divine authority which is not contained in them.[103]

Finally from a letter to the Rev. John Clayton in 1739:

> Permit me to speak plainly. If by catholic principles you mean any other than scriptural, they weigh nothing with me. I allow no other rule whether of faith or practice, than the Holy Scriptures. But on scriptural principles I do not think it hard to justify whatever I do.[104]

I will consider these quotations, as well as others, as I consider Wesley's thoughts on scriptural authority in chapter four. At this point it is sufficient to recognize the similarity in thought and expression between Wesley, and Anglican scholarship of the seventeenth and eighteenth centuries.

As a secondary source of authority for revealing his will, God had provided the church, and the Church of England had fallen heir through continuous connection, to the wisdom and divine grace of the Apostolic Church; the nearest to the Bible and therefore, best able to offer authoritative interpretation. In *The Preface to the Ordinal* (1550), it was claimed the three-fold ministry of bishops, priests, and deacons was validated not only by Scripture but by the "ancient Authors," meaning the early Fathers. The supremacy of Scripture was generally recognized, but appeals to the Fathers occurred even in the Articles.[105]

Henry McAdoo, in his book *The Spirit of Anglicanism*, shows that the appeal to antiquity was not so much an attempt to validate some later teaching or practice, as it was to show what the early church was like and

---

[102] Albert Outler. *The Works of John Wesley. Vol. 1.* (Nashville, Tenn.: Abingdon Press, 1984) 302–03.

[103] *Works* 10:90–1

[104] Frank Baker. *The Works of John Wesley. Vol. 25.* (Nashville, Tenn.: Abingdon Press, 1980) 615.

[105] Robert Grant. *A Short History of the Interpretation of the Bible.* (New York, N.Y. MacMillan Company, 1972) 136.

to show a resemblance to the contemporary church. The desire was not to begin with the present situation and work back to the Fathers, but to take the primacy of Scripture as a starting point. Scripture, they maintained, was best understood and interpreted in the first centuries, and therefore the writers of that period nearest Scripture revealed the teaching of the Church at the beginning, and this should be the pattern for later ages.[106]

For the Anglican Church, the idea of continuity with the early Church Fathers was very important. The belief was held that Scripture was central, but it did not exist in a vacuum apart from the life of the church within which it was formed in the first place. The writings of the Fathers were not a second canon above criticism, but the patristic writings, and decisions of the Councils were believed to show the continuity between the teaching and order of the contemporary church and the early Church.[107]

A statement by Archbishop William Laud shows clearly this sense of continuity between the Primitive Church and the Church of England, as well as a point of comparison with Wesley's views:

> The Church of England is nearest of any Church now in being to the Primitive Church. For that all the positive articles of the present Church of England are grounded upon Scripture, we are content to be judged by the joint and constant belief of the Fathers, which lived within the first four or five hundred years after Christ, when the Church was at its best, and by the Councils held within those times. That Scripture contains all fundamentals is not only held by the Church of England, but was the opinion of the Fathers, and it does not exclude genuine, universal traditions.[108]

Compare Laud's statements with Wesley's:

> From a child I was taught to love and reverence the Scripture, the oracles of God, and next to these to esteem the primitive Fathers, the writers of the first three centuries. Next after the primitive Church, I esteemed our own, the Church of England, as the most scriptural national church in the world.[109]

Finally, it was recognized that God had also placed within human's reason, to recognize divine law and make valid interpretation of scripture.

---

[106] Henry McAdoo. *The Spirit of Anglicanism.* (New York, N.Y.: Charles Scribner's and Sons, 1965) 316–17.

[107] Ibid., 318.

[108] Ibid., 338.

[109] Rupert Davies. *The Works of John Wesley. Vol. 9.* (Nashville, Tenn.: Abingdon Press, 1989) 538.

Thus the church's ordained ministers were custodians of the sacred mysteries and authorized interpreters of the divine law as revealed in the Bible.[110]

Once again, William Laud provided evidence in 1639 which helps to conceptualize the importance and the limitations of reason in Anglican thought, in relation to the Scripture:

> Though reason without grace cannot see the way to heaven, nor believe this Book in which God hath written the way, yet grace is never placed but in a reasonable creature. For the Word of God, and the book containing it, refuses not to be weighed by reason. But the scale is not large enough to contain, nor the weights to measure out, the true virtue and full force of either. Reason, then, can give no supernatural ground into which a man may resolve his faith that Scripture is the Word of God infallibly: yet reason can go so high, as it can prove that Christian religion, which rests upon the authority of this book, stands upon surer grounds of nature, reason, common equity, and justice, than anything in the world which any infidel or mere naturalist hath done, doth, or can adhere unto, against it, in that which he makes, accounts, or assumes as religion himself.[111]

Compare Laud's thoughts with a few of the many quotations we could choose to represent Wesley's views upon the importance, and limitations of reason. In a letter to Dr. Rutherford in 1768:

> It is a fundamental principle with us (Methodists), that to renounce reason is to renounce religion, that religion and reason go hand in hand, and that all irrational religion is false religion.[112]

In "The Case for Reason Impartially Considered" (1781):

> Let reason do all that reason can do: employ it as far as it will go. But at the same time acknowledge it is utterly incapable of giving either faith, hope or love; and consequently of producing either real virtue or substantial happiness. Expect these from a higher source, even from the Father of the spirits of all flesh.[113]

I will consider in great detail Wesley's view of scriptural authority, and his use of tradition and reason in biblical interpretation, in later chapters. At this point, it is clear, that Wesley's views of Scripture were built upon a

---

[110] Frank Baker. *John Wesley and the Church of England*. (London, England: Epworth Press, 1970) 13.

[111] Paul More and Frank Cross. *Anglicanism*. (London, England: SPCK Press, 1957) 102–3.

[112] Rupert Davies. *The Works of John Wesley. Vol. 9*. (Nashville, Tenn.: Abingdon Press, 1989) 382.

[113] Albert Outler. *The Works of John Wesley. Vol. 2*. (Nashville, Tenn.: Abingdon Press, 1985) 600.

solid foundation laid by Anglican scholarship in the seventeenth and eighteenth centuries. It should also be recognized that the Anglican tradition embraced a variety of points of view. One such view was that of the seventeenth century Carolinian divines such as William Laud which helped form the High Churchmanship that Wesley was so familiar with.

However, there were other Anglican churchmen, who could be described as moderates, who perhaps had an impact on Wesley's views. According to John English in his article, "John Wesley and the Anglican Moderates," the moderates should be distinguished from both Puritans and High Churchmen. Unlike the Puritans, they endorsed, in principle, both Episcopal polity, and the Book of Common Prayer. They also could not accept the Calvinistic theology of Puritanism. Here, they were similar to Anglican "Arminian" High Churchmen. However, they rejected episcopacy as of divine right. Furthermore, they wished to revise the Prayer Book in the interest of peace and unity, and asked for a simplification of the Church's doctrine, clearly distinguishing essentials from non-essentials.[114]

A list of the moderate churchmen might include, Ralph Cudworth (1617–1688), Henry Fowler (1632–1714), Henry More (1614–1652), Simon Patrick (1626–1701), John Smith (1618–1652), John Tillotson (1630–1694), John Wilkins (1614–1672), John Worthington (1618–1671), and Edward Stillingfleet (English, 1969, 205). The names of the moderates occur often in the lists of the books which Wesley read and published for his societies. We see, for example, he not only read John Worthington's treatise "The Great Duty of Self-Recognition to the Divine Will," himself, but also read it aloud to a circle of female parishioners in Georgia.[115]

After Aldersgate Wesley published extracts of Worthington's book in his Christian Library. He also published a sermon from Ralph Cudworth in Volume 17, Henry More in 39, Simon Patrick in 20 and 32, John Smith in 19 and 20, and John Tillotson in Volume 45.[116]

How much Wesley was influenced by the moderates is open to debate. He did mention specifically how he changed his mind concerning church order after reading Stillingfleet's *Irenicium*.[117]

---

[114] John English, "John Wesley and the Anglican Moderates of the 17th Century," *Anglican Theological Review 51-3* (1969) 204–5.

[115] Reginald Ward and Richard Heitzenrater. *The Works of John Wesley. Vol. 18.* (Nashville, Tenn.: Abingdon Press, 1988) 419.

[116] John English, "John Wesley and the Anglican Moderates of the 17th Century," *Anglican Theological Review 51–3* (1969) 205.

[117] *Letters* 3:182.

John English summarizes the moderate's views on Scripture, and it is interesting to note the similarity to Wesley's views which will be addressed later. According to English, for the moderates sacred Scripture was the sole rule of both faith and practice. However, different interpretations had given rise to sects and factions. For the moderates, the way to unity in the church was a particular way of regarding the Bible. Since Scripture is the Word of God, and cannot lie, every statement in the Bible was true.[118]

To say every statement was true did not mean that all were equally meaningful. Some statements were clear, while others were obscure and susceptible to different interpretations. The clear and distinct statements were the essentials of the Christian religion, and the basis of the creeds and confessions of all denominations. Disunity came when ungodly men tried to pronounce their opinion as the only correct interpretation of obscure passages. The moderates denounced opinions which were imposed on men's conscience. An example could be found in Edward Stillingfleet's *Irenicum: A Weapon Salve for the Church's Wounds on the Divine Right of Particular Forms of Church Government discussed and Examined.*[119]

The moderates believed that there were certain biblical propositions whose meanings were clear to all Christians. To those who were given greater capacities, more was expected in the way of understanding. However, all Christians were expected to study the Bible and anticipate that God would clarify difficult passages.[120]

The moderates also felt that all churches were more or less corrupt. That is, every church had opinions which were supposed to be essentials. Being good Protestants, the moderates felt the Roman Church was the most corrupt, and the Church of England was the least infected.[121]

The moderates also believed that the Church of England's separation from the Church of Rome was legitimate, while the separation of Nonconformists was not. Separation was permissible only under limited circumstances, such as if a doctrine clearly contradicts Scripture, or if an uncertain opinion had to be acknowledged in order to be in communion with a particular church.[122]

In later chapters I will note the similarities of some of Wesley's expressed views to those of the moderates. How greatly they influenced him is

---

[118] John English, "John Wesley and the Anglican Moderates of the 17th Century," *Anglican Theological Review* (1969) 214.

[119] Ibid., 215.

[120] Ibid., 215.

[121] Ibid., 216.

[122] Ibid., 217.

debatable, but there are clear parallels on certain subjects, such as the essentials of Scripture and separation from the Church of England. Wesley saw no reason to separate as long as the church did not abandon her Articles. It must be remembered however, that just because Wesley gave approval to certain books written by moderates, that does not mean he unqualifiedly endorsed their views. Each view must be examined individually.

In closing, it is clear that Wesley pondered the relationship between churchman and Scripture even before his ordination. On October 6, 1727 he transcribed a sermon on II Corinthians 2:17 entitled, "On Corrupting the Word of God," affirming the central authority of the Bible in Christian doctrine and chastising those who abused it. By this time Wesley's lifelong method of approaching the Scripture had been settled. The Bible was an authoritative handbook of doctrine, but it must be handled with scrupulous honesty to text and context lest the Word of God be corrupted.[123] Note the following quotation from this sermon:

> (III) 1. If we then have spoken the Word of God, the genuine unmixed Word of God, and that only; 2, if we have put no unnatural interpretations upon it, but have taken the known phrases in their common obvious sense, and where they were less known explained Scripture by Scripture; 3, if we have spoken the whole Word as occasion offered, though rather the parts that seemed most proper to give a check to some fashionable vice or to encourage the practice of some unfashionable virtue; and 4, lastly, if we do this plainly and boldly, though with all the mildness and gentleness that the nature of things will bear than, believe ye our works if not our word—or rather, believe them both together. Here is all a preacher can do.[124]

Here we see at age 24 Wesley's strongly developed view of the authority of Scripture, as well as an early statement of his interpretive principles. These views line up with the classical Anglican view which calls for obedience to God's will as revealed in the Bible. We see that Wesley continued to believe that not only did the Church of England have the correct view of Scripture, but its view of Scripture was one of the elements that made it the true church. In his *Journal* on February 6, 1740 he paraphrases the Nineteenth Article, though he calls it the Twentieth:

> Our Twentieth Article defines a true church, 'a congregation of faithful people, wherein the true Word of God is preached and

---

[123] Frank Baker. *John Wesley and the Church of England.* (London, England: Epworth Press, 1970) 20.

[124] Albert Outler. *The Works of John Wesley. Vol. 4.* (Nashville, Tenn.: Abingdon Press, 1987) 250.

the sacraments duly administered.' According to this account the Church of England is that body of faithful people (or holy believers) in England, among whom the pure Word of God is preached and the sacraments duly administered.[125]

Thus we see that Wesley followed the Anglican position in recognizing Scripture as the final authority, but he also recognized that, "scarce ever was an heretical opinion invented or revered but Scripture was quoted to defend it."[126] Wesley again followed the Anglican position of recognizing the importance of tradition and reason in interpreting Scripture. This must be recognized if we are to understand how the Anglican Triad (Scripture, reason, tradition), became the Wesleyan Quadrilateral (Scripture, reason, tradition and experience). It should be noted that all do not agree with this four-fold division. Scott Jones, for example, feels that Wesley should be more accurately understood as "conceiving religious authority to have five components: Scripture, reason, Christian antiquity, experience, and the Church of England.[127] I will discuss this division more fully in later chapters, as well as the manner in which Wesley struggled to develop his own views of these sometimes competing interpretive authorities. Wesley would continue to depend upon his Anglican heritage, but for him the Scripture would become the norm to be placed above all other authorities.

---

[125] Reginald Ward and Richard Heitzenrater. *The Works of John Wesley. Vol. 19.* (Nashville, Tenn.: 1990) 138.

[126] Albert Outler. *The Works of John Wesley. Vol. 4.* (Nashville, Tenn.: 1987) 247.

[127] Scott Jones, "John Wesley's Conception and Use of Scripture" (Ph.D. diss., Southern Methodist University, 1992).

2

The Formation of Wesley's Views on Scripture

Part 2

The Influence of Patristic Writings

During his stay at Oxford, Wesley earned the nickname "Mr. Primitive Christianity."[1] That Wesley's views on a variety of topics were greatly influenced by his study of the Church Fathers is undeniable. Dr. Ted Campbell, in his book *John Wesley and Christian Antiquity*, traces possible influences of Patristic writers upon Wesley over a wide range of issues concerning both doctrine and polity. For example, he discusses how Wesley used the Church Fathers in discussing the centrality of Christian experience (58–61), the human condition (62), divine initiative and human response (62–65), sin and repentance in believers (64), and holiness and perfection (65–66). In chapter 5 Campbell discusses how Wesley was influenced in more practical areas such as, the new persecution of his followers (83), miraculous signs (83–85), Christian societies (86–87), the order of the ministry and the power of ordination (89–93), baptism (95), the eucharist (96), vigils and fasts (98), and the love feast (97).[2] Thus we see, according to Campbell, there was scarcely any area in theology or practice which was not influenced in some manner by Wesley's studies of patristics.

Campbell is not alone in pointing out the influence of the Church Fathers on Wesley's thought. Gordon Rupp in his article "Son of Samuel:

---

[1] Frank Baker. *John Wesley and the Church of England*. (London, England: Epworth Press, 1970) 34.

[2] Ted Campbell. *John Wesley and Christian Antiquity*. (Nashville, Tenn.: Kingswood Books, 1991) 58–97.

John Wesley Church of England Man," quotes Alexander Knox when he states that Wesley's "standard of Christian virtue was pure and exalted. He formed his views in the school of the Greek Fathers, and in that of their closest modern followers the Platonic divines of the Church of England."[3]

In considering a critical doctrine, such as the concept of Christian perfection, Albert Outler maintains that Wesley's insistence in using the word perfection was an illustration of his indebtedness to the Greek Fathers. He understood the word in its Greek connotation as a dynamic concept, and not in the Latin sense of a static stage of grace. Outler goes on to state that in the persons of "Macarius" and "Ephraem Syrus," Eastern spirituality furnished Wesley with two of his chief sources for the doctrine of Christian perfection.[4]

It is not my intention to explore all the possible influences of primitive Christianity on Wesley's thought. I am concerned however, with how Wesley's study of the Church Fathers may have affected his view of biblical authority and interpretation. With that thought in mind, I wish to explore the background influences that helped develop Wesley's high view of patristic studies. Also, I will provide an overview that demonstrates Wesley's high regard for the Church Fathers, and demonstrate briefly his use of the authority of the early church. Finally, I wish to examine various Church fathers that Wesley is known to have read, comparing some of their comments on inspiration, authority, infallibility and interpretation of Scripture, with those of Wesley, searching for commonality. In chapters eight and nine I will focus exclusively on Wesley's interpretive principles, and at that point I will consider more closely the manner in which Wesley used tradition in the interpretation of Scripture.

One note of caution should be given at this point. The attempt to trace influences across 1400 to 1600 years of Church history is a formidable task. Even if a similarity in views on the Bible can be shown between Wesley and Origen, for example, it cannot be automatically assumed that Wesley drew his views from Origen. Perhaps Wesley developed the view on his own, or it came from Pietistic sources, Roman Catholic mystics, or Puritan authors. Seeing similarities in Wesley's views with that of the early Church Fathers is enlightening and important, but demonstrating this is the specific source of Wesley's view would be much more difficult. This would require examination of all possible sources of that particular view. In this chapter I will merely examine certain of the Church Father's views and

---

[3] Kenneth Rowe. *The Place of Wesley in Christian Tradition*. (Metuchen, N.J.: The Scarecrow Press, 1976) 52.

[4] Albert Outler. *John Wesley*. (Oxford, England: Oxford University Press, 1964) 10.

comments on Scripture for similarities and possible sources of influence in Wesley's perspectives.

Background Influences

The Family

As was noted in chapter one, both of Wesley's parents came from dissenting backgrounds, but eventually returned to the Church of England. Like many who had taken this pilgrimage, they had a strong attachment to the established church, and would be classified as "High Church." Those who were High Church would view the Church of England as the true church, being the only reformation church with an Episcopal order received from apostolic succession. The concept of ecclesiastical order was based upon the writing of the Early Church Fathers, as well as doctrine, worship, and liturgy. Almost from the cradle Wesley received a spirit of Anglicanism that revered the early church. This affected his views of the church, its ministry, its worship, its doctrine and discipline.[5]

From his father Wesley received a particular impetus to study Christian antiquity. Two documents of Samuel, both read by John, show this interest in ancient Christianity. First, a pamphlet entitled "The Young Student's Library," containing extracts and abridgments of the most valuable books printed in England and in the foreign journals, included a list of recommended readings. Included was Eusebius' *Ecclesiastical History*, *The History of the General Councils*, *A Summary of Councils*, William Beveridge's *Synodikon*, and a list of other readings of the Church Fathers.[6]

The second example is Samuel's "Advice to Young Clergymen." This article was published by John the year his father died, and included a ten page section specifically concerned with early Christian studies.[7]

Charterhouse

While at Charterhouse, the schoolmaster was Dr. Thomas Walker, and the usher was Andrew Toake. Dr. Walker was esteemed for his knowledge of Hebrew, Greek, and Latin. The school emphasized the classical tradition of education, and was greatly appreciated by Wesley who had almost a sense of reverence for classical authors and ancient times. Toake, must have em-

---

[5] Luke Keefer, "John Wesley, Disciple of Early Christianity," (Ph.D. diss., Temple University, 1982).

[6] Frank Baker. *John Wesley and the Church of England* (Oxford, England: Oxford University Press, 1970) 11.

[7] Ted Campbell, "John Wesley and Christian Antiquity," (Ph.D. diss., Temple University, 1991).

phasized the same in his teaching, for later Wesley was known as a classical scholar of distinction at Oxford.[8]

Wesley's days at Charterhouse contributed to his primitivism by emphasizing an admiration for things ancient, as well as giving Wesley a knowledge of Greek and Hebrew to study in the original languages. Also, these Anglican clergymen instilled within Wesley the Anglican regard for the early centuries of the church.[9]

Oxford

Christian antiquity was the focus of great debate and study in British Christianity in John Wesley's day, and had been for at least a century. By the time Wesley arrived at Oxford, the great patristic revival which distinguished the university in the seventeenth century had died down, but patristic studies were still an important part of his education. The university's libraries were filled with scholarly editions of ancient Christian works, learned histories of Christian centuries, and hosts of tracts and books claiming Christian antiquity, and the Church Fathers, as being on their side.[10] Oxford had long been a center of patristic studies, as well as being a stronghold of conservative Anglicanism which emphasized the early Christian writers in its defense.[11] The need of the Anglican Church to justify itself as a truly apostolic church fostered the patristic search for what Thomas Ken called, "The faith preferred by the whole church before the disunion of the East and West."[12]

Among Wesley's mentors at Oxford were the great scholars of the seventeenth century revival of patristic studies, William Beveridge and Robert Nelson, as well as Jeremy Taylor, George Bull, Thomas Ken, John Kettlewell, George Hickes, John Sharp, George Smallridge, and others. According to Albert Outler, "The common interests of all these men was their rootage in Christian tradition more primitive, (and in their eyes, more truly catholic), than the corruptions of the 'papists,' or the exaggerations of the 'protestants.'"[13]

There were vast library resources at Oxford. After Wesley took a serious turn in his studies, there were numerous volumes he could study

---

[8] Luke Keefer, "John Wesley Disciple of Early Christianity," (Ph.D. diss., Temple University, 1982).

[9] Ibid

[10] Ted Campbell. *John Wesley and Christian Antiquity*. (Nashville, Tenn.; Kingswood Books, 1991) 9.

[11] Ibid., 26.

[12] Albert Outler. *John Wesley*. (Oxford, England: Oxford University Press, 1964) 45.

[13] Ibid., 45.

that would enlighten him about the early centuries of the church. As long as Wesley held his fellowship at Lincoln College he would return often for study and retreat. Here he would read the works of churchmen whose entire system was built upon the thought of the first five centuries. Luke Keefer comments:

> One needs only to observe the records of his reading, provided by his diaries for these years, to discover how much he took advantage of Oxford's resources, frequently copying out sections from books that were of later use to him.[14]

While at Oxford in 1725 Wesley drew up a plan of study which he tried to follow. Monday and Tuesday were to be reserved for Greek and Roman history and literature; Wednesday for logic and ethics; Thursday for Hebrew and Arabic; Fridays for Metaphysics and Natural philosophy; Saturdays for the composition of oratory and poetry; and Sunday for divinity.[15]

In the divinity studies on Sunday, Wesley showed an inclination towards the Fathers. A review of his readings reveals his study of Johann Ernst Grabes' *Spicilegium Patrum*, William Wake's *Apostolic Epistles and Fathers*, William Reeve's *Apologies of Justin Martyr, Tertullian*, and *Minucius Felix*, and William Cave's *Primitive Christianity*.[16]

Keefer also speculates, that based upon Wesley's later knowledge, he must have read John Jewel's *Apologia Ecclesiae Anglicanae* defending the church against Rome by its appeal to the Bible and the Fathers for support of Anglican doctrine. He seems also to have read Richard Hooker's *Laws of Ecclesiastical Polity* appealing to Scripture and reason in tracing the ecclesiastical order which better represents the values of the early church. Wesley's ability in later years, to refer to a wide range of Early Fathers, indicates an immersion in them during this period.[17]

From these writers, as well as the influence of his tutors mentioned in the last chapter, George Wigan, Henry Sherman, and Jonathan Colley, Wesley learned the three canons of Anglican dogma; Scripture, tradition, and reason. Later Wesley added another arm, that of experience. At this point in his development however, Wesley would be trained that the

---

[14] Luke Keefer, "John Wesley Disciple of Early Christianity," (Ph.D., diss., Temple University, 1982).

[15] Luke Tyerman. *The Life and Times of the Reverend John Wesley. Vol. 1.* (New York, N.Y.: Harper Bros., 1870) 55–56.

[16] V. H. H. Green. *The Young Mr. Wesley.* (New York, N.Y.: St. Martin's Press, 1961) 305–319.

[17] Luke Keefer, "John Wesley Disciple of early Christianity," (Ph.D. diss., Temple University, 1982).

Scripture was supreme, but was open to abuse. Church tradition, which Wesley understood to be an unbroken line from the earliest ages, could provide guidance. Since the Fathers were the closest to the apostolic age, their interpretation of Scripture would be more valid than that of later times. This estimation of the early church would affect his view of biblical interpretation, though we shall see his high regard of the early church would be tempered somewhat during his missionary experience in Georgia.

As noted in chapter one, Wesley became a "man of one book," when he joined the Holy Club. This involved a study of Scripture in the original language. Also, the Holy Club exhibited a strong interest in the early church. According to Wesley, their interest was in "taking the Bible as interpreted by the Primitive Church, and our own, for their whole and sole rule of faith."[18]

The members of the Holy Club felt the commands and examples of the first century Christians applied to the eighteenth century Church as well. Wesley's contemporaries often used the argument "the times have changed," to accommodate the Bible to their lives, rather than their lives to the Bible, as the Holy Club was attempting.[19]

Richard Heitzenrater in his book *Diary of an Oxford Methodist*, comments that the devotional piety practiced in the Holy Club centered around meditation, self-examination, prayer and Bible reading. He further states that these mystical practices were part of a tradition that went back to the Early Fathers of the church.[20]

Wesley was encouraged in his patristic research by John Clayton, a Fellow of Brasenose College, who became a member of the Holy Club in 1732. A friendship was established that would influence Wesley over the next six years. Wesley evidently sought his advice even after he left Oxford for a chaplaincy at the collegiate church in Manchester.

Clayton was a competent patristic scholar who awakened Wesley to a renewed study of the Fathers. It was also Clayton who convinced Wesley and the Holy Club to focus upon primitive ecclesiastical practices, such as observing the Wednesday and Friday stationary fasts of the primitive church. In his *Journal* Wesley records, "The next year (1732), I began ob-

---

[18] Rupert Davies. *The Works of John Wesley. Vol. 9.* (Nashville, Tenn.: Abingdon Press, 1989) 368.

[19] Luke Keefer, "John Wesley Disciple of Early Christianity," (Ph.D. diss., Temple University, 1982).

[20] Richard Heitzenrater. *Diary of an Oxford Methodist.* (Durham, N.C.: Duke University Press, 1985) 18.

serving the Wednesday and Friday fasts, commonly observed in the ancient church, tasting no food till three in the afternoon."[21]

In his sermon "Cause of the Inefficacy of Christianity" (1789), Wesley writes:

> While we were at Oxford the rule of every Methodist was (unless in case of sickness) to fast every Wednesday and Friday in the year, in imitation of the primitive church, for which they had the highest reverence.[22]

The emphasis upon both the ancient church, and the keeping of stations was reinforced during the summer of 1733 when John Clayton introduced Wesley to Dr. John Byron and Dr. Thomas Deacon. Dr. Deacon was one of the non-juring priests, or high churchmen, who refused to take the oath to the government. Deacon was John Clayton's bosom companion and Wesley's chosen councilor.[23]

Deacon enlisted Wesley's service in preparing his *Complete Collection of Devotions, taken from the Apostolical Constitutions, the Ancient Liturgies, and the Common Prayer Book of the Church of England*. When Wesley returned from the visit he was filled with zeal for the ancient church, and for the stations.[24]

An example of Clayton's and Deacon's advice to Wesley, concerning the stations and the primitive church, can be seen in John Clayton's letter to Wesley in 1733:

> Rev. and Dear Sir- I have been thinking upon the two points which you prepared in your last, and must acknowledge myself to be utterly unable to form any judgment upon them which will be serviceable to you.
>
> My own rule is to spend an hour every Friday looking over my diary, and observing the difference between it, and the preceding week; after which, I examine the resolutions set down in the account of my last weekly examination, and inquire how I have kept them, and then see what others are necessary to be formed, which I write down at the end of my diary every week, that so they may be materials for my subsequent examinations.

---

[21] Reginald Wad and Richard Heitzenrater. *The Works of John Wesley. Vol. 18.* (Nashville, Tenn.: Abingdon Press, 1988) 244.

[22] Albert Outler. *The Works of John Wesley. Vol. 4* (Nashville, Tenn.: 1987) 94.

[23] Luke Tyerman, *The Oxford Methodists*. (London, England: Harper and Brothers, 1873) 39.

[24] Frank Baker. *John Wesley and the Church of England*. (London, England: Epworth Press, 1970) 31.

> As to your question about Saturday. I can only answer it by giving an account how I spend it. I do not look upon it as a preparation for Sunday, but as a festival itself; and, therefore, I have continued festival prayer for the three primitive hours, and for morning and evening, from the Apostolic Constitutions, which, I think, I communicated to you whilst at Oxford. I look upon Friday as my preparation for the celebration of both the Sabbath and the Lord's day; the first of which I observe much like a common saint's day, or as one of the inferior holidays of the Church. I bless God, I have generally contrived to have the Eucharist celebrated on Saturdays as well as other holidays, for the use of myself and the sick people whom I visit.
>
> Dr. Deacon offers his humble service to you, and lets you know that the worship and discipline of the primitive Christians have taken up so much of his time that he has never read the Fathers with a particular view of their moral doctrines, and therefore, cannot furnish you with the testimonies you want out of his collection. However, if you will give me a month's time, I will try what I can do for you.[25]

Clayton and Dr. Deacon also interested John and Charles Wesley in the study of the *Apostolic Constitutions* and the *Ecclesiastical Canons* prompting Wesley's interest in primitive liturgies. Wesley's *A Collection of Forms of Prayer for Every Day of the Week*, his earliest publication, resulted from this inspiration.[26]

Georgia

An interesting view of Wesley's dependence on the Church Fathers during his missionary experience can be seen in a quote from August Spangenburg who met Wesley on his arrival:

> Above all he believes that all reference in Scripture of doubtful interpretation must be decided, not by reason, but from the writings of the first three centuries, e.g., infant baptism, foot washing, fast days, celibacy, and many others.[27]

It seems, at this point, that the authority of the Early Church Fathers was almost as important to Wesley as the Scriptures themselves, with rea-

---

[25] Luke Tyerman. *The Oxford Methodists*. (London, England: Harper and Brothers, 1873) 31–33.

[26] Luke Keefer, "John Wesley Disciple of Early Christianity," (Ph.D. diss., Temple University, 1982).

[27] Frank Baker. *John Wesley and the Church of England*. (London, England: Epworth Press, 1970) 43.

son a distant third. It was in Georgia, however, that Wesley's view on the authority of the Church Fathers began to change.

Wesley, while in Georgia, read extensively among the Church Fathers. Luke Keefer in his dissertation entitled "John Wesley, Disciple of Early Christianity," lists the following authors and readings based upon Wesley's *Journal*. Wesley read Church Fathers such as Macarius, Ephraem Syrus, Clement of Rome, Irenaeus, Clement of Alexandria, Polycarp and Cyprian.

Among the collections he read were Clarendon's *Constitutions*, Echard's *Ecclesiastical History*, Claude de Fleury's *Catechism*, *History of the Church*, *Moeurs de Israelites*, and the book which affected him most *Manners of Ancient Christians*. He also read Cave's *Primitive Christianity*, Hickes' *Christian Priesthood*, and Beveridge's *Synodikon*.[28]

Wesley had owned a copy of *Synodikon* since 1731, and had certainly read portions of it earlier than 1734–35, when he probably concentrated on the Apostolic Canons, which occupied the first fifty-seven pages of Vol. I. The text and ancient commentary were presented in parallel columns of Greek and Latin. It was this study which began to convince Wesley he had given too much authority to Christian tradition, in relation to the Bible. I will consider this change of opinion as it relates to Wesley's views on biblical interpretation in chapter nine. To summarize his change of view however, Wesley stated that the *Synodikon* convinced him that the General councils erred, "and that things ordained by them as necessary to salvation have neither strength nor authority unless they be taken out of Holy Scripture."[29]

An Overview of Wesley's Use of the Writings of the Church Fathers

Wesley's special regard for the Apostolic Fathers can be observed in a number of ways. It has already been noted what a voracious reader Wesley was, particularly as it applied to the teachings of the Fathers. V. H. H. Green, in his book *The Young Mr. Wesley* notes:

> Wesley read the writings of the Fathers of the early church in Grabe's *Spicilegium*. He also studied Wake's *Apostolic Epistles and Fathers*, Reeve's *Apologies of Christian Martyrs*, St. Augustine's *Confessions*, Lactantius, Vincent of Lerin's *Commonitorium*, and more recent

---

[28] Luke Keefer, "John Wesley Disciple of Early Christianity," (Ph.D. diss., Temple University, 1982).

[29] Reginald Ward and Richard Heitzenrater. *The Works of John Wesley. Vol.18.* (Nashville, Tenn.: Abingdon Press, 1988) 171.

works on the early church like William Cave's *Primitive Christianity*, and Marshall's *Penitential Discipline of the Primitive Church*.[30]

We've seen how Wesley's reading continued in Georgia, particularly as it related to the impact of reading William Beveridge's *Synodikon*. His interest did not waver after the beginning of the Revival. He continued to study and refer to the early Christian writings. An examination of Wesley's writings after 1737 contains over 150 references to early Christian writings including the following:

Augustine	Basil
Athanasian Creed	Chrysostom
Athenagoras	Clement of Alexandria
Clement of Rome	Ignatius of Antioch
Cyprian	Jerome
Dionysius of Alexandria	Justin Martyr
Ephraem Syrus	Macarius of Egypt
Eusebius	Origen
Polycarp	Tertullian

A complete list can be found in pages 125–34 of Ted Campbell's *John Wesley and Christian Antiquity*.[31]

Another evidence of Wesley's high regard for the Early Church Fathers can be seen by examining his *A Christian Library*. His first volume began with a translation of "Spiritual Homilies," attributed to St. Macarius the Egyptian. The 29th volume published in 1753 included an abridgment of Anthony Horneck's *Happy Ascetic*, and the 31st volume in 1753 included an abridgment of Cave's classic work *Primitive Christianity*.[32]

The preface of *A Christian Library* gives clear insight into how highly Wesley viewed the writings of the Fathers. In the preface he proclaims that he had edited and published:

> such a collection of English divinity, as (I believe), is all true, all agreeable to the Oracles of God; as is all practical, unmixed with controversy of any kind, and all intelligible to plain men; such as

---

[30] V. H. H. Green. *The Young Mr. Wesley.* (New York, N.Y.: St. Martin's Press, 1961) 274.

[31] Ted Campbell. *John Wesley and Christian Antiquity.* (Nashville, Tenn.: Abingdon Press, 1991) 125–34.

[32] Ibid., 45.

is not superficial, but going down to the depth, and describing the height of Christianity; and yet not mystical, not obscure to any of those who are experienced in the ways of God.[33]

Wesley began his Christian library with a:

> 'Preface to the Epistles of the Apostolic Fathers,' in which he presents and commends, the writings of Clement of Rome, Ignatius, and Polycarp as those who delivered 'the pure doctrine of the Gospel; and what Christ and his Apostles taught, and what these holy men had themselves received from their own mouths.' Having 'the advantage of living in the apostolic times, of hearing the holy Apostles and conversing with them,' and having been chosen by them for leadership in the nascent church we 'cannot with any reason doubt what they deliver. but ought to receive it, though not with equal veneration, yet with only little less regard than we do the sacred writings of those who were their masters and instructors' and ' as worthy of a much greater respect than any composers which have been made since.' As 'persons of consummate piety adorned with all those Christian virtues which they so affectionately recommended to us' they were 'in all the necessary parts of it. so assisted by the Holy Ghost, as to be scarce capable of mistaking.'[34]

This quotation shows clearly Wesley's more developed view of the Christian Fathers, having a position of authority nearest the Scripture, but subordinate to Scripture. He believed that the early Christian writers stood closest to the Apostles, and were especially endowed with the Holy Spirit. With this understanding it is easy to see how Wesley would question in his "Address to the Clergy" (1756):

> Can any who spends several years in those seats of learning, be excused, if they do not add to that of the languages and sciences, the knowledge of the Fathers? The most authentic commentators on Scripture, as being both nearest the fountain, and eminently endowed with that Spirit by whom all Scripture was given. It will be easily perceived, I speak chiefly of those who wrote before the Council of Nice. But, who would not likewise desire to have some acquaintance with those that followed them? With St. Chrysostom, Basil, Jerome, Austin, and above all, the man of a broken heart, Ephraeum Syrus?[35]

---

[33] Robert Chiles. *Scriptural Christianity: A Call to John Wesley's Disciples.* (Grand Rapids, Mich.: Francis Asbury Press, 1984) 68.

[34] Ibid., 69.

[35] *Works* 10:484.

Wesley's Writings Compared to Select Writings of the Church Fathers

By referring to the appendix in Ted Campbell's *John Wesley and Christian Antiquity*, we can find a complete list of all the Church Fathers mentioned by Wesley, by name or inference, in his writings. At this point I compare some of Wesley's statements on Scripture, with select quotations from Church Fathers Wesley is known to have read. I do not expect one to one correspondence, but it could be helpful in considering similarity of thought, when searching for underlying influences upon Wesley's view of Scripture.

For the purpose of comparison, I will consider three areas; the inspiration infallibility, and interpretation of Scripture. Under each category I give quotations from the Church Fathers, followed by select quotations from Wesley. Each of these areas will be considered in more detail in later chapters.

The Inspiration of Scripture

Origen from *On First Principles:*

> On this account we must explain to those who believe, that the sacred books are not the works of men, but that they were composed and have come down to us as a result of the inspiration of the Holy Spirit, by the will of the Father of the universe through Jesus Christ.[36]

> On this point the entire church is unanimous, that while the whole law is spiritual, the inspired meaning is not recognized by all, but only by those who are gifted with the grace of the Holy Spirit in the words of wisdom and knowledge.[37]

Wesley from his *Explanatory Notes Upon the New Testament*:

> All Scripture is inspired by God. The Spirit of God not only once inspired those who wrote it, but continually inspires, supernaturally assists those who read it with earnest prayer.[38]

From "A Letter to the Right Reverend the Lord Bishop of Gloucester" (1763):

---

[36] Origen. *Origen on First Principles*. (New York, N.Y.: Harper and Rowe, 1966) 272.
[37] Ibid., 5.
[38] John Wesley. *Explanatory Notes Upon the New Testament*. (London, England: Epworth Press, 1948) 794.

I do firmly believe (and what serious man does not), we need the same Spirit to understand the Scripture which enabled the holy men of old to write it.[39]

Gregory of Nyssa in *Against Eunomius Book VII*:

Thus it is only by the power of the Spirit that holy men were under divine influence and inspired, and every Scripture is for this reason said to be 'given by inspiration of God.'[40]

Wesley in "The Law Established Through Faith II"(1750):

We know that all 'Scripture given by the inspiration of God is profitable' either 'for doctrine' or 'for reproof,' either 'for correction' or 'for instruction in righteousness'; and 'that the man of God,' in the process of the work of God in his soul, has need of every part thereof, that he 'may' at length 'be perfect, thoroughly furnished unto all good works'.[41]

Origen:

Further, if only one ponders over the prophetic sayings with all the attention and reverence they deserve, it is certain that in the very act of reading and diligently studying them his mind and feelings will be touched by a divine breath, and he will recognize that the words he is reading are not the utterances of man, but the language of God.[42]

Wesley in the preface to *The Explanatory Notes Upon the New Testament*:

This is what we now style the Holy Scripture: this is that 'Word of God which remaineth forever': of which, though 'heaven and earth pass away, one jot or tittle shall not pass away.'[43]

Wesley later in the preface quotes Martin Luther saying:

'Divinity is nothing but a grammar of the language of the Holy Ghost'.[44]

---

[39] Gerald Cragg. *The Works of John Wesley. Vol. 11.* (Nashville, Tenn.: Abingdon Press, 1989) 509.
[40] Phillip Schaff and Henry Ware. *A Select Library of Nicene and Post-Nicene Fathers of the Christian Church. Vol. 5.* (Grand Rapids, Mich.: Erdmanns Publishing House, nd) 193.
[41] Albert Outler. *The Works of John Wesley. Vol. 2.* (Nashville, Tenn.: Abingdon Press, 1985) 37.
[42] Origen. *Origen on First Principles.* (New York, N.Y.: Harper and Rowe, 1966) 267.
[43] John Wesley. *Explanatory Notes Upon the New Testament.* (London, England: Epworth Press, 1948) 9.
[44] Ibid., 9.

Augustine:

> It is the Spirit of God who 'speaks through the mouth of the prophets and guides the pen of the Apostles'.[45]

Justin Martyr in *Dialogue with Trypho*:

> There existed long before this time, certain men more ancient than all those who are esteemed philosophers, both righteous and beloved of God, who spoke by the Divine Spirit, and foretold events which would take place, and which are now taking place. They are called prophets. These alone both saw and announced the truth to men, neither reverencing nor fearing any man, not influenced by desire for glory, but speaking those things alone which they saw, and which they heard, being filled with the Holy Spirit. For they did not use demonstrations in their treatises, seeing that they were witnesses to the truth above all demonstrations, and worthy of belief, and those events which have happened, and those which are happening, compel you to assent to the utterances made by them, although indeed, they were entitled to credit an account of the miracles which they performed, since they both glorified the Creator, the God and Father of all things, and proclaimed His son, the Christ (sent) by Him.[46]

Wesley, like Augustine and Justin Martyr, felt that God had spoken through the lips of the prophets. In his sermon "The Witness of Our Own Spirit" he proclaims the Old and New Testaments were, "All which the prophets and the 'holy men of old' wrote 'as they were moved by the Holy Ghost.'"[47]

In *The Explanatory Notes Upon the New Testament* he proclaims:

> 10. Concerning the Scripture in general, it may be observed, the Word of the living God, which directed the first patriarchs also, was in the time of Moses committed to writing. To this were added, in several succeeding generations the inspired writings of the other prophets. Afterwards what the Son of God preached, and the Holy Ghost spake by the apostles, the apostles and evangelists wrote.[48]

---

[45] Eugene Portalie. *A Guide to the Thought of St. Augustine.* (London, England: Burns and Oates, 1960) 122.

[46] Alexander Robert and James Donaldson. *The Ante-Nicene Fathers. Vol. 1.* (Christian Literature Publishing, 1885) 198.

[47] Albert Outler. *The Works of John Wesley. Vol. 1* (Nashville, Tenn.: Abingdon Press, 1984) 303.

[48] John Wesley. *Explanatory Notes Upon the New Testament.* (London, England: Epworth Press, 1948) 8–9.

Wesley also agreed with Justin Martyr that the fulfillment of prophecy was a proof of divine inspiration as he states in his essay "A Clear and Concise Demonstration of the Divine Impartation of the Holy Scripture."[49] As he states in his *Journal* in 1738:

> Are the New Testament prophecies fulfilled? This I next set myself to examine. I read them carefully over, and could not but see every event answered the prediction; so that the more I compared one with another, the more firmly I was convinced that 'all Scripture was given by inspiration of God.'[50]

The Infallibility of Scripture

Irenaeus from his "*Against the Heresies*":

> But if we cannot find the solution of every scriptural difficulty we should not seek another God, for that were gross impiety. All such matters we should leave in the hands of God, who has made us, being duly aware that the Scriptures are perfect having been uttered by the Word of God and His Holy Spirit.[51]

Clement of Rome from the "*Ist Epistle to the Corinthians*":

> Look carefully into the Scripture which are the true utterances of the Holy Spirit. Observe that nothing of an unjust or counterfeit character is written in them.[52]

Augustine:

> It is the Spirit of God who 'speaks through the mouth of the prophets and guides the pens of the Apostles.'
>
> Every absolute statement of Scripture, even those the author conceived without revelation, becomes a true revelation for the reader because it is guaranteed by the Word of God, who inspired it. Therefore, any error in the Bible is impossible. If you think you have come across a false statement it is because either 'the text is incorrect or the interpreter made a mistake, or you did not understand.'[53]

---

[49] *Works* 11:484.

[50] Reginald Ward and Richard Heitzenrater. (Nashville, Tenn.: Abingdon Press, 1988) 273–74.

[51] Alexander Roberts and James Donaldson. *The Ante-Nicene Fathers. Vol. 1.* (The Christian Literature Publishing CO., 1885) 399.

[52] Allen Menzies. *The Ante-Nicene Fathers. Vol. X.* (The Christian Literature Publishing Co., 1886) 242.

[53] Eugene Portalie. *A Guide to the Thought of St. Augustine.* (London, England: Burns and

Wesley in his *Journal* in 1776:

> Nay, If there be any mistakes in the Bible, there may as well be a thousand. If there is one falsehood in that book it did not come from the God of truth.[54]

Interpretation—The Use of Context

Irenaeus from "*Against the Heresies*":

> But they alter the scriptural context and connection, and dismember the truth as much as they can. This whole system in which they make light of the Scripture and wrest them to their purposes has fallen through like an unsubstantiated dream. For, as we have said, they collect words and sayings at haphazard, and give them unnatural and unreal connection.[55]

Wesley, from his sermon "On Corrupting the Word of God" (1727):

> a second method of corrupting it—by mixing it with false interpretations. And this is done, sometimes, by repeating the words wrong; and sometimes by repeating them right, but putting a wrong sense upon them, one that is either strained or unnatural, or foreign to the writers intention in the place from whence they are taken, perhaps contrary either to his intentions in that very place, or to what he says in some other place, or to what he says in some other part of his writings. And this is easily effected; any passage is easily perverted by being recited simply, without any of the preceding or following verses. By this means it may seem to have one sense, when it will be plain by observing what goes before and what follows after that it really has the direct contrary.[56]

Interpreting Scripture by Scripture

Clement of Alexandria from "*The Stromata or Miscellanies*":

> But if it is not enough merely to state the opinion, but if what is stated must be confirmed, we do not wait for the testimony of men, but we establish the matter by the voice of the Lord, which is the surest of all demonstrations or rather is the only demonstration.

Oates, 1960) 122.
[54] *Journals* 6:117.
[55] Hugh Kerr. *Readings in Christian Thought.* (Nashville, Tenn.: Abingdon Press, 1966) 28.
[56] Albert Outler. *The Works of John Wesley.* Vol. 4. (Nashville, Tenn.: Abingdon Press, 1987) 247.

> But the truth is not found by changing the meaning (for so people subvert all true teaching), but in the consideration of what perfectly belongs to and becomes the Sovereign God, and in establishing each of the points demonstrated in the Scripture again from similar Scripture.[57]

Tertullian from "*Against Praxeas*":

> They would have the entire revelation of both Testaments yield to these three passages, whereas the only proper course is to understand the few statements in light of the many.[58]

Wesley from his tract "Popery Calmly Considered":

> And Scripture is the best expounder of Scripture. The best way, therefore, to understand it, is carefully to compare Scripture to Scripture, and learn thereby the true meaning of it.[59]

Interpreting Scripture Literally

Origen from "*Origen on First Principles*":

> Accordingly he who reads in an exact manner must, in obedience to the Saviour's precept which says, 'Search the Scripture,' carefully investigate how the literal meaning is true and how far it is impossible, and to the utmost of his power must trace out from the use of similar expressions, the meaning scattered everywhere through Scripture of that which when taken literally is impossible.[60]

Wesley from *A Plain Account of Christian Perfection*:

> Try all things by the written word and let all bow down before it. You are in danger of enthusiasm every hour, if you depart ever so little from Scripture, yea, or from the plain, literal meaning of any text, taken in connection with the context.[61]

In comparing the writings of these Church fathers with Wesley on select topics concerning Scripture, it is not my intention to maintain that Wesley copied directly. However, since Wesley states in his writings that

---

[57] Alexander Roberts and James Donaldson. *The Ante-Nicene Fathers. Vol. 2* (The Christian Literature Publishing Co., 1885) 552.
[58] Ibid., 3:615.
[59] *Works* 10:142.
[60] Origen. *Origen on First Principles*. (New York, N.Y.: Harper and Rowe, 1966) 296.
[61] John Wesley. *A Plain Account of Christian Perfection*. (Kansas City, Mo.: Beacon Hill Press, 1971) 97.

he had read from these Fathers, it is interesting to note the similarity in thought and expression. It would be foolhardy to ignore the possible impact the reading of the Early Church Fathers had upon the development of Wesley's thoughts.

Conclusion

As has been noted, Wesley's concern for the early church spanned almost his entire life, from his days at Oxford until his last days. Wesley had a great desire to recover "Primitive Christianity." During his days at Oxford he earned the nickname "Mr. Primitive Christianity."[62] Wesley shared the classical Anglican tradition of the restitution of early Christianity, not as an institution or an organization, but as a personal experience. He searched for patterns, beliefs, even virtues which he wished to see restored to the Christianity of his age. He also used Christian antiquity in an apologetic manner to defend what he perceived as correct beliefs and practices in the church. For example, Wesley founded the Methodist Societies for the very practical reason of helping individuals follow divine grace, but the fact that it conformed to the pattern of the ancient church, Wesley felt was a sign of its rightness.[63] In "A Plain Account of the People Called Methodists" (1749) he remarks upon founding a "society." "Upon reflection I could not but observe, this is the very thing which was from the beginning of Christianity."[64]

Wesley also appealed to Christian antiquity to validate practices he felt agreed with Scripture, but were not prescribed by Scripture. For example, in a letter to John Clark in 1756 he remarks concerning the concept of the Episcopal form of government :

> As to my judgment, I still believe 'the Episcopal form of Church government to be both scriptural and apostolical:' I mean, well agreeing with the practice and writings of the Apostles. But that it is prescribed in Scripture I do not believe.[65]

Finally, and most importantly, Wesley ascribed special authority to the Church Fathers as interpreters of Scripture. For Wesley, the Bible was the supreme authority. However, there were times Scripture needed interpre-

---

[62] Frank Baker. *John Wesley and the Church of England*. (London, England: Epworth Press, 1970) 34.

[63] Ted Campbell. *John Wesley and Christian Antiquity*. (Nashville, Tenn.: Kingswood Books, 1991) 111.

[64] Rupert Davies. *The Works of John Wesley. Vol. 9*. (Nashville, Tenn.: Abingdon Press, 1989) 258.

[65] *Letters* 3:182.

tation. In chapters 8 and 9, it will be seen that Wesley used a number of secondary sources, such as reason and experience in interpreting the Bible. However, when considering Wesley's interpretive principles, one must not ignore the role of tradition. The time came, during his missionary stay in Georgia, when Wesley recognized that the Early Church Fathers were men subject to error. Then he would warn against putting too much emphasis upon church tradition, and would warn that Christian antiquity was only a subordinate authority to Scripture. Wesley would state to William Dodd in 1756, "But I try every church and doctrine by the Bible."[66]

Still, it was never easy for Wesley to depart from established church tradition, especially if it was grounded in antiquity. He continued to give great weight to the Early Fathers in interpreting Scripture. For example, in writing to John Smith in 1746 Wesley makes the comment concerning the "testimony of the Spirit":

> . . . and then let me know what kind of proof it is which you expect in a question of this nature over and above that of Scripture, as interpreted by the writers of the earliest Christian Church.[67]

I believe Luke Keefer catches the heart of Wesley's thought on this matter when he states that for Wesley anything novel in religion was not true. Christianity was forever the same. The best interpretation of difficult passages of Scripture was to be found by studying the Early Church Fathers, who were taught by the Apostles, who in turn were taught by Christ. Wesley held to the primitive sense of Scripture not to the rationalistic reinterpretation of his age.[68]

To close this section, I will quote from Wesley's letter to Dr. Conyers Middleton in 1749. Middleton had written his "Free Inquiry," in which he spoke very disparagingly of the Primitive Fathers. In fact, according to Wesley, Middleton considered that "all the primitive Fathers were fools or knaves, and most of them one and the other."[69] Wesley's long response gives an overview of his reverence for the Primitive Fathers. In his conclusion he states:

> 11. All this may be allowed concerning the primitive Fathers; I mean particularly Clemens Romanus, Ignatius, Polycarp, Justin Martyr, Irenaeus, Origen, Clemens Alexandrius, Cyprian; to whom I would

---

[66] Ibid., 3:172
[67] Frank Baker. *The Works of John Wesley.* Vol. 26. (Nashville, Tenn.: Abingdon Press, 1982) 203.
[68] Luke Keefer, "John Wesley Disciple of Early Christianity," (Ph.D. diss., Temple University, 1982).
[69] *Works* 10:1.

add Macarius and Ephraem Syrus. I allow that some of these had not strong natural sense, that few of them had much learning, and none the assistance which our age enjoys in some respects above all that went before.

Hence I doubt not but whoever will be at the pains of reading over their writings for that poor end, will find many mistakes, many weak suppositions, and many ill-drawn conclusions.

12. And yet I exceedingly reverence them, as well as their writings, and esteem them very highly in love. I reverence them, because they were Christians, such Christians as are above described. And I reverence their writings, because they describe true, genuine Christianity, and direct us to the strongest evidence of the Christian doctrine.[70]

The Influence of the Missionary Trip to Georgia

During Wesley's trip to Georgia and subsequent missionary work there was a continuation of his high view of scriptural authority, particularly in his preaching, and the continued discipline of his individual and corporate Bible study. Though Wesley may have considered his missionary endeavour a failure, for our purpose we see the continued development of his scriptural views. His emphasis on the preaching of Scripture is clear in his description of his motivation for going to Georgia in a letter to Dr. Burton in 1735:

> My chief motive to which all the rest are subordinate is the hope of saving my own soul. I hope to learn the true sense of the gospel of Christ by preaching it to the heathen. They have no comments to construe away the text, no vain philosophy to corrupt it, no luxurious, sensual, covetous ambitious expounders to soften its unpleasing truths, to reconcile earthly mindedness and faith, the Spirit of Christ and the spirit of the World.[71]

He continues in the letter to Dr. Burton to show his confidence in the Word of God, "Why, that if you add the loss of life to the rest, so much the greater is the gain. For though the grass withereth, and the flower fadeth, the Word of God shall stand forever."[72]

---

[70] *Works* 10:79.

[71] *Journals* 8:288.

[72] Ibid., 289.

The Formation of Wesley's Views on Scripture: Part 2

On the journey to Georgia Wesley and his companions continued the disciplined regimen of Bible study developed in the Holy Club. In his *Journal* describing the journey Wesley states:

> We now began to be a little regular. Our common way of living was thus: from four in the morning till five, each of us used private prayer. From five to seven we read the Bible together, carefully comparing it (that we might not lean to our own understanding) with the writings of the earliest ages.[73]

One of Wesley's fellow travelers, Benjamin Ingham, wrote his mother describing how he and Wesley read nine to ten chapters of the Old Testament a day completing it before arrival in Georgia.[74] He also states in his letter :

> He (Wesley), held no principles but what he believed to be revealed in the Word of God: and in the interpretation of the Word he always judged the most literal sense, unless when the literal sense of one Scripture contradicted some other.[75]

Wesley describes his method of preaching in his *Journal* on April 11, 1736.

Here once again we see the priority the Scripture held in his life and ministry, even at this point in his spiritual development which might be considered prior to his own conversion at Aldersgate:

> I preached at the new storehouse (Frederica), on the first verse of the Gospel for the day, 'Which of you convinceth me of sin? And if I say the truth, why do you not believe me?' There was a large congregation, whom I endeavored to convince of unbelief, by simply proposing the conditions of salvation as they are laid down in Scripture and appealing to their own hearts whether they believed they could be saved on no other terms.[76]

This is probably a fair description of Wesley's preaching in America. Wesley could assume, with an ease impossible today, that he and his congregation shared a common belief in the final and supreme authority of all

---

[73] Reginald Ward and Richard Heitzenrater. *The Works of John Wesley. Vol. 18.* (Nashville, Tenn.: Abingdon Press, 1988) 138.

[74] William Arnett, "John Wesley—A Man of One Book," (Ph.D. diss., Drew University, 1954).

[75] Luke Tyerman. *The Life and Times of the Reverend John Wesley. Vol. 1..* (New York, N.Y.: Harper Bros., 1870) 176.

[76] Reginald Ward and Richard Heitzenrater. *The Works of John Wesley. Vol. 18.* (Nashville, Tenn.: Abingdon Press, 1988) 156.

Scripture. Therefore, after selecting a text he could expound that text and challenge them to an instant personal decision.[77] Wesley states in a letter to Mary Chapman in 1737:

> I feed my brethren in Christ, as he giveth me power, with the pure unmixed milk of His Word. And those who are as little children receive it, not as the word of man, but as the Word of God.[78]

As was mentioned in the last section another important development in Wesley's view of Scripture, was the decision he had gone too far in ascribing the writing of the Church fathers a level equal to Scripture. At this point let me merely point out that Wesley stated on his homeward voyage from Georgia that he had made the mistake of "Making antiquity a co-ordinate (rather than a subordinate) rule with Scripture."[79]

The Mystic Influence

As we consider the biblical and spiritual development of John Wesley, we discover the influence of the mystical writers and movements intertwined throughout Wesley's developmental views of Scripture and his Aldersgate experience. It is difficult to discuss these influences in a neat chronological framework. In looking closely at these influences I find them blanketing his Oxford, missionary and Aldersgate experiences and reaching beyond them into the future. Both Wesley's biblical and spiritual development were greatly influenced by encounters with writers such as William Law and Jeremy Taylor, movements such as the Moravians, and individuals such as Peter Boehler.

In considering John Wesley's Oxford experience it seems certain the importance of the Bible was reinforced by the reading of Jeremy Taylor's, *The Rules and Exercises of Holy Living*. Taylor repeatedly returned for his fundamental authority to the Word of God which he confined to the Bible.[80] Martin Schmidt states, "It was certainly significant for John Wesley's development that in this book he was so strongly directed to the Bible."[81]

---

[77] W. C. Dougherty. *John Wesley the Preacher*. (London, England: Epworth Press, 1955) 14.

[78] Frank Baker. *The Works of John Wesley. Vol. 25*. (Oxford, England: Oxford University Press, 1980) 504.

[79] Reginald Ward and Richard Heitzenrater. *The Works of John Wesley. Vol. 18*. (Nashville, Tenn. Abingdon Press, 1988) 212–13.

[80] Allen Coppedge. *John Wesley in Theological Debate*. (Wilmore, Ky.: Wesley Heritage Press, 1987) 28.

[81] Martin Schmidt. *John Wesley a Theological Biography. Vol. 2 Part 2*. (Nashville, Tenn.: Abingdon Press, 1972) 76–77.

In the Moravians Wesley found a group of people who wished to attain to New Testament standards of religious piety and inward experience. Wesley's encounter with Peter Bohler was important, not only in helping him to obtain his own "heart warming experience," but in laying the groundwork for the fourth leg of the Quadrilateral; experience. In his dealing with Bohler, Wesley was pointed once and again to Scripture to discover whether instantaneous conversion experience was valid. In his *Journal* in 1738 Wesley records:

> The next morning I began the Greek Testament again, resolving to abide by the 'law and the testimony,' and being confident that God would hereby show me(whether) this 'doctrine was of God.'[82]

Again describing this same period Wesley state:

> But I could not comprehend what he spoke of an 'instantaneous' work. I could not understand how this faith should be given in a moment; how a man could at once be thus turned from darkness to light, from sin and misery to righteousness, and joy in the Holy Ghost. I searched the Scriptures again touching this very thing, particularly the Acts of the Apostles: but to my utter astonishment found scarce any instance there of other than instantaneous conversions-scarce any other so slow as that of St. Paul, who was three days in the pangs of the new birth.[83]

Thus we see, from the Moravians Wesley learned to make the New Testament not simply the standard for external conduct or a formula for religion, but a standard for experiential religion of the inner life.[84]

Interestingly enough Wesley would later break with the mystics over the very issue of Scripture. Wesley felt the mystics placed experience above the Scriptures. In 1741 John warned his brother Charles against this practice, "As yet I dare in no wise join with the Moravians: (1), because their whole scheme is mystical, not scriptural, refined in every point above what is written."[85]

Later in a letter to Thomas Hartley in 1764 he writes:

> Yet at the same time I cannot but bewail your vehement attachment to the Mystic writers; with whom I conversed much for sev-

---

[82] Reginald Ward and Richard Heitzenrater. *The Works of John Wesley. Vol. 18.* (Nashville, Tenn.: Abingdon Press, 1988) 232.

[83] Ibid., 234.

[84] William Pellowe, "John Wesley's Use of the Bible," *Methodist Review 106* (1923) 358.

[85] Frank Baker. *The Works of John Wesley. Vol. 26.* (Nashville, Tenn.: Abingdon Press, 1982) 56.

eral years, and whom I then admired perhaps more than you do now. But I found at length an absolute necessity of giving up either them or the Bible.[86]

Finally note one last example in a letter from John Wesley to the Editor of the London Chronicle in 1760:

> It is true that Mr. Law, whom I love and reverence now, was once 'a kind of oracle' to me. He thinks I am still 'under the power' of my 'own spirit' as opposed to the Spirit of God. If I am, yet my censure of the Mystics is not at all owing to this, but to my reverence for the oracles of God, which, while I was fond of them, I regarded less and less; till at length, finding I could not follow both, I exchanged the Mystic writer for the scriptural.[87]

These last two quotes show quite clearly the early influence of the Mystics upon Wesley's views, and his later break with the writers and movements.

The Influence of Aldersgate

> In the evening I went very unwillingly to a society in Aldersgate Street, where one was reading Luther's *Preface to the Epistle to the Romans*. About a quarter before nine, while he was describing the change which God works in the heart through faith in Christ, I felt my heart strangely warmed. I felt I did trust in Christ, Christ alone, for salvation; and an assurance was given me, that he had taken away my sins, even mine, and saved me from the law of sin and death.[88]

Was Wesley converted at Aldersgate? Many have debated that point, and the answer may well depend upon one's definition of conversion. My intent is not to answer the question of Wesley's "conversion," but instead concentrate upon the effect his "heart warming experience," had upon his views and use of the Bible. However, I would be remiss if I did not point out, regardless of one's definition of conversion, clearly something dramatic happened to Wesley in 1738. Prior to Aldersgate, Wesley felt he was not a Christian, in the New Testament sense of the word. On January 8, 1738, on his way back from Georgia, Wesley recorded this critical self-analysis:

---

[86] *Letters* 4:234.
[87] Ibid., 4:106.
[88] Reginald Ward and Richard Heitzenrater. *The Works of John Wesley. Vol. 18.* (Nashville, Tenn.: Abingdon Press, 1988) 249–50.

By the most infallible of proofs, inward feeling, I am convinced,

1. Of unbelief, having no such faith in Christ as will prevent my heart from being troubled, which it could not be, if I believed in God, and rightly believed also in Him (i.e. Christ).

2. Of pride, throughout my life past, inasmuch as I thought I had what I find I have not.

3. In gross irrecollection, inasmuch as in a storm I cry to God every moment; in a calm, not.

4. Of levity and luxuriancy of spirit, recurring whenever the pressure is taken off, and appearing by my speaking words not tending to edify; but most, by my manner of speaking of my enemies.

'Lord, save, or I perish!' Save me,

1. By such a faith as implies peace in life and death;

2. By such humility as may fill my heart from this hour forever, with a piercing uninterrupted sense, *Nihil est quod hactenus feci*, having evidently built without foundation.

3. By such a recollection as may cry to thee every moment, especially when all is calm, Give me faith or I die; give me a lowly spirit; otherwise *Mihi non sit suave vivere*.

4. By steadiness seriousness, sobriety of spirit, avoiding as fire every word that tendeth not to edifying, and never speaking of any who oppose me or sin against God, without all my own sins in array before my face.[89]

Upon arrival in England he states:

> I went to America to convert the Indians; but Oh! Who shall convert me?
> Who, what is he that will deliver me from this evil heart of unbelief? I have a fair summer religion. I can talk well; nay, and believe myself, while no danger is near: but let death look me in the face, and my spirit is troubled. Nor can I say, 'To die is gain!'[90]

According to his own words, he went reluctantly to the meeting at Aldersgate, and heard the reading of Martin Luther's *Preface to the Epistle to*

---

[89] Ibid., 208–09.
[90] Ibid., 211.

the Romans. It is not known what portion of the Preface so affected Wesley. An examination of the Preface shows it is not just an introduction to the book but a summary of the whole meaning of the gospel message. Luther writes

> Faith alone justifies us and fulfills the law, and this because faith brings in the spirit gained by the merits of Christ. The spirit in turn gives us the happiness and freedom at which the law aims; and this shows that good works really proceed from faith.[91]

William Jones suggests, in the introduction to Luther's Preface, that Wesley, "Must have felt that Luther was speaking directly to his spiritual condition."[92]

This seems like a clear possibility when we hear Luther state:

> To outward appearance, you observe the law scrupulously, condemning those who do not observe it, and being quick to teach one and all. Granted that in appearance and conduct, you observe the law, owing to your fear of punishment or hope of reward, yet you do nothing from free choice and out of love for the law, but unwillingly under compulsion; were there no law you would rather do something else.[93]

Wesley may have felt Luther wrote those words just to describe him. At any rate, at some point in the reading he felt his heart "strangely warmed," and from this point on he was a changed man. Elmer Clark in his book *What Happened at Aldersgate* suggests that after Aldersgate Wesley had a new message and preached with new power. If Wesley's heart had not been "strangely warmed" we might never have heard of him. Wesley was thirty-five, in his thirteenth year of ministry, and had done nothing to separate himself from other churchmen. Without Aldersgate there would have been no revival or Methodism, at least at this time.[94]

This is not to say his previous years of training at home, Oxford, or in Georgia, meant little in making Wesley the man he was. In fact, Wesley's actual beliefs were probably little different after Aldersgate, than they were before. As mentioned earlier in this chapter, Wesley's views on Scripture had gone through a lengthy incubation prior to May, 1738. I believe Wesley's

---

[91] Martin Luther. *Martin Luther's Preface to the Epistle of St. Paul to the Romans.* (Nashville, Tenn.: Methodist Evangelistic Materials, 1962) 5.

[92] Ibid., 1.

[93] Ibid., 4.

[94] Elmer Clark. *What Happened at Aldersgate?* (Nashville, Tenn.: Methodist Publishing House, 1938) 39.

views on the inspiration and authority of Scripture were already firmly established prior to that dramatic night at Aldersgate. Wesley from his youth had been a diligent student of the Bible. For years he had mentally agreed to the truth of the gospel. But these truths had never really gripped him, or came to the place where they dominated his life. With Aldersgate Wesley became dominated by a new passion, a desire to bring souls to a saving knowledge of Jesus Christ.[95] Wesley and his followers became convinced that "by grace we are saved by faith" and that "justification by faith was the doctrine of the church as well as the Bible."[96] It is significant that 18 days after Wesley's experience at Aldersgate, he preached at Oxford his famous sermon, "Salvation By Faith," on June 11, 1738. Tyerman observes it is from this point in his life that Wesley's chief aim, virtually his only aim, was to explain the plan of scriptural salvation to the people. Most of his sermon texts have an immediate bearing on this subject.[97]

Wesley had been a great student of the Bible, but he discovered the Bible was not an end in itself. It was God's Word for man's guidance, spiritual nurture, encouragement, discipline in Christ and final salvation. It was God's grand instrument to show people how to live here and how to get to heaven in the world to come. Wesley's primary concern in interpreting the Bible was to lift up the doctrine of salvation.[98]

From this point on in Wesley's life it is difficult to separate his views and use of the Bible from his passion for souls, for it is in evangelism that the Bible asserted its supremacy as never before.[99] Wesley was bound to follow the Bible, and it was the Bible that commanded him to preach the gospel, even if it involved invading another man's parish. A quotation from a letter on this issue originally thought written to James Hervey, but more likely written to John Clayton, summarizes well how interconnected were Wesley's views on biblical authority and his passion to preach:

> Permit me to speak plainly. If by catholic principles you mean any other than scriptural, they weigh nothing with me. I allow no other rule, whether of faith or practice, than the Holy Scriptures. But on scriptural principles I do not think it hard to justify whatever I do. God in Scripture commands me, according to my power, to in-

---

[95] William Arnett, "John Wesley-A Man of One Book." (Ph.D. diss., Drew University, 1954).

[96] *Works* 8:349.

[97] Luke Tyerman. *The Life and Times of the Reverend John Wesley. Vol. 1* (New York, N.Y.: 1870) 234.

[98] Mack Stokes. *The Bible in the Wesleyan Heritage.* (Nashville, Tenn.: Abingdon Press, 1979) 11.

[99] William Arnett, "John Wesley–A Man of One Book," (Ph.D. diss., Drew University, 1954).

struct the ignorant, reform the wicked, confirm the virtuous. Man forbids me to do this in another's parish; that is in effect to do it at all; seeing I have no parish of my own, nor probably ever shall. Whom then shall I hear? God or man? If it be just to obey man rather than God, judge you. A dispensation of the gospel is committed to me, and woe to me if I preach not the gospel. But where shall I preach it upon the principles you mention?[100]

Wesley, of course, preached before Aldersgate and certainly it was his desire to center his message on the Bible. This connection was always obvious and present. With Aldersgate however, we see a flame being lit that would rage into the blaze of the Wesleyan Revival and result in over 42,000 sermons. We cannot say for certain, that without Aldersgate Wesley would not have developed into the prolific Bible preacher he became. The facts, however, speak for themselves. Wesley before Aldersgate produced no revival, while Wesley after Aldersgate did. We must recognize that Aldersgate changed John Wesley, and this change was not only in his personal spiritual experience. The Aldersgate experience became a driving force that greatly influenced both Wesley's message and method directly influencing his use of the Holy Scriptures.

---

[100] Frank Baker. *The Works of John Wesley.* Vol. 25. (Oxford, England: Oxford University Press, 1980) 615.

3

John Wesley's View on Scriptural Authority

Part 1

As we move beyond the development of Wesley's views of the Scripture to the consideration of the manner in which he studied and used the Bible in his life and ministry, there is one important area which must first be explored. The question must be asked, to what extent did John Wesley consider the Bible to be the ultimate source and authority of his preaching and teaching? Wesley would rejoice to depict himself as "a man of one Book,"[1] but what exactly did Wesley mean by this statement? We know for example, that Wesley also emphasized experience, tradition, and reason in the Wesleyan Quadrilateral. Where exactly did the Scripture fit into this equation? Wesley certainly had faith in the Scripture, but did he consider the Bible the underlying foundation of all faith and doctrine?

Before attempting to answer these questions, I will outline my approach over the next two chapters. In this chapter I will begin by making some overall comments on Wesley's views, buttressed with his own comments. Next, I will consider the ways in which Wesley's view of Scripture reflected or differed from those of the Reformers, most specifically Martin Luther and John Calvin.

In chapter four, I will continue the investigation by comparing Wesley's views with those of other eighteenth century Protestant groups. I will touch briefly once again upon his roots in Anglicanism, but I will also make brief comparisons with both the Quakers and the Puritans.

In perhaps the most important portion of chapter four, I will once again allow John Wesley to speak for himself describing not only his faith

---

[1] *Letters* 4:299.

in the Bible and his willingness to be known as a "Bible Bigot"[2] but also his desire for the Methodist movement to be built on this same foundation. I also wish to stress the extent to which Wesley considered the Bible the ultimate authority, by indicating how he held the Bible to be the source of all doctrine and the standard of all judgment.

Finally, I wish to mention the reasons why Wesley had such a strong view of the authority and the importance of the Scriptures. These views can be summarized by noting that they were from God, and that they had a salvific purpose.

A Summary of Wesley's View on Scriptural Authority

It is safe to say, based on Wesley's own comments, that Wesley viewed the Bible as the ultimate authority in matters of faith and practice. To Wesley, the Scriptures were always first. The Bible was not simply the first of books to him; it was in a category all to itself and its authority was decisive. Wesley offered no teaching until he had convinced himself that its foundation was well set in the Book of God.[3] To Wesley, there was only one source of authority, one way to know the will of God, and God had written it in a Book. In the preface to his *Sermons on Several Occasions* (1746) Wesley explains:

> 5. To candid, reasonable men I am not afraid to lay open what have been the inmost thoughts of my heart. I have thought, I am a creature of a day, passing through life as an arrow through the air. I am a spirit come from God, and returning to God; just hovering over the great gulf, till a few moments hence I am no more seen—I drop into unchangeable eternity! I want to know one thing; the way to heaven—how to land safely on that happy shore. God himself condescended to teach the way: for this very end He came from heaven. He hath written it down in a book. Oh, give me that book! At any price give me the Book of God. I have it. Here is knowledge enough for me. Let me be—*homo unius libri*.[4]

Wesley in his sermon "On God's Vineyard" (1787) makes it clear that from the very beginning of the Holy Club, there was only one standard of judgment and one rule of faith, the Word of God:

---

[2] Reginald Ward and Richard Heitzenrater. *The Works of John Wesley. Vol. 22.* (Nashville, Tenn.: Abingdon Press, 1993) 42.

[3] W. E. Sangster. *The Path to Perfection.* (Nashville, Tenn.: Abingdon Press, 1943) 33.

[4] Albert Outler. *The Works of John Wesley. Vol. 1.* (Nashville, Tenn.: Abingdon Press, 1984) 105.

> From the very beginning, from the time four young men united together, each of them was *homo unius libri*- a man of one Book. God taught them all to make His Word 'a lantern unto their feet, and a light in all their paths' (Ps. 119:105). They had one, and only one rule of judgment with regard to all their tempers, words, and actions, namely the oracles of God. They were one and all determined to be 'Bible Christians.' They were continually reproached for this very thing, some terming them in derision 'Bible Bigots,' others 'Bible Moths'—feeding they said upon the Bible as moths do upon cloth. And indeed unto this day it is their constant endeavour to think and speak as the Oracles of God.[5]

When Wesley was challenged for authority on any question, his first appeal was to the Holy Bible, always in the sense of Article VI of the Thirty-Nine Articles of the Anglican Church. This does not mean that Wesley was not aware that Scripture alone may not always settle every controversial point. Wesley would appeal to the primitive church and to Christian tradition as a complementary witness to the Scripture. He also insisted on the use of reason, yet did not ignore the importance of Christian experience. As I will show in chapter nine Wesley believed in a four-fold theological method, the Wesleyan Quadrilateral, that profited from the wisdom of tradition, accepted the discipline of critical reason, and stressed Christian experience, and yet Scripture was always pre-eminent. Scripture was always the primary source, with other forces merely dynamic interactive aids to interpreting Scripture.[6] I will consider how all these forces inter-relate in a later chapter. Suffice it to say, that for Wesley neither the united testimony of the ancient church fathers and reformers, nor critical reason, nor religious experience, was sufficient to prove or disprove any doctrine not found in Scripture. Wesley's unequivocal stance will become much clearer as we progress through this chapter. At this point let me quote from Wesley's "A Roman Catechism With a Reply Thereto":

> For as all faith is founded upon divine authority, so there is now no divine authority but the Scriptures; and therefore no one can make that to be of divine authority which is not contained in them.[7]

In a letter which Telford believes Wesley wrote to Thomas Whitehead in 1748, Wesley explains the differences between Christianity and

---
[5] Albert Outler. *The Works of John Wesley. Vol. 3.* (Nashville, Tenn.: Abingdon Press, 1986) 504.
[6] Albert Outler, "The Wesleyan Quadrilateral in Wesley," *Wesleyan Theological Journal Vol. 20.* (1985) 17–18.
[7] *Works* 10:91.

Quakerism by considering statements from Robert Barclay. Both Wesley and Barclay believed that knowledge of God was revealed by the Spirit. However, Barclay felt:

> 'Yet these revelations are not to be subjected to the examination of the Scripture as to a touchstone.' Here there is a difference. The Scriptures are the touchstone whereby Christians may examine all, real and supposed, revelations. In all cases they appeal to the law and the testimony, and try every spirit thereby.[8]

As we see, Wesley was content to base all of his convictions and faith upon the Bible. If anyone could show what he taught, preached or believed was contrary to revelation, he was quite prepared to change. Again, from the preface to his *Sermons*:

> But I trust wherein soever I have mistaken, my mind is open to conviction. I sincerely desire to be better informed. I say to God and man, 'What I know not, teach thou me.' Are you persuaded you see more clearly than me? It is not unlikely that you may. Then treat me as you would desire to be treated upon a change of circumstances. Point me out a better way, than I have yet known. Show me it is so by the plain proof of Scripture.[9]

In summary, Wesley continually expressed the Bible to be the only standard of truth and the only model of pure religion. He went out of his way to emphasize that the basis of his work from beginning to end was the Word of God.[10] The Bible was the pervasive influence upon Wesley's preaching, teaching, letters and *Journal*, as I will show in chapter five. The Bible was the determining factor in his own religious concerns. Quite consistently Wesley quoted the Bible as the source of his convictions and nothing apart from it.[11] Most importantly, Wesley believed that all doctrine and truth was ultimately based upon the Word of God. In his sermon "The Witness of Our Own Spirit" (1746) he states:

> But the Christian rule of right and wrong is the Word of God, the writings of the Old and New Testament: all which the prophets and 'holy men of old' wrote as 'they were moved by the Holy Ghost;' 'all' that 'Scripture' was 'given by inspiration of God,' which is in-

---

[8] *Letters* 2:117.

[9] Albert Outler. *The Works of John Wesley. Vol. 1.* (Nashville, Tenn.: Abingdon Press, 1984) 107.

[10] A. Skevington Wood. *The Burning Heart.* (Grand Rapids, Mich.: Wm. B. Eerdmann's Pub. Co., 1967) 210.

[11] Martin Schmidt. *John Wesley a Theological Biography. Vol. 2. Part.1.* (Nashville, Tenn.: Abingdon Press, 1972) 183.

deed 'profitable for doctrine,' or teaching the whole will of God;' 'for reproof' of what is contrary thereto, 'for correction' of error; for 'instruction (or training us up) in righteousness,' II Timothy 3:16.[12]

All of these affirmations of Wesley's strong views on the authority of Scripture will be further amplified later in chapter five. There, I will once again quote from Wesley's own words concerning his faith in Scripture, and the ultimate authority of the Bible as the fountain of all truth and doctrine and the ultimate standard of judgment.

Wesley's View of Scripture and the Reformers

Concerning his views on *"sola fide"* Wesley was one with the Reformers and was in the middle of the road within the broad stream of Protestants.[13] Colin Williams in his book *John Wesley's Theology Today*, concludes that Wesley was one with the Reformers in his principle of Sola Scriptura, in that Scripture is the final authority in matters of faith and practice, not that tradition and experience had no value, but in these further sources of insight must be congruous with the revelation recorded in Scripture.[14]

At this point let us go beyond generalizations to specifics, and consider how closely Wesley's views resembled those of the great Reformers, Martin Luther and John Calvin.

Wesley and Luther

When considering the Reformers it should be recognized that they differed from Aquinas and most of the ancient exegetes in their insistence on the right of the text, as literally interpreted, to stand alone. Robert Grant in his book, *A Short History of Interpretation*, states:

> Scripture for the Reformers is not one of several pillars which uphold the house of faith: it is the sole foundation. The Church was not the arbiter of the meaning of Scripture, for Scripture, the Word of God, was the Church's judge.[15]

---

[12] Albert Outler. *The Works of John Wesley. Vol. 1.* (Nashville, Tenn.: Abingdon Press, 1984) 302–03.

[13] George Allen Turner. *Inspiration and Interpretation.* (Grand Rapids, Mich.: Wm B. Eerdmann's Pub. Co., 1957) 157–58.

[14] Colin Williams. *John Wesley's Theology Today.* (Nashville, Tenn.: Abingdon Press, 1960) 157–58.

[15] Robert Grant. *A Short History of the Interpretation of the Bible.* (New York, N.Y.: MacMillan Company, 1972) 129.

The Reformers insisted on a literal, grammatical, historical understanding of the Bible, recognizing the necessity of the guidance of the Spirit. Luther's views certainly fall within the parameters thus far discussed. His famous announcement at Worms underlines his view of the authority of Scripture:

> Unless I am convinced by testimony of Scripture or by clear reason (for I do not trust either the Pope or in councils alone, since it is well known that they have often erred and contradicted themselves)—I am bound by the Scripture I have quoted, and my conscience is captive to the Word of God. I cannot and will not retract anything, since it is neither safe, nor right, to go against conscience.[16]

Luther believed in the grammatical and historical interpretation of Scripture, not as an end in itself, but instead as a means to focus on Christ; "Christ is the point in the circle from which the whole circle is drawn."[17]

Luther also introduced the subjective element of experience into interpretation, "Experience is necessary for the understanding of the Word. It is not merely to be repeated as known, but to be lived and felt."[18]

At the same time, Luther recognized that experience was not enough for the accurate interpretation of Scripture. It is also essential that the Holy Spirit brings illumination to the mind of the exegete; "God must say to you in your heart, this is God's Word."[19]

Already we can see a similarity between some of Luther's and Wesley's views. At this point I will look more closely at some of the critical issues such as the inspiration and authority of Scripture, infallibility, and the interpretation of Scripture, including the use of reason and church tradition. I wish to discover if I can agree with Archbishop Soederblom's assessment that Wesley might be called "the Anglican version of Luther."[20]

Inspiration and Authority

When considering Luther's and Wesley's views upon the inspiration and authority of Scripture, one finds some striking similarities, but also at least one striking difference. First, let us consider some of the similarities.

---

[16] *Luther* 32:112.

[17] Robert Grant. *A Short History of the Interpretation of the Bible.* (New York, N.Y.: MacMillan Company, 1972) 131.

[18] Ibid., 132.

[19] Ibid., 132.

[20] Franz Hildebrandt. *From Luther to Wesley.* (London, England: Lutterworth Pub., 1951) 15.

Both Luther and Wesley believed in the divine inspiration of Scripture, and it was from this inspiration that Scripture derived its authority. The following quotations from both Luther and Wesley clearly show this confidence.

Luther:

> The Scriptures, although they also were written by men, are not of men, nor from men, but from God.[21]

Wesley commenting on II Timothy 3:16 in his *Explanatory Notes Upon the New Testament:*

> All Scripture is inspired by God. The Spirit not only once inspired those who wrote it, but continually inspires, supernaturally assists those who read it with earnest prayer.[22]

Luther in his *Lectures on the Psalms*:

> To hear or read the Scripture is nothing else than to hear God. It cannot be otherwise, for Scriptures are divine. In them God speaks and they are His Words.[23]

Wesley in the preface to his *Sermons*:

> God himself condescended to teach the way. For this very end, He came from Heaven. He hath written it down in a book. Oh give me that Book. At any price give me the Book of God.[24]

Luther in 1524 wrote:

> He is called a prophet who has received this understanding directly from God without further intervention, into whose mouth the Holy Ghost has given words. For He (the Spirit) is the source and they have no other authority than God.[25]

Wesley in his sermon "The Witness of Our Own Spirit" (1746) defines the Word of God as:

> The writings of the Old and New Testament: all which the prophets and the 'holy men of old' wrote 'as they were moved by the Holy

---

[21] *Luther 35:153*

[22] John Wesley. *Explanatory Notes Upon the New Testament.* (London, England: Epworth Press, 1948) 794.

[23] M. Reu. Wartburg. *Luther and the Scriptures.* (Columbus, Ohio.: Wartburg Press, 1944) 17.

[24] Albert Outler. *The Works of John Wesley. Vol. 1.* (Nashville, Tenn.: Abingdon Press, 1984) 105.

[25] M.Reu Wartburg. *Luther and the Scriptures.* (Columbus, Ohio.: Wartburg Press, 1944) 1952.

Ghost;' all that 'Scripture which was given by inspiration of God,' and which is indeed 'profitable for doctrine,' or 'teaching the whole will of God;' 'for reproof' of what is contrary thereto:' for correction of error,' and for instruction (or training up) in righteousness.'[26]

While Luther and Wesley accepted the inspiration of the Holy Ghost, they also recognized that God used the authors as individual instruments, expressing their thoughts and feelings in their own words.

Luther:

> But it is forgivable when the Holy Spirit, speaking through Paul, sins a little against the rules of grammar. He speaks with great fervor, and anyone who is fervent when he speaks cannot be precise about following the rules of grammar and the principles of rhetoric.[27]

Wesley in his comments on Acts 15:7 in his *Explanatory Notes Upon the New Testament*:

> For how really soever they were inspired, we need not suppose their inspiration was always so instantaneous and express as to supersede any deliberation in their own minds, or any consultation with each other.[28]

Since the Scriptures are divinely inspired, they are also authoritative. For both Luther and Wesley no other authority was equal to the prophetic and apostolic witness of Scripture. This meant that Scripture alone was sufficient to establish and substantiate the articles of faith. As Paul Althaus states about Luther's views, in his book *The Theology of Martin Luther*, and it could be equally said about Wesley:

> The Scriptures offer all that is necessary to salvation. Christians need no other truth for their salvation beyond what is proclaimed in Scripture. No dogma or rule of the Church not already contained in Scripture is necessary for salvation.[29]

---

[26] Albert Outler. *The Works of John Wesley. Vol. 1.* (Nashville, Tenn.: Abingdon Press, 1984) 302–03.

[27] *Luther* 26:92.

[28] John Wesley. *Explanatory Notes Upon the New Testament.* (London, England: Epworth Press, 1948) 455.

[29] Paul Althaus. *The Theology of Martin Luther.* (Philadelphia, Pa.: Fortress Press, 1966) 5.

The following quotations from both Luther and Wesley will both confirm Althaus' opinion, as well as continue to show similarities in the views of these two giants of the church.

Luther:

> All articles are sufficiently established in the Holy Scriptures, so that it is not necessary to establish any beyond this.[30]

> Nothing should be asserted in questions of faith without Scriptural precedent.[31]

Wesley in "A Roman Catechism With a Reply Thereto":

> For as all faith is founded upon divine authority, so there is now no divine authority but the Scriptures, and therefore no one can make that to be divine which is not contained in them.[32]

In a letter to Thomas Church in 1746:

> The ultimate appeal must always be to Scripture. The Apostles substantiated their assertions from the sacred writings, and I must do the same.[33]

Luther:

> No one is bound to believe more than what is based in Scripture.[34] For what is asserted without the Scripture may be held as opinion, but need not be believed.[35]

Wesley writing to Ann Bolton in 1789:

> Enjoin nothing that the Bible does not clearly enjoin, forbid nothing it does not clearly forbid.[36]

In his *Journal* in 1744:

> We cannot indeed say or do either more or less than we apprehend consistent with the written Word of God.[37]

---

[30] *Luther* 34:111.
[31] *Luther* 32:238.
[32] *Works* 10:90–91.
[33] *Letters* 2:244.
[34] *Luther* 32:96.
[35] *Luther* 36:29.
[36] *Letters* 8:192.
[37] Reginald Ward and Richard Heitzenrater. *The Works of John Wesley. Vol 20.* (Nashville,

From the "Sermon on the Mount XII":

> Believe nothing they say unless it is clearly confirmed by plain passages of the Holy Writ.[38]

Luther:

> This conflict between the Scriptures and the doctrines of men cannot reconcile. Therefore, because these two forms of doctrine contradict one another we allow even young children to judge here whether we are to give up the Scripture, in which the one Word of God is taught from the beginning of the world, or whether we are to give up the doctrine of men, which were newly discovered yesterday and which change daily.[39]

Wesley in a letter to Joseph Benson in 1788 writes:

> You will observe that it is dangerous on such subjects to depart from Scripture either as to language or sentiment. I believe that most controversies which have disturbed the Church have arisen from people's wanting to be wise above what is written, not contented with what God has plainly revealed there.[40]

Another manner in which to discern the importance of scriptural authority for both Luther and Wesley, and also point out their similarities, would be to consider some of their usages of Scripture. For example, in the development of their theologies it is clear that neither Wesley nor Luther had a desire to say anything particularly original. Instead, they felt their commission was accurately to exegete the Scripture. Perhaps for this reason, neither of the men felt a need, unlike Calvin, to produce a systematic theology.

Paul Althaus describes Luther's philosophy well when he states:

> All Luther's theological thinking presupposes the authority of Scripture. His theology is nothing more than an attempt to interpret the Scripture. Its form is basically exegesis. He wrote no dogmatic, nor an ethics, nor a Summa-not like Calvin's *Institutes*.[41]

Tenn.: Abingdon Press, 1991) 16.

[38] Albert Outler. *The Works of John Wesley. Vol. 1* (Nashville, Tenn.: Abingdon Press, 1984) 683.

[39] *Luther* 35:153.

[40] *Letters* 8:89.

[41] Paul Althaus. *The Theology of Martin Luther*. (Philadelphia, Pa.: Fortress Press, 1966) 3.

Compare this quotation with Albert Outler's comments in his introduction to Wesley's writings in his volume of *The Library of Protestant Thought:*

> (Wesley) seems never to have felt the impulse to produce anything resembling a comprehensive exposition of his theological ideas, and this may have been just as well. Short doctrinal summaries are scattered throughout his writings, and these give ample evidence that his thought was consciously organized around a stable core of basic coordinated motifs. But there is no extended development of his system, for the simple reason that there never seems to be a practical need for such a theology.[42]

Another obvious similarity between Luther and Wesley was their use of Scripture in their sermons and other writings. Again Althaus comments concerning Luther, that his sermons were, "saturated with quotations and were largely exegetical in character." He goes on later to comment that "There is no precedent for the way in which Luther, as an exegete and as a preacher, thinks in constant conversation with Scripture."[43]

Luther may have had no precedent, but he certainly had a follower. In chapter five I will show just how fully Wesley incorporated Scripture into his sermons, *Journal,* and *Letters,* but for now I will to quote from Franz Hildebrandt, from his book *From Luther to Wesley,* when he states:

> . . . sermons, letters, journals, show on every page the man who speaks in biblical terms, argues in biblical ways, and thinks in biblical categories; at no point is he nearer to Luther and farther from contemporary English theology.[44]

One final similarity between Luther and Wesley, in reference to the authority of Scripture, can be seen in their agreement that Scripture did not derive its authority from the church. The church did not authenticate Scripture; instead the Scripture authenticated the church. Luther states quite clearly where the authority lies:

> It is not the Word of God because the church says so, but because God's Word says so, therefore is the church. The church does not make the Word, but is made by the Word.[45]

---

[42] Kenneth Rowe. *The Place of Wesley in the Christian Tradition.* (Metuchen, N.J.: The Scarecrow Press, 1976) 72.

[43] Paul Althaus. *The Theology of Martin Luther.* (Philadelphia, Pa.: Fortress Press, 1966) 3–4.

[44] Franz Hildebrandt. *From Luther to Wesley.* (London, England: Lutterworth Press, 1951) 26.

[45] M. Reu Wartburg. *Luther and the Scriptures.* (Columbus, Ohio. Wartburg Press, 1944) 35.

> The Queen must rule and everyone must obey, and be subject to her. The Pope, Luther, Augustine, Paul, or even an angel from heaven-these should not be masters, judges, or arbiters, but only witnesses, disciples, and confessors of Scripture.[46]

Wesley expresses the same concept when he states in his essay "Popery Calmly Considered, "In all cases the church is to be judged by the Scripture, not the Scripture by the Church."[47]

This is not to say that for Wesley or Luther the church, or tradition, had no place in biblical interpretation. However, the church was clearly seen as a secondary authority.

Before leaving this section on biblical authority, I must comment on one clear difference in Luther's and Wesley's views. While they both believed mightily in the authority of Scripture, they were not in complete agreement upon what constituted Scripture. As was shown in the last chapter, Wesley willingly accepted Article Six of the Thirty-Nine Articles, which defined the canonical books of the Old and New Testaments. The Article differentiated between the canonical and apocryphal books of the Old Testament and acknowledged, "All the Books of the New Testament, as they are commonly received, we do receive and account them Canonical."[48]

Luther however, held a different view. While he would maintain strenuously the authority of the canonical books, he was not ready to classify all the commonly accepted books as canonical. The most well known example of this distinction can be seen in his comments concerning the Epistle of James. In his preface to the epistle he writes:

> But to state my opinion, though without imposing it to anyone, I consider that it is not the writing of any apostle. Therefore St. James' Epistle is really an epistle of straw compared to them, for it has nothing of the nature of the gospel about it.[49]

It should be recognized that Luther's problem with the Epistle of James probably centered on its seeming contradiction of the Apostle Paul's message of justification by faith. For Luther, "All genuine books agree in preaching Christ. This is the true test of all books when we see whether they preach Christ."[50] All books should be distinguished on the basis of their closeness or distance from the center of the Scripture, the gospel. So,

---

[46] *Luther* 26:58.
[47] *Works* 10:142.
[48] *Book of Common Prayer,* 1977, 868–9.
[49] *Luther* 35:395–96.
[50] Paul Althaus. *The Theology of Martin Luther.* (Philadelphia, Pa.: Fortress Press, 1966) 83.

Luther accepted the canon established by the early church, but not without distinction. It is clear that Luther did not view James on the same level of canonicity. He also had questions about Hebrews, Jude and Revelation. In his translation of the Bible he placed a space between them and the other books, and in the index of his 1534 Bible, they are dealt with on the same level as the Old Testament Apocrypha.[51] Concerning these books Luther states, "They have from ancient times had a different reputation, and do not belong to the true and certain chief books of the New Testament."[52]

Perhaps the most important point to recognize here, is that regardless of the accuracy of Luther's views about James and the other books, this did not affect his overall view of the authority of Scripture, at least as it compares with Wesley. They both felt the canonized Scripture was inspired and had authority. Their difference was not in their view of authority, but in their opinion as to which books belonged in the canon.

Interpreting the Bible

In comparing Luther's and Wesley's views on biblical interpretation some fascinating similarities surface. I will spend two later chapters discussing Wesley's interpretive principles in detail, but for now I will merely attempt to compare and contrast their views.

Interpreting the Bible by the Spirit. Luther clearly felt that the correct and only way to interpret the Scripture was in the Spirit of the author. As Paul Althaus states concerning Luther's views:

> The fact that the Scripture is the final authority precludes any outside source interpreting it. Self-validation necessarily includes self-interpretation.[53] Luther recognized that sinful man, apart from Christ, cannot understand the Scripture. He also would not accept Rome's view that the church was the final interpreter, or the enthusiast's view that there was some particular gift to interpretation.[54] Instead, Luther knew that only man moved by the Spirit of God can interpret the Scripture, "For the Spirit is necessary to understand all of Scripture, as well as every part of it."[55]

---

[51] M. Reu Wartburg. *Luther and the Scriptures.* (Columbus, Ohio.: Wartburg Press, 1944) 44–45.

[52] *Luther* 35:394

[53] Paul Althaus. *The Theology of Martin Luther.* (Philadelphia, Pa.: Fortress, Press, 1966) 76.

[54] Ibid., 76–78.

[55] M. Reu Wartburg. *Luther and the Scriptures.* (Columbus, Ohio.: Wartburg Press, 1944) 78.

> No prophecy is a matter of ones own interpretation. Be governed by this and do not think you can interpret Scripture with your own reason and wisdom. The Holy Spirit Himself must expound Scripture, otherwise, it must remain unexpounded.[56]

Wesley would certainly agree with Luther's contention. Consider a quotation from a letter to the Bishop of Gloucester in 1762:

> I do firmly believe (and what serious man does not), we need the same Spirit to understand the Scripture which enabled the holy man of old to write it.[57]

> The Spirit of God once inspired those who wrote it, but continually inspires, and supernaturally assists those who read it with earnest prayer.[58]

The Scripture Interprets Itself. Both Luther and Wesley made strong statements on allowing the Bible to interpret itself.

Luther:

> Scripture is therefore its own light. It is a grand thing when Scripture interprets itself.[59]

Wesley in "Popery calmly Considered":

> And Scripture is the best expositor of Scripture. The best way, therefore, to understand it, is to carefully compare Scripture with Scripture, and learn the true meaning of it.[60]

Both Luther and Wesley spoke of interpreting according to the analogy of Scripture, or as Wesley referred to it, "interpreting Scripture by Scripture, according to the analogy of faith."[61] However, as we shall discover later in chapters eight and nine, Wesley did not define the analogy of faith, or Scripture, as narrowly as Luther. Wesley felt the Bible should be approached as a whole, and that various texts should be seen as a part of a

---

[56] *Luther* 30:166.

[57] Gerald Cragg. *The Works of John Wesley. Vol. 11.* (Nashville, Tenn.: Abingdon Press, 1989) 509.

[58] John Wesley. *Explanatory Notes Upon the New Testament.* (London, England: Epworth Press, 1948) 794.

[59] M. Reu Wartburg. *Luther and the Scriptures.* (Columbus, Ohio.: Wartburg Press, 1944) 77.

[60] *Works* 10:142.

[61] Albert Outler. *The Works of John Wesley. Vol. 2* (Nashville, Tenn.: Abingdon Press, 1985) 501.

single theology[62] He felt there was an interconnectedness of Scripture and warned Hannah Ball in 1772 ". . . not to build your faith on a single text of Scripture, and much less on a particular sense of it."[63]

While Wesley emphasized that there were a number of grand truths that run through the Scripture, the analogy of faith which cannot be ignored, Luther's view was much more focused. For Luther, the analogy of Scripture was nothing less than the analogy of the Gospel. For Luther, all Scripture must be interpreted Christocentrically. Christocentric interpretation was gospel centered interpretation, which was understood in terms of the gospel of justification by faith alone.[64]

For Luther, all Scripture had to be clearly seen in terms of the gospel, and all Interpretation, of individual passages must be subordinate to that. If any particular passage of Scripture seemed to oppose the evangelical interpretation it did not have the authority of the Word of God. As we saw earlier, it was this belief that enabled Luther to oppose the Epistle of James, because he felt that it contradicted the doctrine of justification by faith. Therefore Luther felt free to say:

> Away with James. His authority is not enough to cause me to abandon the doctrine of faith and to deviate from the authority of the other apostles and the entire Scripture.[65]

While I am confident that Wesley would not deny the importance of Christ as an interpretive principle, he did not define the analogy of faith as narrowly as Luther.

Interpreting the Bible by Context. A closely connected concept to the importance of Scripture interpreting Scripture would be the importance of using context in interpretation. This was emphasized by both Luther and Wesley:

Luther:

> That is not the right way to interpret Scripture, to collect statements from different parts of the Bible without regard for logical order or context. But that is what is commonly done, and it leads to nothing

---

[62] Wayne McCowen and James Massey. *Interpreting God's Word Today: An Inquiry Into Hermeneutics From a Biblical, Theological Perspective.* (Anderson, Ind.: Warner Press, 1988) 752.

[63] *Letters* 5:328.

[64] Paul Althaus. *The Theology of Martin Luther.* (Philadelphia, Pa.: Fortress Press, 1966) 79.

[65] M. Reu Wartburg. *Luther and the Scriptures.* (Columbus, Ohio.: Wartburg Press, 1944) 81.

but errors, therefore keep in mind the whole of Scripture, compare the contradictory passages and as the two cherubim facing one another find the harmony of their mutual diversity in the center of the *propitiatorium*, that is in the true understanding of Christ.[66]

Wesley in his sermon "On Corrupting the Word of God" (1727) comments that the Scripture should be explained by Scripture:

> (III) 1. If then we have spoken the Word of God, the genuine unmixed Word of God, and that only; 2. If we have put no unnatural interpretation upon it, but (have) taken the known phrases in their common, obvious sense, and where they were less known explained Scripture by Scripture.[67]

Interpreting Scripture Literally. For both Luther and Wesley, the idea that Scripture best interprets itself also included the realization the Scripture is best interpreted literally whenever possible. The literal interpretation should be laid aside only if it becomes clear that a literal translation is impossible.

Luther:

> Where the Holy Spirit established something that must be believed, there we must not evade the natural meaning of the words, nor wrest them from the connection in which they stand unless an express and clear article of faith compels us to arrange or interpret the statement otherwise. If we acted differently, what would become of the Bible?[68]

> The Holy Spirit is the plainest writer and speaker in heaven, and earth, and therefore His words cannot have more than one, and that very simplest sense, in which we call the literal, ordinary sense.[69]

Wesley: to Samuel Furley in 1755:

> The general rule of interpreting Scripture is this: the literal sense of every text is to be taken, if it is not contrary to some other texts.

---

[66] Ibid., 11.

[67] Albert Outler. *The Works of John Wesley. Vol. 4.* (Nashville, Tenn.: Abingdon Press, 1987) 251.

[68] M. Re Wartburg. *Martin Luther and the Scriptures.* (Columbus, Ohio. Wartburg Press, 1944) 51–52.

[69] *Luther* 39:178.

But in that case the obscure text is to be interpreted by those which speak more plainly.[70]

Reason, Tradition, and Experience in Biblical Interpretation

When considering Wesley's interpretive principles, one cannot ignore what has been called the Wesleyan Quadrilateral. This involves the relationship between Scripture, tradition, reason, and experience. It is interesting to note that Luther also comments on the use and misuse of tradition, reason, and experience in biblical interpretation. What is quite clear, however, is that both Luther and Wesley placed these only as secondary authorities next to Scripture.

Reason

Luther and Wesley maintained since man is fallen, reason is not sufficient to draw men to God without the assistance of revelation. Wesley makes it clear that reason is only to be a "handmaiden of faith, the servant of revelation."[71] Reason had its place, but it must be recognized that it also had limitations in that reason, in and of itself, could not produce faith. In "The Case for Reason Impartially Considered" (1781) Wesley insists:

> Let reason do all that reason can: employ it as far as it will go. But at the same time acknowledge it is utterly incapable of giving either faith, or hope or love; and consequently of producing either real virtue or substantial happiness. Expect these from a higher source, even from the Father of the spirits of all flesh.[72]

Luther speaks even more strongly against the use of reason apart from God. Luther felt that God's Word and reason were in sharp opposition to one another. Reason rejected what the Word preached and faith confessed as nonsense. Therefore Luther could say:

Reason despises faith.[73]

> The teaching of human experience and reason are far below divine law. The Scriptures expressly forbid us to follow our own reason, Deut.12.[74]

---

[70] Frank Baker. *The Works of John Wesley. Vol. 26.* (Oxford, England: Oxford University Press, 1982) 557.
[71] *Journals* 5:492.
[72] Albert Outler. *The Works of John Wesley. Vol. 2.* (Nashville, Tenn.: Abingdon Press, 1985) 600.
[73] *Luther* 34:160.
[74] Hugh Kerr. *A Compend of Luther's Theology.* (Philadelphia, Pa.: Westminster Press, 1943) 4.

Arguments based on reason determined nothing, but because the Holy Ghost says it is true, it is true.[75]

Reason is not useless in interpreting Scripture, but the fleshly reason of man must be enlightened by the Holy Spirit. Reason then can be of value:

Luther:

Reason in godly men is something different since it does not fight with faith, but rather aids it.[76]

Wesley once again in "The Case For Reason Impartially Considered" (1781) asks, "Is it not reason (assisted by the Holy Spirit), which enables us to understand what the Holy Spirit declares?"[77]

Tradition

I have already noted that Luther and Wesley agreed that Scripture did not derive its authority from the church. This did not mean that the writings of the church fathers, or the rulings of the church held no value, but they were certainly considered only a secondary authority.

Luther:

It will not do to make articles of faith out of holy father's words nor works.[78]

But everyone indeed knows that at times they (the fathers) have erred as men will; therefore I am ready to trust them only when they approve opinions from Scripture, which has never erred.[79]

This is the real act, to gather Scripture correctly. The father who can do this best, is the best father. One should read all the books, of all the fathers, with caution, not believing them but rather watching out whether they also cite clear passages and illumine Scripture with Scripture.[80]

---

[75] M. Reu Wartburg. *Luther and the Scriptures.* (Columbus, Ohio.: Fortress Press, 1944) 15.
[76] Ibid., 71.
[77] Albert Outler. *The Works of John Wesley. Vol. 2* (Nashville, Tenn.: Abingdon Press, 1985) 588.
[78] *Luther* 32:231.
[79] Ibid., 32:11.
[80] Ibid., 39:165.

We have already discovered how committed Wesley was to the writings of the early church fathers. His commitment was to the point that he felt God delivered him from the "error" of giving too much authority to the writings of antiquity.[81] In chapter nine I will consider in detail Wesley's use of tradition in biblical interpretation. At this point let me merely state that Wesley was perfectly willing to check his interpretation against the writings of the church fathers. However, he warned against overemphasizing the teachings of the church against that of Scripture. There was no question where the final authority rested as he shows in "A Roman Catechism With a Reply Thereto":

> As long as we have the Scripture, the church is to be referred to the Scripture and not the Scripture to the church.[82]

"The Advantage of the Members of the Church of England Over Those of the Church of Rome":

> I lay down this undoubted truth-the more the doctrine of any Church agrees with the Scripture, the more ready ought it to be received. And, on the other hand, the more the doctrine of any Church differs from the Scripture, the greater cause we have to doubt of it.[83]

Experience

Paul Althaus believes that, though perhaps to a lesser extent than Wesley, Luther emphasized experience. According to Althaus, Luther believed that the authority of the Word of God which confronts us in Scripture, establishes itself in our heart through experience. When it came to the heart and center of the gospel, the message of sin and grace, Luther appealed not only to Scripture, and the consensus of the church, but also to his own experience in spiritual matters. There can be no doubt that experience was one of the principles of his theology.[84]

> Thus Luther could say, "I am at least partly informed concerning Holy Writ, and besides I have, to some extent, tested these spiritual matters in experience."[85]

---

[81] Reginald Ward and Richard Heitzenrater. *The Works of John Wesley. Vol. 18* (Nashville, Tenn.: Abingdon Press, 1988) 212.

[82] *Works* 10:94.

[83] Ibid., 10:133.

[84] Paul Althaus. *The Theology of Martin Luther.* (Philadelphia, Pa.: Fortress Press, 1966) 8.

[85] *Luther* 32:258.

Wesley emphasized experience more than Luther, but only in a confirmatory capacity, not as an equal or verifier of Scripture.

Luther and Infallibility. J. Theodore Mueller in his book *Luther and the Bible* states:

> Luther unfailingly asserts the inerrancy of Scripture over against the errancy of human historians and scientists. He writes, 'The Scriptures have never erred'.[86] Luther certainly maintained that the Scriptures were without error and should be accepted as such, "The saints were subject to error in their writings and to sin in their lives, Scripture cannot err."[87]

In commenting on the testimony of the church Luther maintained:

> But everyone indeed knows, that at times they have erred as men will; therefore, I am ready to trust them only when they give me evidence for their opinion from Scripture which has never erred. This St. Paul bids me to do in I Thes. 5:21 when he says, 'Test everything, hold fast what is good.' St. Augustine writes of St. Jerome to the same effect.
>
> I have learned to do only those books that are called the Holy Scriptures the honor of believing firmly that none of their writings have erred. All others I read as not to hold what they say to be the truth unless they prove it to me by Holy Scripture or clear reason.[88]

As can be seen from this last quotation, if we are to talk about infallibility of Scripture, Luther would be sure to apply this concept only to those books that he felt were canonical:

> I have ascribed this honor (namely infallibility), to books which are termed canonical, so that I carefully believe not one of the authors erred.[89]

As I have discussed, Luther distinguished the books of the canon based upon how closely they stayed to the gospel message. As long as the preaching of Christ was not obscured, the Scripture was an infallible author to which all should submit. For example, concerning the book of Genesis, Luther maintained that the Holy Spirit speaks of the seventh day, and men

---

[86] Harold Lindsell. *The Battle for the Bible.* (Grand Rapids, Mich.: Zondervan Publishers, 1976)

[87] M. Reu Wartburg. *Luther and the Scriptures.* (Columbus, Ohio.: Wartburg Press, 1944) 35.

[88] *Luther* 32:11.

[89] M. Reu Wartburg. *Luther and the Scriptures.* (Columbus, Ohio.: Wartburg Press, 1944) 24.

are to bow down to His authority, "Do the Holy Ghost the honor of realizing he is more learned than you are."[90]

The problems of the Bible as they related to natural science, history, anthropology, or philosophy were of little importance to Luther. His faith allowed him to criticize the Bible on specific details, while he continued to accept it as an infallible book, inspired by the Holy Spirit.[91]

Luther did not ignore apparent contradictions in the Bible, any more than Wesley did. He was troubled by issues such as the arrangement of the Law of Moses, the order of the prophecies of Jeremiah, the difficulties of arranging the different gospel passages, and the accounts of the cleansing of the temple. Luther attempted to give possible explanations to solve these problems and concluded:, "When discrepancies occur in the Holy Scripture and we cannot harmonize them, let it pass, it does not endanger the article of faith."[92]

Luther did not ignore the problems, but his faith in the Scripture was such that it did not disillusion him if he could not find the answer to seeming contradictions.

In comparing Luther's view of infallibility with Wesley's we do discover clear similarities. Wesley also spoke of the infallibility of Scripture in "The Means of Grace" (1746), "All Scripture is given by inspiration of God (consequently, all Scripture is infallibly) true."[93]

However, the issue becomes, what did Wesley mean by infallibility, and how broadly should this term be applied to Scripture? I believe Wesley would apply the term to all the Old and New Testament Books, not excluding certain books as Luther might. However, Wesley also had to deal with issues such as seeming contradictions. In chapter seven I will deal specifically with the issue of Wesley and infallibility, and at that point other similarities, and differences, between Luther and Wesley might emerge.

Conclusion

In comparing the views of Martin Luther and John Wesley on Scripture it would appear that the similarities outweigh the differences. I believe a quotation by Franz Hildebrandt in his book *From Luther to Wesley* summarizes it well when he states that there are:

---

[90] Ibid., 86.
[91] Paul Althaus. *The Theology of Martin Luther.* (Philadelphia, Pa.: Fortress Press, 1966) 83.
[92] Ibid., 83.
[93] Albert Outler. *The Works of John Wesley. Vol. 1.* (Nashville, Tenn.: Abingdon Press, 1984) 388.

Obvious differences, as different as the two centuries and countries in which they lived. Nevertheless, it is true to say that at no point was English church history so clearly touched by Luther as it was in John and Charles Wesley; and again no real Reformation has occurred since Luther, except in Methodism.[94]

Wesley and Calvin

In comparing Calvin's views upon Scripture with Wesley's, and to a lesser extent Luther's, we discover once again some real similarities. As with Luther, I propose to consider such areas as the inspiration and authority of Scripture and the interpretation of Scripture. I intend to make one change in the format however. To this point, in comparing Wesley to both the church fathers and Luther, I have quoted Wesley in different areas as a point of comparison. Rather than repeating these quotations, I will, for the most part, only make reference to the similarities, and then develop Wesley's view much more fully in later chapters.

Inspiration and Authority

In beginning to consider Calvin's views, one must realize that he devoted his life to the interpretation of Scripture. Donald McKim in his book, *Readings in Calvin's Theology*, notes that Calvin wrote commentaries on the Pentateuch, Job, Psalms, Isaiah, and the whole New Testament except II and III John and Revelation. His lectures, sermons, correspondence, and his *Institutes of the Christian Religion*, were all saturated with Scripture.[95]

Clearly there is a similarity with Wesley in the scriptural saturation of sermons and correspondence. A closer look also reveals similarities in views upon authority and inspiration.

Calvin, like Wesley, felt that the authority of Scripture came from the fact that it is God who speaks it; "Thus the highest proof of Scripture derives in general from the fact that God in person speaks it."[96]

Calvin at different times referred to Scripture as, "the Word of God,"[97] which has "flowed to us from the very mouth of God by the ministry of men."[98]

---

[94] Franz Hildebrandt. *From Luther to Wesley.* (London, England: Lutterworth, 1951) 15.
[95] Donald McKim. *Readings in Calvin's Theology.* (Grand Rapids, Mich.: Baker Book House, 1984) 146.
[96] *Calvin* 1:78.
[97] Ibid., 1:74.
[98] Ibid., 1:80.

At times it almost appears that Calvin embraces a view that the writers were so overwhelmed by the Holy Spirit that they were nothing but, "sure and genuine scribes of the Holy Spirit."[99] In his commentary on II Timothy 3:16 Calvin states:

> Whoever then wishes to profit in the Scripture, let him, first of all, lay down this as a settled point, that the Law and the Prophets are not a doctrine delivered according to the will and pleasure of men, but dictated by the Holy Spirit.[100]

According to Donald McKim, most interpreters would reject the idea that Calvin held to a mechanical dictation theory, in light of his other statements stressing the involvement of the whole personality of the biblical writer.[101] Instead, his training as a humanist gave him the concept of accommodation. His view of accommodation, in which God accommodated Himself to man's limited understanding, was similar to Wesley's. Thus Calvin believed:

> In Scripture the divine God has bridged the infinite gulf between Himself and humanity by condescending to talk and act in human forms. Human authors, divinely appointed, expressed God's message about Himself in human words and thought forms.[102]

Calvin, like Wesley, did not seem to emphasize the mode of inspiration as much as the result of inspiration. It was clear to Calvin the biblical writers were not writing on their own, but were moved by the Spirit:

> . . . the truth cries out openly that these men who were previously contemptible among folk, suddenly beginning to discourse so gloriously of the heavenly mysteries, must have been instructed by the Spirit.[103]

So, for Calvin, the inspiration of Scripture and the authority of Scripture are closely linked, for Scripture's primary source of authority is that it comes from God:

---

[99] Ibid., 2:1157.
[100] John Calvin. *Calvin's Commentary Vol. XXI*. (Grand Rapids, Mich.: Baker Book House, 1979) 249.
[101] Donald McKim. *Readings in Calvin's Theology*. (Grand Rapids, Mich.: Baker Book House, 1984) 60.
[102] Ibid., 54.
[103] *Calvin* 1:91.

Scriptures attain full authority among believers only when men regard them as having sprung from heaven, as if they were the living Word of God heard.[104]

Calvin believed there were different avenues which proved that the Scripture was from God, and therefore authoritative. For example, in Vol. I of his *Institutes*, Calvin discussed the following topics as evidence that Scripture comes from God; Scripture's unique majesty and impressions, miracles and prophecies, the simplicity, heavenly character and authority of the New Testament, the universal content of the church, and the faithfulness of the martyrs.[105] This section emphasizes some of the same points Wesley makes in his "A Clear and Concise Demonstration of the Divine Impartation of the Holy Scriptures."[106]

Calvin also felt that merely reading the Scriptures would convince men of the divine inspiration and authority of the Word of God:

> Now this power which is peculiar to Scripture is clear from the fact that of human writing, however artfully polished, there is none capable of affecting us at all comparably. Read Demosthenes or Cicero, read Plato, Aristotle and others of that tribe. They will, I admit, allure you, delight you, move you, enrapture you in wonderful measure. But betake yourself from them to the sacred readings; then, in spite of yourself, so deeply will it affect you, so penetrate your heart, so fix itself in your very marrow, that, compared with the deep impression, such vigor as the orator and philosopher have will nearly vanish. Consequently, it is easy to see that the Sacred Scriptures, which so far surpass all gifts and graces of human endeavour, breathe something divine.[107]

Wesley emphasizes this same point in commenting on the Song of Solomon in his *Explanatory Notes Upon the Old Testament* when he refers to "the quality of the penman who was confessedly a man inspired by God," and comments on the "singular efficacy of it upon the hearts of sober and serious persons."[108] He also emphasizes the same points in his *A Compendium of Natural Philosophy*.

---

[104] Ibid., 1:74.

[105] Ibid., 1:81–92.

[106] *Works* 11:484.

[107] *Calvin* 1:82.

[108] John Wesley. *Explanatory Notes Upon the Old Testament*. (Salem, Ohio.: Schmul Publishers, 1975) 3:1925.

Yet all these proofs of the inspiration and authority of Scripture are not enough. For Calvin, Scripture authenticates itself, with the help of the internal testimony of the Holy Spirit:

> We ought to seek our convictions in a higher place than human reasons, judgments, or conjectures, that is, in the secret testimony of the Spirit.[109]
>
> For as God alone is a fit witness of Himself in His Word, so also the Word will not find acceptance in men's hearts before it is so sealed by the inward testimony of the Spirit.[110]
>
> Let this point therefore stand: that those whom the Spirit has inwardly taught, truly rest upon Scripture, and that Scripture indeed is self-authenticated; hence it is not right to subject it to proof and reasoning. Therefore illumined by His power, we believe neither by our own, nor by anyone else's judgment that Scripture is from God; but above human judgment we affirm with utter certainty (just as if we were gazing upon the majesty of God Himself) that it has flown to us from the very mouth of God by the ministry of men.[111]

Since Scriptural authority came from God, Calvin accepted, as did Luther and Wesley, that authority was not conferred by the church. Instead, Calvin urges that the church was built upon the foundation of the prophets and the apostles. Indeed, "If the teaching of the prophets and apostles is foundational, these must have had authority before the church began to exist."[112]

Also, since all authority must ultimately be based upon Scripture, then the Bible must be the source of knowledge for salvation and all doctrine, "No one can get even the slightest taste of right and sound doctrine, unless he is a pupil of Scripture."[113]

Any straying from Scripture can only lead to disaster:

> If we turn aside from the Word, as I have just now said, though we may strive with strenuous haste, yet, since we got off track, we shall never reach the goal.[114]

---

[109] *Calvin* 1:78.
[110] Ibid., 1:79.
[111] Ibid., 1:80.
[112] Ibid., 1:75.
[113] Ibid., 1:72.
[114] Ibid., 1:73.

Wesley would certainly agree with Calvin on this point. As he states in his letter to William Dodd in 1756:

> I therein build on no authority, ancient or modern, but the Scripture. If this supports any doctrine, it will stand, if not the sooner it falls the better.[115]

Calvin and Biblical Interpretation

To understand Calvin's interpretative principles, they must be examined in the light of his training as a Christian humanist. One important intent of the Christian humanist was a wish to return to the classical sources of the faith, particularly the Bible and the early church theologians, to find out what Christ intended Christianity to be. We have seen how important the desire to return to "Primitive Christianity" was to Wesley in chapter two.

Calvin was exposed to the new method of legal research, which aimed to discover the intent of the ancient law codes in the original context, rather than relying on textbooks and traditional commentaries. He clearly adopted this view in his desire to study the culture in which a passage of Scripture was written. Circumstances and context were main ingredients if one wished to interpret the Bible.[116]

Wesley would certainly have agreed with Calvin's comments on the importance of context in interpreting Scripture:

> there are many statements in Scripture the meaning of which depends upon context."[117]

> In order to understand (Jesus' remark on swearing) correctly, it is necessary to understand the occasion which prompted Him to speak as He did.[118]

Another emphasis on interpretation, which Wesley shared with Calvin, was the desire to interpret the Bible in the simplest, most literal fashion. This was one reason Calvin so appreciated Chrysostom whose:

---

[115] *Letters* 3:157.

[116] Donald McKim. *Readings in Calvin's Theology.* (Grand Rapids, Mich.: Baker Book House, 1984) 48–49.

[117] *Calvin* 2:1346.

[118] Donald McKim. *Readings in Calvin's Theology.* (Grand Rapids, Mich.: Baker Book House, 1984) 49.

Supreme concern was always not to turn aside even to the slightest degree from the genuine, single sense of Scripture and to allow himself no liberties by twisting the plain meaning of words.[119]

Closely connected with Calvin's desire for literal interpretation, was his emphasis on brevity and simplicity. Calvin, like Wesley, was not interested in empty speculation, but wished to discover the relevance of a certain portion of Scripture, and deliver it in as succinct a manner as possible.[120]

Calvin:

> . . . we must leave those empty speculations on such unimportant things as the 'natural orders, and the number of angels.'[121]

Wesley in his preface to his *Sermons*:

> I design plain truth for plain people. Therefore of set purpose I abstain from all nice and philosophical speculations.[122]

For Calvin, as we have seen and shall see further with Wesley, it was the plain, literal, natural meaning of Scripture which was most important:

> Galatians 4:22—Let us know, then, that the true literal meaning of Scripture is the natural and simple one.[123]

Finally, it should be noted for Calvin that the internal testimony of the Holy Spirit was necessary, not only to confirm the inspiration and authority of Scripture, but to aid in exegesis. Hans Frei in his book *The Eclipse of the Biblical Narrative* writes, "Calvin we noted speaks about the internal testimony of the Spirit as enlightening the heart and mind to see what the text says in any one case."[124]

Wesley agrees, as we see in his letter to the Bishop of Gloucester (1763):

---

[119] Ibid., 65.

[120] Ibid., 66.

[121] *Calvin* 1:164.

[122] Albert Outler. *The Works of John Wesley. Vol. 1* (Nashville, Tenn.: Abingdon Press, 1984) 104.

[123] John Calvin. *Calvin's Commentary Vol. XXI.* (Grand Rapids, Mich.: Baker Book House, 1979) 136.

[124] Hans Frei. *The Eclipse of the Biblical Narrative.* (New Haven, Conn.: Yale University Press, 1974) 35.

I do firmly believe (and what serious man does not), we need the same Spirit to understand the Scripture which enabled the holy men of old to write it.[125]

Conclusion

In comparing John Calvin's and John Wesley's views upon Scripture, even to a small degree, we find some obvious similarities. In fact, in at least one interpretive aspect, I believe Wesley may have been closer to Calvin than to Luther. Robert Grant in his book, *A Short History of Interpretation,* states that Calvin had a more objective type of interpretation than Luther. According to Grant, for Calvin, "Scripture itself is the authority for Christian belief, rather than any Christocentric interpretation of Scripture.[126] I believe I have shown in my comparison of Wesley and Luther that Wesley's view would fall closer to Calvin's concept of Scriptural authority.

---

[125] Gerald Cragg. *The Works of John Wesley. Vol. 11.* (Nashville, Tenn.: Abingdon Press, 1989) 509.

[126] Robert Grant. *A Short History of the Interpretation of the Bible.* (New York, N.Y.: MacMillan Company, 1972) 133.

4

John Wesley's View on Scriptural Authority

Part 2

Wesley's View of Scripture and Eighteenth Century Protestantism

IN HIS attitude toward the Scriptures Wesley differed little from most other eighteenth century Protestants. In his sermon "On Faith" (1788) Wesley clearly places himself with other Protestants in describing how their faith is based upon the revealed Word of God.

> The faith of the Protestants, in general, embraces only those truths as are necessary to salvation which are clearly revealed in the oracles of God. Whatever is plainly declared in the Old and New Testament is the object of their faith. They believe neither more nor less than what is manifestly contained in, and provable by, the Holy Scriptures. The Word of God is 'a lantern unto their feet and a light in all their paths.' They dare not, on any pretence, go from it to the right hand or the left. The written Word is the whole and sole rule of their faith, as well as practice. They believe whatsoever God has declared, and profess to do whatsoever He hath commanded. This is the proper faith of Protestants: by this they will abide and no other.[1]

Wesley and the Puritans

A number of studies have been made to explore the similarities between Wesley and the English Puritan tradition. Robert Monk in his book *John Wesley and His Puritan Heritage* outlines in pages 15–24 his attempt to

---

[1] Albert Outler. *The Works of John Wesley.* Vol. 3. (Nashville, Tenn.: Abingdon Press, 1986) 496.

examine the resemblance between Wesley and the Puritan ethos, especially the similarities of their teachings concerning the outward manifestations of the Christian life. Monk goes on to point out that in discussing the possible influences of Puritanism upon Wesley's thought, particularly as it relates to Scripture, it must be recognized that the Puritan movement included persons from a wide variety of theological, ecclesiastical, and political positions. This term could refer to some who:

> . . . remained in the Established Church, the Separatists such as the Baptists, some Independents who chose to separate from the Established Church, and Presbyterians and Independents who were finally forced out by the Act of Uniformity of 1662.[2]

What linked these groups together was a desire to purify and renew Christian thought and life, a conviction of an experiential relationship with God revealed in Christ and finally, most important for my purpose, a conviction of religious authority based upon Scripture which becomes the primary guide of faith and action.[3]

In his refusal to recognize any other norm of truth but Scripture, Wesley clearly placed himself in line with the Puritans. This is one of the reasons why the Puritans so appealed to Wesley and why he appreciated their writings. He commended them because:

> Next to God himself they honor His word. They are mighty in the Scripture, equal to any of those who went before them, and far superior to most that have followed them. They prove all things hereby. Their continual appeal is to the Law and Testimony. Nor do they easily form a judgment of a thing till they have weighed it in the balance of the sanctuary.[4]

In considering Puritan influences upon Wesley there are two primary areas to be investigated; his own Puritan ancestry, and the influence of his readings. First, Wesley had an illustrious Puritan heritage, though it is not clear how aware he was of his ancestor's views, or how much influence they had on him in his early development. On his father's side, Wesley's great-grandfather Bartholomew Wesley was ejected from the Church of England in 1662. Wesley's grandfather, John Wesley, was arrested in 1660 for "diabolically railing in the pulpit against the late king and his posterity, and

---

[2] Robert Monk. *John Wesley: His Puritan Heritage*. (Nashville, Tenn.: Abingdon Press, 1966) 27.

[3] Ibid., 27.

[4] A. Skevington Wood. *The Burning Heart*. (Grand Rapids, Mich.: Wm. B. Eerdmanns Pub. Co., 1967) 210.

praising Cromwell, also, for false doctrine, professing to speak with God."⁵ He was removed from his church in 1667.

Wesley's maternal grandfather father, Dr. Samuel Annesley, refused to conform and in 1662 was ejected. He was one of the acknowledged leaders of the London Non-conformists.⁶

It is not difficult to understand that John did not learn much about his Puritan ancestry from his father or mother. Both Samuel and Susannah were converts from the Dissenters back to the Established Church. Samuel had attended a dissenting academy in London, but in 1683 he left the dissenters and entered Exeter College, Oxford. In 1688 he graduated, was ordained and married Susannah. However, in spite of their fervor as first generation converts, Luke Keefer in his dissertation entitled "John Wesley, Disciple of Early Christianity" observes, "One cannot jump out of one's skin by change of denomination, and Samuel and Susannah Wesley carried much of their Puritan heritage into their Anglicanism."⁷

In fact, Keefer believes the influence may have been stronger because it was subconscious. Values are modeled without an attempt to tie them to a specific truth. Therefore he believes the primary method in which the Puritan tradition was infused into Methodism was through the family life of the Epworth rectory.⁸

Even with Keefer's statement, it seems that if Wesley had only to depend upon parental information and enthusiasm he would never have developed sympathy for his Puritan ancestry. It is clear that his sympathy did develop, as can be seen in this letter from John to Charles in 1768 concerning the possibility of one or more of Charles' sons entering the ministry:

> It is highly probable one of the three will stand before the Lord. But, so far as I can learn, such a thing has scarce been for these thousand years before, as a son, father, grandfather, *atavus tritavus*, preaching the gospel, nay and the genuine gospel in a line.⁹

As Frank Baker points out, the important fact to note here is that Wesley states that his ancestors proclaimed the "genuine" gospel, revealing

---

⁵ Frank Baker. *Wesley's Puritan Heritage.* (London, England: London Quarterly and Holborn Press, 1962) 182.

⁶ Ibid., 182.

⁷ Luke Keefer, "John Wesley, Disciple of Early Christianity" (Ph.D. diss., Temple University, 1982).

⁸ Ibid.

⁹ *Letters* 5:76.

his strong sympathy for his Puritan forebears, who for conscience' sake had defied the discipline of church and state.[10]

What may have had a greater influence on John Wesley's views of the Puritans and their beliefs was his exposure to Puritan writings. As early as 1739 Wesley read Neal's *History of the Puritans*. In 1747 he returned to this writing and commented:

> I stand amazed, First, at the execrable spirit of persecution, which drove these venerable men out of the church, and in which Queen Elizabeth's clergy were as deeply tinctured as ever Queen Mary's were: Secondly, at the weakness of the holy confessors, many of whom spent so much of their time, and strength in disputing about surplices and hoods, or kneeling at the Lord's Supper.[11]

That Wesley was familiar with Puritan literature, and was influenced by them is clear from his inclusion of Puritan writers in his *A Christian Library*. In 1748 Wesley began a correspondence entitled "To a Friend," with an idea of obtaining a list of dissenting writings to be included:

> I have often thought of mentioning to you, and a few others, a design I have had for some years of printing a little library, perhaps of four score or one hundred volumes, for the use of those that fear God. My purpose was to select whatever I had seen most valuable in the English language, and either abridge or take the whole tracts, only a little corrected or explained, as occasion should require. Of these I could print ten or twelve, more or less a year, on a fine paper, and large letter, which should be cast for the purpose . . .
>
> As soon as I am able to purchase a printing press and types, I think of entering on this design. I have several books now ready; and a printer who desires nothing more than food and raiment. In three or four weeks I hope to be in London, and if God permits, to begin without delay. [12]

Eventually Wesley published 50 volumes in his *A Christian Library*. Robert Monk, in listing the authors of the first edition, lists 32 of the 72 authors as Puritan. In the second edition of the library, Puritan materials make up 7200 pages compared with the Church of England material with

---

[10] Frank Baker. *Wesley's Puritan Heritage*. (London, England: London Quarterly and Holborn Press, 1962) 181.

[11] Ibid., 184.

[12] Frank Baker. *The Works of John Wesley*. Vol.26. (Oxford, England: Oxford University Press, 1982) 323.

3900 pages. In fact, the Puritan writers comprise nearly one half of the collection representing the largest single tradition of writers.[13]

Wesley explained why he included the large number of Puritan writings in the preface to his Puritan material in his *A Christian Library:*

> After an account of the lives and sufferings and deaths of those holy men who sealed the ancient religion with their blood, I believe nothing would either be more agreeable or more profitable to the serious reader then some extracts from the writing of those who sprung up, as it were, from the ashes. These breathe the same spirit, and were, in a lower degree, partakers of the same sufferings. Many of them took joyfully the spoiling of their goods, and all had their names cast out as evil, and thereby made a byword and receiver of reproach. I have endeavored to rescue from obscurity a few of the most eminent of these. I say a few for there is a multitude of them which it would be tedious even to name. Nor have I attempted to abridge all works of these few, for some of them are immensely voluminous. The works of Dr. Goodwin alone would have suffered to fill fifty volumes. I have therefore selected what I conceived would be of most general use, and most proper to form a complete body of Practical divinity.[14]

Frank Baker concludes that Wesley throughout the years realized that he had a close spiritual affinity with the Puritans, and his Puritan blood was in part responsible for his resolution to preach the "genuine gospel" no matter what the established church might say.[15]

In comparing Wesley and the Puritans more specifically on their view and use of Scripture, Luke Keefer states it well when he says:

> While many churchmen would have been content to rest on the interpretive comments of the fathers, the Puritans and Wesley opted for the more primitive voice of the Scriptures alone. This is one reason why Puritan divines excelled at biblical exegesis, an area of supreme interest for Wesley as his *Notes Upon the Old and New Testaments* demonstrates.[16]

---

[13] Robert Monk. *John Wesley: His Puritan Heritage.* (Nashville, Tenn.: Abingdon Press, 1966) 255–64.

[14] Ibid., 36.

[15] Frank Baker. *Wesley's Puritan Heritage.* (London, England: London Quarterly and Holburn Review, 1962) 186.

[16] Luke Keefer, "John Wesley, Disciple of Early Christianity," (Ph.d. diss., Temple University, 1982).

Wesley and the Quakers

Where Wesley differed in his views of the Bible from some other Protestant groups was chiefly in the areas of emphasis. According to Turner, Wesley and the Methodists stood midway between the Calvinists and the Friends in their general view of the Bible. To the Calvinist the Bible was the written Word of God through the Holy Spirit. There was little emphasis upon the Witness of the Spirit except in connection with the printed page. Calvin stated, "The very office of the Holy Spirit is to confirm within us what God has promised in His Word."[17] For the Friends, the Spirit could be received without the medium of the written Word to a greater extent then was accepted in most communions.

Wesley certainly shared some similarities with the Quakers, but their views usually went beyond his. A good example would be in the emphasis on the desire for "primitive Christianity." William Penn wrote a tract calling "Quakerism a new nickname for old Christianity." He wanted to make clear the ideal of basic Christianity or Christianity without frills. He coined the phrase "Primitive Christianity revived."[18] This certainly resembles Wesley's views on this subject.

The Quakers, even more than Wesley, emphasized experience. In their movement, God was real and personal and must be experienced. According to Elton Trueblood in his book *The People Called Quakers*, "It is the experience of the changed life that is true verification. The Quakers placed a strong emphasis on the doctrine of the Holy Spirit."[19]

Again, another similarity would be the emphasis on interpreting Scripture literally. The Quakers wished to take Scripture in plain words. However, the Quakers went much further in this emphasis than Wesley. They made fun of the biblical studies of Puritan pastors who spent, "so many years at Oxford and Cambridge to know what unlearned men, fishermen, ploughmen, and herdsmen did when they spoke forth the Scriptures."[20]

Like Wesley, the Quakers also felt that Scripture could only be interpreted correctly with the help of the Spirit. However, it was also at this point that the Quakers went well beyond where Wesley would be willing to follow. Their stress was on the immediacy of the Spirit, and the intuitive

---

[17] George Allen Turner. *Inspiration and Interpretation.* (Grand Rapids, Mich.: Wm. B. Eerdmann's Pub. Co., 1957) 157.

[18] D. Elton Trueblood. *The People Called Quakers.* (New York, N.Y.: Harper and Rowe Publishers, 1966) 64.

[19] Ibid., 67.

[20] Hugh Barbour. *The Quakers in Puritan England.* (New Haven, Conn.: Yale University Press, 1964) 157.

grasp of the truth. Thus the Friends could be found waiting in silence for the "inner light" brought by the Spirit.

George Fox, who was not an intellectual on the level of the reformers but was more of a mystic, maintained that the revelation of God never ended. The Book of Life was never closed. Man's soul was essentially prophetic.[21] Fox had a high opinion of the Bible, but he wished to emphasize the "inner light" without minimizing biblical faith. Maximin Piette in his book *John Wesley and the Evolution of Protestantism,* summarizes the Quaker's view stating that truth could not be found in State, Church, dissidents, or the Church of Rome. Truth could only be found in the Word of God, revealed by the inner light. This inner light, the Quakers claimed, was the true way to discover the meaning of the Bible and the works necessary for salvation."[22]

However, the stressing of the "inner light" had obvious dangers. There is always a temptation to forget or neglect biblical foundations. Almost of necessity the Bible takes a secondary role to the light within. Quakers did not expect the Spirit to contradict biblical revelation, but they did feel the Scripture and the leading of light were parallel. The Spirit worked with a power apart from Scripture to lead men to truth.

The Quakers believed that emphasizing the Light of Christ would save them from the temptation to idolize the Bible. According to Elton Trueblood, the Quakers felt they could not:

> . . . claim the Bible as their fundamental basis of faith, for that would be making the Scriptures more important than Christ. This is why the Quakers did not speak of the Bible as the Word of God. It is Christ alone who is the Word. The words of the Bible are good words, but they are not superior to the Eternal Word from which they came.[23]

The Quakers, but not Wesley, believed that the authors of the Bible could be mistaken. They believed that the church and the Pope were not infallible. However, they did not seem as aware of the dangers of error in their own leadership by the Spirit. Robert Barclay maintained for example, "We then trust to and confide in this Spirit, because we know and certainly

---

[21] Rufus Jones. *George Fox—Seeker and Friend.* (London, England: George Allen and University Press LTD., 1930) 77.

[22] Maximin Piette. *John Wesley ad the Evolution of Protestantism.* (London, England: Sheed and Ward, 1937) 172.

[23] Elton Trueblood. *The People Called Quakers.* (New York, N.Y.: Harper and Rowe Publishers, 1966) 79.

believe it can only lead us aright, and never mislead us."[24] While Wesley would agree that the Spirit of God is the real source of divine truth, he would not have agreed with Robert Barclay's statement that divine revelation is not subject to "the outward testimony of the Scripture, or of the reason of man, as to the more noble or certain rule or touchstone."[25] For Wesley, the "Scriptures are the touchstone."[26] Thus we see the primary differences were in the view of the Holy Spirit and His work, rather than in views upon the Bible.

Wesley and the Anglicans

If we compare Wesley's view of Scripture and authority with that of his own church it is clear that any differences are primarily in emphasis, not in the fundamentals. I have already emphasized, in the first chapter, the strong dependence Wesley had upon the Church of England, and the tremendous influence the church had upon the development of Wesley's scriptural views. The Sixth Article was a critical foundation in Wesley's view of the Bible. The Anglican Church in turn aligned itself with Classical Protestantism in commitment to "sola scriptura."[27] Wesley in turn was committed to the doctrines of his church.

It must be remembered however, that while Wesley followed the Anglican position recognizing Scripture as the final authority, he also recognized the importance of tradition and reason in interpreting Scripture as did Anglicanism. Thomas Tenison, Archbishop of Canterbury when the Wesley brothers were born, had defined the Protestant theological method as the "cogent use of Scripture, reason and tradition."[28] Even after Wesley, Francis Paget could affirm "that the distinctive strengths of Anglicanism rest upon its equal loyalty to the unconflicting rights of reason, Scripture and tradition."[29] It was within this framework that Wesley developed his own views on scriptural authority and interpretation.

While we recognize Wesley's dependence on and sympathy with Anglican Theology, we must also point out his distinctive position in that

---

[24] Ibid., 88.

[25] George Allen Turner. *Inspiration and Interpretation.* (Grand Rapids, Mich.: Wm B. Erdmann's Pub. Co., 1957) 158.

[26] *Letters* 2:117.

[27] Allen Coppedge. *John Wesley in Theological Debate.* (Wilmore, Ky.: Wesley Heritage Press, 1987) 63.

[28] Albert Outler, "The Wesleyan Quadrilateral in Wesley," *Wesleyan Theological Journal 20* (1985) 10.

[29] Ibid., 10.

Wesley would later add experience to the traditional Anglican Triad. It might be said that Wesley was attempting to incorporate the notion of conversion into Anglican tradition.[30] Equally as important it must be noted that whether in dealing with the Anglican Triad or the Wesleyan Quadrilateral, Holy Scripture was clearly superior and unique.

Wesley's Faith in the Bible

In the reading of Wesley's works I was amazed to find over 125 quotations that related in some form to Wesley's faith in the Bible. The difficulty arises in determining the method in which to present this material in an informative and interesting manner, without merely stringing together long lists of quotations. In this section I will provide examples from Wesley's writings of his belief in the Bible and his desire to be a Bible or Scriptural Christian. Also it will be shown how determined Wesley was that the Methodist movement be worthy of those same titles. The crowning portion will be Wesley's proclamation of the Bible as the ultimate source of all doctrine and the ultimate standard of judgment.

How strong was Wesley's belief in the Bible? He makes it quite clear, that he believes all that is in the Bible, and in fact is sure of nothing but Scripture. In a letter to the Reverend Mr. Venn in 1763 he states:

> If any one will convince me of my errors I will heartily thank him. I believe all the Bible as far as I understand it, and am ready to be convinced. If I am a heretic I became such by reading the Bible.[31]

In "The Principles of a Methodist Farther Explained" (1746) he states, "What will you believe? I hope no more than is written in the Book of God. And thus far you might venture to believe even without miracle."[32]

In his *Journal* in 1774 Wesley wrote, "I read Dr. Wilson's tract on 'The Circulation of the Blood.' What are we sure of but the Bible?"[33] On another occasion he remarked:

> After having sought for truth with some diligence for half a century, I am at this day (1768) hardly sure of anything but what I learn

---

[30] Ibid., 11.
[31] *Letters* 4:216.
[32] Rupert Davies. *The Works of John Wesley. Vol. 9.* (Nashville, Tenn.: Abingdon Press, 1989) 220.
[33] Reginald Ward and Richard Heitzenrater. *The Works of John Wesley. Vol. 22.* (Nashville, Tenn.: Abingdon Press, 1993)

from the Bible. Nay, I positively affirm I know nothing else so certainly that I would dare stake my salvation upon it.[34]

Wesley's belief and confidence in the Bible was so strong, that he felt those who disbelieved the Bible would be gullible enough to believe anything. Even the devil believed in the Bible, how could man disbelieve? In a letter to the "Editor of Lloyd's Evening Post" (1774) Wesley urges:

> I cannot but repeat the observation wherein experience confirms me more and more that they who disbelieve the Bible will believe anything. They may believe Voltaire. They may believe the Shastah. They may believe a man can put himself into a quart bottle.[35]

In his sermon "Of the Church" (1785), "For the devil believes, and cannot but believe, all that is written in the Old and New Testament is true."[36]

In reading Wesley one discovers that he not only was not ashamed, but he delighted in offering himself as a "Bible Bigot," or as a Bible or Scriptural Christian. Consider on May 2, 1766 Wesley says, "My ground is the Bible. Yea, I am a Bible Bigot. I follow it in all things both great and small."[37]

In a letter to Ann Bolton on March 25, 1772 Wesley painted a beautiful picture when he states, "Now you and I are Bigots to the Bible. We think the Bible language is like Goliath's sword, there is none like it."[38]

Wesley leaves no room for doubt when he describes his views in the following quotations. From "Causes of the Inefficacy of Christianity" (1789):

> Here I am: I and my Bible. I will not, I dare not vary from this Book, either in great things or small. I have no power to dispense with one jot or tittle of what is contained therein. I am determined to be a Bible Christian, not almost but altogether. Who will meet me on this ground? Join me on this or not at all.[39]

---

[34] *Journals* 2:470.

[35] *Letters* 6:123.

[36] Albert Outler. *The Works of John Wesley. Vol. 3.* (Nashville, Tenn.: Abingdon Press, 1986) 49.

[37] Reginald Ward. *The Works of John Wesley. Vol. 22.* (Nashville, Tenn.: Abingdon Press, 1993) 42.

[38] *Letters* 5:313.

[39] Albert Outler. *The Works of John Wesley. Vol.* (Nashville, Tenn.: Abingdon Press, 1987) 93.

In a letter to Freeborn Garrettson in 1789:

> If I have a plain Scripture or plain reason for doing a thing well. These are my rules, and my only rules. I regard not whether I had freedom or no. This is an unscriptural expression and a very fallacious rule. I wish to be in every point, great and small, a scriptural, rational Christian.[40]

Wesley was just as determined that the Methodists be Scriptural Christians, as evidenced by the number of occasions in which he proclaimed them such, or called them "back to the Bible." Note for example in 1765 Wesley writes in his "Short History of Methodism" (1765) that he and his associates in 1738 were of one heart and one judgment and "resolved to be Bible Christians at all events and wherever they were to preach, with all their might, plain old Bible Christianity."[41]

On a number of occasions Wesley challenged his associates and followers to be "Bible Christians." To his Joseph Benson in 1777 he proclaims, "We are called to propagate Bible religion through the land, that is faith working by love, holy tempers and holy lives."[42] In a letter to Mary Bishop in 1774 he states, "Most of our little flock at Oxford were tried with this, my brother and I in particular. Nay, but I say, 'To the Bible. To the Bible!"[43] To Joseph Cownley, in 1750, Wesley writes, "Oh keep close to the Bible! Neither you or I is wiser than either St. Peter or St. Paul."[44]

In a letter to an evangelical layman in 1751 he exclaims:

> I think it has likewise done great harm to their hearers, diffusing among them their own prejudice against other preachers; against their ministers, me in particular (of which you have been an undeniable instance), against the scriptural Methodist manner of preaching Christ. So we preached, and so you believed. This is the scriptural way, the Methodist Way, the true way.[45]

Wesley even more clearly lays down his desire that Methodism be a "Bible Religion," in his descriptions and defenses of Methodism in his writings. Wesley made it quite clear in his letters defending the movement that

---

[40] *Letters* 8:112.
[41] Rupert Davies. *The Works of John Wesley. Vol. 9.* (Nashville, Tenn.: Abingdon Press, 1989) 369.
[42] *Letters* 6:291.
[43] Ibid., 128.
[44] Frank Baker. *The Works of John Wesley. Vol.26.* (Oxford, England: Oxford University Press, 1982) 418.
[45] Ibid., 487–89.

Methodism had only one foundation, the Bible, and only one desire, to be Bible Christians. In his *Journal* in 1761 he states:

> The whole ingredients of Methodism, so called, have been discovered in print over and over. And, they are enrolled in a public register, the Bible, from which they extracted them at first.[46]

In "Letter to a Clergyman" (1787):

> Here, then, divide from the Methodists, whom they judge to be going too far. They would have their parishioners moral men- that is, in the plain terms honest heathens; but they would not have them pious men, devoted to God, Bible Christians.[47]

Wesley best expressed his view and vision of the Bible and its authority in relation to the Methodist movement when he attempted a detailed description of the history and character of Methodism in his essays and sermons. For example, in his essay entitled "A Short History of Methodism" (1765) he writes, "They endeavour to live according to what they preach, to be plain Bible Christians."[48]

Wesley gave a more extended description of Methodism's dependence on the Bible in his sermon "On Laying the Foundation of a New Church" (1777):

> Such was the rise and such has been the progress of Methodism from the beginning to the present time. But you will naturally ask, what is Methodism? What does this new word mean? Is it not a new religion? This is a very common, nay, almost universal supposition. But nothing can be more remote from the truth. It is a mistake all over. Methodism, so called, is the old religion, the religion of the Bible, the religion of the primitive church, the religion of the Church of England. 2. This is the religion of the Bible, as no one can deny who reads it with any attention. It is the religion which runs through the Old and New Testament. Moses and the prophets, our Blessed Lord, and His apostles proclaim with one voice, 'Thou shalt love the Lord thy God with all thy soul and thy neighbor as thyself' (Matt. 22:37). Love is the fulfilling of the Law (Romans 13:10), the end of the commandment (I Timothy 1:5), of all the commandments which are contained in the Oracles of God. The inward and the outward fruits of this love are also largely described

---

[46] Reginald Ward and Richard Heitzenrater. *The Works of John Wesley.* Vol. 21. (Nashville, Tenn.: Abingdon Press, 1992) 299.

[47] *Letters* 7:391.

[48] Rupert Davies. *The Works of John Wesley.* Vol. 9. (Nashville, Tenn.: Abingdon Press, 1989) 371.

by the inspired writers. So that whoever allows the Scripture to be the Word of God must allow this to be true religion.[49]

Finally, Wesley gives one other very clear description of the distinguishing characteristics of a Methodist in his essay "The Character of a Methodist" (1742). He would certainly include himself in this description as well as his desire for the movement as a whole. Once again his dependence on Scripture is abundantly clear:

> 1. The distinguishing marks of a Methodist are not his opinions of any sort. His assenting to this or that scheme of religion, his embracing any particular set of notions, his espousing the judgment of one man or of another, are quite wide of the point. Whosoever therefore imagines that a Methodist is a man of such or such an opinion is grossly ignorant of the whole affair; and he mistakes the truth totally. We believe, indeed, that all Scripture is given by inspiration of God,' and herein we are distinguished from the Jews, Turks, and Infidels. We believe this written Word of God to be the only and the sufficient rule of both Christian faith and practice, and herein we are fundamentally distinguished from those of the Romish Church. We never therefore willingly distinguish or designedly deviate from the most usual way of speaking unless when we express Scripture truths in Scripture words which we presume no Christian will condemn. Neither do we affect to use any particular expressions of Scripture more frequently than others, unless they are such as are more frequently used by the inspired writers themselves. Therefore neither will any man who knows where of he affirms, fix the mark of a Methodist here, in any actions or customs purely indifferent or undetermined by the Word of God.[50]

The Bible as the Source of All Doctrine and the Ground of All Judgment

Perhaps the strongest expression of Wesley's absolute dependence upon Scripture as the ultimate authority in all matters can be seen by the manner in which he used the Bible as the source of all doctrine and the ground of all judgments. Time and time again in his writings Wesley proclaimed there was no other authority but the Bible, that it was the rule of all actions,

---

[49] Albert Outler. *The Works of John Wesley. Vol. 3.* (Nashville, Tenn. Abingdon Press, 1986) 585–86.

[50] Rupert Davies. *The Works of John Wesley. Vol. 9.* (Nashville, Tenn.: Abingdon Press, 1989) 33–35.

and the source of all doctrine. His constant appeal as we see in his sermon "The Means of Grace" (1746), was to the "Law and the Testimony" and his demand was "where is it written."[51]

In this section I will show how firmly Wesley believed the Bible to be the ultimate authority and the source of all doctrines by a series of quotations. Also included will be a number of appeals to the "Law and the Testimony," and perhaps most importantly, Wesley's appeals to the final judgment bar, "is it written in Scripture?"

John Wesley made it perfectly clear in his writings all he wished to know could be found in the Bible, and there was no other authority but the written Word of God. I discovered over forty quotations that spoke specifically to this issue and have included a portion at this point. Please note that Wesley leaves no doubt where the answer lies when there is a question concerning rules, doctrines or authority. He clearly tells where we can find all we need to know in a letter to Henry Venn (1763), "If I am a heretic I became such by reading the Bible. All my notions I drew from thence, and with little help from men unless in the single point of Justification by Faith."[52]

In his essay entitled, "A Roman Catechism with a Reply Thereto" Wesley makes several strong statements concerning the authority and sufficiency of Scripture:

> The Scripture, therefore, is a rule sufficient in itself, and was by men divinely inspired, at once delivered to the world; and so neither needs nor is capable of any further addition. For as all faith is founded upon divine authority, so there is now no divine authority but the Scriptures, and therefore no one can make that to be of divine authority which is not contained in them.[53]

At this point I will list a few short quotations by Wesley as he elaborates on this issue of Scripture as the complete rule of faith and practice. Wesley proclaims, "I allow no other rule whether of faith or practice than the Holy Scriptures."[54] "The Scriptures are the complete rule of faith and practice, and they are clear in all necessary points."[55] "Enjoin nothing that

---

[51] Albert Outler. *The Works of John Wesley. Vol. 1.* (Nashville, Tenn.: Abingdon Press, 1984) 390.

[52] *Letters* 4:216.

[53] *Works* 10:90–91.

[54] Frank Baker. *The Works of John Wesley. Vol.25.* (Oxford, England: Oxford University Press, 1980) 265.

[55] *Letters* 2:325.

the Bible does not clearly enjoin, forbid nothing it does not clearly forbid."[56] "We cannot say or do either more or less than we apprehend consistent with the written Word of God."[57] Finally from "The Principles of a Methodist Farther Explained" (1746) "I have declared again and again that I make the Word of God the rule of all my actions and that I no more follow any 'secret impulse' instead thereof than I follow Mahomet or Confucius."[58]

As can be seen from some of these shorter quotations from Telford's collection of Wesley's letters, some of the clearest expressions of Wesley's views appear in his correspondence. In a letter to John Smith in 1745 Wesley notes:

> Nay, I know not that implicit faith was due to any or all of the Apostles put together. They were to prove their assertions by the written Word. You and I are to do the same. Without such proof I ought no more to have believed St. Peter himself than St. Peter's (pretended) successor. I receive the Written word as the whole and sole rule of my faith.[59]

In a letter to William Dodd in 1756 he states:

> I therein build on no authority, ancient or modern, but the Scripture. If this supports any doctrine, it will stand; if not, the sooner it falls the better. Neither the doctrine in question, nor any other, is anything to me unless it be the doctrine of Christ and His apostles. If, therefore, you will please to point out to me any passages in that sermon which are either contrary to Scripture or not supported by it, and to show that they are not, I shall be full as willing to oppose as ever I was to defend them. I search for truth, plain Bible truth, without any regard to the praise or dispraise of men.[60]

In his famous letter, originally thought to be to James Hervey, but now considered more likely to be John Clayton (1739), in which Wesley announced the "World was his Parish," he shows that he was bound by no other principle but Scripture in regard to the invasion of another man's parish:

> Permit me to speak plainly. If by catholic principles you mean any other than scriptural, they weigh nothing with me. I allow no other

---

[56] Ibid., 8:192.
[57] Reginald Ward and Richard Heitzenrater. *The Works of John Wesley. Vol. 20.* (Nashville, Tenn.: Abingdon Press, 1991) 16.
[58] Rupert Davies. *The Works of John Wesley. Vol. 9.* (Nashville, Tenn.: Abingdon Press, 1989) 198.
[59] *Letters* 2:44.
[60] Ibid., 3:157.

> rule whether of faith or practice, than the Holy Scriptures. But on scriptural principles I do not think it hard to justify whatever I do. God in Scripture commands me according to my power to instruct the ignorant, reform the wicked, confirm the virtuous. Man forbids me to do this in another's parish; that is in effect to do it at all; seeing I have now no parish of my own, nor probably ever shall. Whom then shall I hear, God or man? If it be just to obey man rather than God, judge you. A dispensation of the gospel is committed to me; and woe to me if I preach not the gospel. But where shall I preach it upon the principles you mention?[61]

Thus Wesley showed his belief that the Bible was the complete rule of faith, the rule of all actions, the ultimate authority. Another example of how seriously he believed these statements is evidenced by the way in which he based all doctrine upon Scripture. As previously noted in the letter to John Smith (1746), Wesley proclaimed "The ultimate appeal must always be to the Scripture."[62] Time and time again Wesley maintained that the foundation of all doctrine was the Bible. In a letter to the Reverend Mr. Downes in 1759 answering charges against the Methodists he states, "They 'search the Scriptures' and hereby try every doctrine whether it be of God. And what is agreeable to Scripture they embrace, what is contrary to it they reject."[63] Later in 1772 in "Some remarks to Mr Hill" he states "Every doctrine must stand or fall by the Bible."[64]

For Wesley the written Word of God was the whole rule of faith. Every doctrine, every imagination was to be judged against the Bible. In a letter to William Dodd in 1756, "I try every church and every doctrine by the Bible. This is the Word by which we are judged in that day."[65] From his *Journal* in 1744 we read, "We cannot indeed say or do either more or less than we apprehend consistent with the written Word of God."[66] In a letter to John Smith in 1745 "(2). an imagination that a doctrine not provable by Scripture might nevertheless be proved by miracles. I believe not. I receive the written Word as the whole and sole rule of my faith."[67]

---

[61] Frank Baker. *The Works of John Wesley. Vol. 25.* (Nashville, Tenn.: Abingdon Press, 1980) 615.

[62] *Letters* 2:244.

[63] Rupert Davies. *The Works of John Wesley. Vol. 9.* (Nashville, Tenn.: Abingdon Press, 1989) 363.

[64] *Works* 10:412.

[65] *Letters* 3:172.

[66] Reginald Ward and Richard Heitzenrater. *The Works of John Wesley. Vol. 20.* (Nashville, Tenn.: Abingdon Press, 1991) 16.

[67] Frank Baker. *The Works of John Wesley. Vol. 26.* (Oxford, England: Oxford University Press, 1982) 155.

Perhaps no word from Wesley would better summarize his conviction of the authority of Scripture as the ultimate rule of right and wrong than this quotation from his sermon "The Witness of Our Own Spirit" (1746):

> But the Christian rule of right and wrong is the Word of God, the writings of the Old and New Testament: all which the prophets and 'holy men of old' wrote 'as they were moved by the Holy Ghost', all that 'Scripture' which was' given by inspiration of God' and which is indeed 'profitable for doctrine; or teaching the whole will of God, 'for reproof' of what is contrary thereto; 'for correction' of error; and 'for instruction' (or training us up) in righteousness (II Timothy 3:16).
>
> This 'is a lantern unto a' Christian's feet', and a 'light in all his paths.' This alone he receives as his rule of right and wrong, of whatever is really good or evil. He esteems nothing good but what is here enjoined, either directly or by plain consequence. He accounts nothing evil but what is here forbidden, either in terms or by undeniable inference. Whatever the Scripture neither forbids nor enjoins (either directly or by plain consequence) he believes to be of an indifferent nature, to be in itself neither good nor evil: this being the whole and sole outward rule whereby his conscience is to be directed in all things.[68]

In reading Wesley it is clear that he showed his belief in the ultimate authority of the Bible more specifically than just speaking in generalities of it being the source and the judgment bar of all doctrine. When specific doctrinal questions or issues arose, Wesley's admonition was to appeal to the "Law and Testimony." In a letter to Thomas Whitehead in 1748:

> The Scriptures are the touchstone whereby Christians examine all, real or supposed revelations. In all cases they appeal to the law and the testimony and try every spirit thereby.[69]

How were Christians to test the spirits and discern if they were from God? The answer was not found in dreams or visions which might not be from God, instead they must be "brought to a certain test, the Law and the Testimony."[70] What about discerning the will of God? Again the answer was not to be found in dreams, visions, or impressions as he reveals in his sermon "The Nature of Enthusiasm" but by, "consulting the oracles

---

[68] Albert Outler. *The Works of John Wesley. Vol. 1.* (Nashville, Tenn.: Abingdon Press, 1984) 302–03.

[69] *Letters* 2:117.

[70] Reginald Ward and Richard Heitzenrater. *The Works of John Wesley. Vol. 19.* (Nashville, Tenn.: Abingdon Press, 1990) 73.

of God. 'To the law and to the testimony.' This is the general method of knowing what is 'the holy and acceptable will of God.'"[71]

Note the appeals to Richard Morgan Sr. in the following two letters, the first from 1732 and the second from 1734:

> To the law and testimony we appeal, whereby we ought to be judged. If by these it can be proved that we are in error, we will immediately and gladly retract it.[72]

> The question then must be determined some way; and for an infallible determination of it to the law and testimony we appeal. At that tribunal we ought to be judged. If the oracles of God are still open to us, by them must every doubt be decided. And should all men contradict them we could only say, 'Let God be true and every man a liar.'[73]

For a final example consider Wesley's warning in his "Sermon On the Mount XII" (1750):

> And see that you bring whatever you hear 'to the law and to the testimony.' Receive nothing untried, nothing till it is weighed in 'the balance of the sanctuary.' Believe nothing they say unless it is clearly confirmed by plain passages of Holy Writ.[74]

Another prime example of how firmly Wesley held to the authority of the Bible can be seen in the numerous occasions in which he appealed directly to passages of Scripture. To Wesley, if a word or doctrine was found in the Scripture and not misused in some form, it was authoritative and should be followed. If it was not found in the Scripture he wanted nothing to do with it.

Consider first how Wesley felt bound to preach and teach doctrines, if they were based on the authority of Scripture. He felt one obligation, to preach and teach the Word of God. If it was Scripture, it was authoritative and it must be expounded. In 1772 Wesley expounded on I Corinthians 13. He noted it was love that the congregation lacked, but they did not

---

[71] Albert Outler. *The Works of John Wesley. Vol. 2.* (Nashville, Tenn.: Abingdon Press, 1985) 54.
[72] Frank Baker. *The Works of John Wesley. Vol. 25.* (Oxford, England: Oxford University Press, 1980) 343.
[73] Frank Baker. *The Works of John Wesley. Vol. 25.* (Oxford, England: Oxford University Press, 1980.) 380
[74] Albert Outler. *The Works of John Wesley. Vol. 1.* (Nashville, Tenn.: Abingdon Press, 1984) 683.

want to be told so, "But I cannot help that. I must declare just what I find in the Book."[75]

In his sermon on "Satan's Devices" (1750), Wesley clearly proclaims the authority of the Word of God even if man abused Scripture:

> But the abuse of this or any other scriptural doctrine does by no means destroy its use. Neither can the unfaithfulness of man perverting his right way 'make the promise of God of none effect.' No 'let God be true and every man a liar.' The Word of the Lord shall stand.[76]

Note the manner in which Wesley showed that all pastoral authority was based upon Scripture, but that authority did not go beyond Scripture itself, in his sermon "On Obedience to Pastors" (1785):

> Whatever they desire of him to do, he does: if it be not forbidden in the Word of God. Whatever they desire him to refrain from, he does so; if it be not enjoined in the Word of God. I speak all this on supposition (though that is a supposition not to be made), that the Bible was silent on this head; that the Scripture said nothing concerning dress and left it to everyone's own discretion. But if all other texts were silent, this is enough, 'Submit yourselves to them that are over you in the Lord.'[77]

What if the doctrine, subject or issue was controversial? For Wesley, they could not be denied if they were scriptural. In his sermon "On Faith" (1788) Wesley states:

> Indeed sceptics may ask, 'How do disembodied spirits know each other?' I answer plainly, 'I cannot tell.' But I am certain that they do. That is as plainly proved from one passage of Scripture, as it could be from a thousand. Did not Abraham and Lazarus know each other in Hades even afar off? The Scripture therefore clearly decides this question.[78]

Note how Wesley in his sermon, "The Witness of the Spirit I" (1746), continually calls the hearers to Scripture, in the effort to distinguish God's voice from other presuppositions:

> How then may the real testimony of the Spirit with our spirit be distinguished from this damning presupposition? 3. I answer, the

---

[75] *Sermons* 5:488.
[76] Albert Outler. *The Works of John Wesley. Vol. 2.* (Nashville, Tenn.: Abingdon Press, 1985) 147.
[77] Ibid., 3:379–83.
[78] Ibid., 4:197.

Holy Scriptures abound with marks whereby the one may be distinguished from the other. For the Scriptures lay down the clear obvious marks. For instance the Scripture describes repentance. Again the Scriptures describe the being born of God. The Scripture describes the joy of the Lord. Once more the Scriptures teach, 'This is the Love of God,' (the sure mark thereof), 'that we keep His commandments.'[79]

There was no more controversial issue Wesley had to deal with than his position on holiness, specifically the doctrine of Christian Perfection. It would have been much easier to drop the whole concept, but he refused because it was scriptural. In "A Farther Appeal to Men of Reason and Religion, Part 1" (1745) he maintains:

> 10. Many of those who are perhaps as 'zealous of good works' as you think I have allowed you too much. Nay my brethren, but how can we help allowing it, if we allow the Scriptures to be from God? For is it not written, and do not you yourselves believe; 'Without holiness no man shall see the Lord?' And how, then, without fighting about words, can we deny that holiness is a condition of final acceptance? And as, to the first acceptance, or pardon, does not all experience as well as Scripture prove that no man ever yet truly 'believed the gospel' who did not first repent.[80]

In his *Plain Account of Christian Perfection* Wesley reiterates quite forcefully the doctrine he preached and why he preached it:

> 'This is Mr. Wesley's doctrine. He preaches perfection!' He does; yet this is not his doctrine, any more than it is yours, or anyone's else, that is a minister of Christ. For it is His doctrine, peculiarly, emphatically His; it is the doctrine of Jesus Christ. These are His words, not mine: 'Ye shall therefore be perfect, as your Father who is in heaven is perfect' (Matthew 5: 48). And who says ye shall not; or at least, not till your soul is separated from the body?
>
> It is the doctrine of St. Paul, the doctrine of St. James, of St. Peter, and St. John; and no otherwise Mr. Wesley's than it is the doctrine of every one who preaches the pure and the whole Gospel. I tell you, as plain as I can speak, where and when I found this. I found it in the oracles of God, in the Old and New Testament; when I read them with no other view or desire,

---

[79] Ibid., 1:277–81.
[80] Gerald Cragg. *The Works of John Wesley. Vol. 11.* (Nashville, Tenn.: Abingdon Press, 1989) 116.

but to save my own soul. But whosoever the doctrine, is I pray you, what harm is there in it?[81]

Just as firmly as Wesley determined to preach all doctrines found in the Scripture, he was as steadfastly opposed to preaching any idea or doctrine not found in Scripture. The authority was to be found in the Word of God. If it could not be found in Holy Writ, it was not worth considering. Wesley summarizes this thought well in a letter to Joseph Benson in 1788:

> You will observe that it is dangerous on such subjects to depart from Scripture either as to language or sentiment. I believe that most controversies which have disturbed the Church have arisen from people's wanting to be wise above what is written, not contented with what God has plainly revealed there.[82]

Another good example can be seen from Wesley's visit to Bristol in 1740. Here Wesley was approached by a man who wished to know if a person could be saved without the faith of assurance. Wesley's answer showed how strongly he held to the doctrine, but also how careful he was not to go beyond the bounds of Scripture:

> (1) I cannot approve of your terms because they are not scriptural. I find no such phrases as either 'faith of assurance' or 'faith of adherence' in the Bible.[83]

On this same issue of assurance, Wesley wrote in a letter to Rev. Arthur Bedford in 1738, "I dare not affirm so much of this assurance, or that 'it is given to very few,' for I believe it is given to none at all. I find it not in the Book of God."[84] Again to Samuel Walker in 1756, "Assurance is a word I do not use because it is not scriptural."[85] Wesley refused to accept any concept or doctrine not clearly shown in Scripture. It did not matter if this issue was unconditional election,[86] heresy or schism,[87] submitting to parish

---

[81] John Wesley. *A Plain Account of Christian Perfection*. (Kansas City, Mo.: Beacon Hill Press, 1971) 117.

[82] *Letters* 8:89.

[83] Reginald Ward and Richard Heitzenrater. *The Works of John Wesley. Vol. 19*. (Nashville, Tenn.: Abingdon Press, 1990) 136.

[84] Frank Baker. *The Works of John Wesley. Vol.25*. (Oxford, England: Oxford University Press, 1980) 563.

[85] *Letters* 3:222.

[86] *Works* 9:210.

[87] *Letters* 3:182.

authority,[88] the consecration of churches,[89] or any other issue. Where was it found in Scripture?

Another clear example of this allegiance to the Word of God can be seen in Wesley's sermon "The Marks of the New Birth" (1748):

> But some men will say, 'True, whosoever is born of God doth not commit sin, habitually.' Habitually! Whence is that? I read it not. It is not written in the Book of God. God plainly saith, 'he doth not commit sin' I John 3:9. And thou addest 'habitually.' Who art thou that mendest the Oracles of God. Thou 'addest to the Words of this Book'. Beware, I beseech thee lest God 'add to thee all the plagues that are written therein' Rev. 22:18.[90]

Wesley issues his rallying cry once again in a letter to William Law in 1756:

> But I would gladly know by what authority you give us this touchstone, and how you prove it to be infallible. I read nothing like it in the Oracles of God. Where does the Bible speak this?[91]

How much more strongly could Wesley make his views known than in the comments seen in the following three sermons? In "The Means of Grace" (1746) he states quite unequivocally, "I pray, where is this written? I expect you should show me plain Scripture for your assertion, otherwise I dare not receive it, because I am not convinced you are wiser than God."[92]

In his sermon "On the Wedding Garment" (1790), Wesley speaks concerning a statement made by John Calvin:

> 6. Another elegant writer, now I trust with God, speaks strongly to the same effect in the preface to his comment on St. Paul's Epistle to the Romans, 'We certainly,' says he, 'shall need a better righteousness than our own, wherein to stand at the bar of God on the day of judgment.' I do not understand the expression. Is it scriptural? Do we read it in the Bible? Either in the Old Testament or the New? I doubt, it is an unscriptural, awkward phrase, which has no determinate meaning.[93]

---

[88] Albert Outler. *The Works of John Wesley.* Vol. 3. (Nashville, Tenn.: Abingdon Press, 1986) 377.
[89] Rupert Davies. *The Works of John Wesley.* Vol. 9.(Nashville, Tenn.: Abingdon Press, 1989) 537.
[90] Albert Outler. *The Works of John Wesley.* Vol. 1. (Nashville, Tenn.: Abingdon Press, 1984) 420.
[91] *Letters* 3:365.
[92] Albert Outler. *The Works of John Wesley.* Vol. 1. (Nashville, Tenn.: Abingdon Press, 1984) 390.
[93] Ibid., 4:142.

Finally, I believe Wesley's message, "On Knowing Christ After the Flesh" (1789), is a clear example of his desire to stay true to the authority of Scripture and scriptural expressions. Wesley comments on the practice of using the phrases, "our dear Lord, our dear Savior":

> Is there any Scripture, any passage either in the Old or New Testament which justifies this manner of speaking? Does any of the inspired writers make use of it, even in the poetical Scriptures?. Therefore I still doubt whether any of the inspired writers ever addresses the word to either the Father or the Son. Hence, I cannot but advise all lovers of the Bible, if they use the expression at all, to use it very sparingly, seeing the Scripture affords neither command or precedent for it. And surely 'if any man speaks' either in preaching or prayer 'he should speak as the Oracles of God' I Peter 4:11.[94]

The Sources of Scriptural Authority

In closing this chapter I believe it has been shown that John Wesley had a tremendous confidence and a dogmatic allegiance to the authority of Scripture. Some would feel that this view ignores common sense. None the less, for Wesley, the Bible was the ultimate authority on all matters of faith and practice. The Bible was the source of his convictions, the only standard of truth and the model of pure religion. The Bible was the source of all doctrine, the standard of all judgment. Whatever was in the Bible was to be believed, whatever was absent was to be rejected. John Wesley was perfectly willing to be known as a "Bible Bigot," and he wished the Methodist movement no better title. In reading Wesley it does not appear his views changed radically throughout his life. In accepting these statements a question still might be asked, "Why was Wesley so confident in the authority of the Bible?" The answer is simply because the Bible was from God. If it is asked, "Why was Wesley so insistent that all doctrine, teaching and preaching be centered upon the Scripture," the answer would be because the Bible was the means God had chosen to bear the message of redemption.

Ultimately for John Wesley, the Bible derived its authority from divine inspiration. The Bible had ultimate authority because the Bible was from God. In an "Earnest Appeal to Men of Reason and Religion" (1744), Wesley writes, "We believe the Scripture to be of God. According to the light we have, the Scripture is of God and while we believe this we dare not turn aside from it, to the right hand or the left."[95]

---

[94] Ibid., 102.
[95] *Works* 8:6.

In his sermon "Dives and Lazarus" (1788), Wesley wrote, "I warn you in His name that the Scriptures are the real Word of God."[96]

In chapter six I will take an in depth look at Wesley's view of the inspiration of Scripture. At this point however, it must be said, a clear understanding of his belief in, and emphasis and use of the Bible cannot be obtained without a realization that for Wesley the Bible's ultimate authority came from the fact that all Scripture is inspired by God.

> We believe, indeed that 'all Scripture is given by inspiration of God' (II Timothy 3:16), and herein are we distinguished from Jew, Turks, and infidels. We believe this written Word of God to be the only and the sufficient rule both of Christian faith and practice; and herein we are fundamentally distinguished from those of the Romish Church.[97]

To truly appreciate Wesley's faith in the authority of Scripture we must acknowledge his use of Scripture. Actions speak louder than words, and for Wesley the primary purpose of Scripture is to function as a means of bearing the message of redemption. The Bible has a saving purpose and that is its reason for being. The Bible is a practical book that contains the way to holiness and heaven. We should recall this powerful quotation from the preface to his *Sermons*:

> I want to know one thing, the way to heaven—how to land safe on that happy shore. God himself has condescended to teach the way: for this very end He came from heaven. He hath written it down in a book. O give me that book. At any price give me the Book of God. I have it. Here is knowledge enough for me. Let me be '*homo unius libri*'.[98]

The authority of Scripture was based firmly in the work of Christ, the testimony of the Holy Spirit, and the reliability of Scripture as a channel through which the Spirit applied the grace of salvation.[99]

Wesley's use of Scripture as the source and life of his ministry showed how emphatically he believed the absolute authority and total reliability of the Bible. Dr. Wilber Dayton in his article "The Bible in the Wesleyan Tradition" states it well when he says:

---

[96] Albert Outler. *The Works of John Wesley. Vol. 4.* (Nashville, Tenn.: Abingdon Press, 1987) 16.

[97] Rupert Davies. *The Works of John Wesley. Vol. 9.* (Nashville, Tenn.: Abingdon Press, 1989) 33–34.

[98] Albert Outler. *The Works of John Wesley. Vol. 1.* (Nashville, Tenn.: Abingdon Press, 1984) 105.

[99] Larry Shelton. "John Wesley's Approach to Scripture in Historical Perspective," *Wesleyan Theological Journal 16* (1981) 39.

It is that plain and simple. The Scriptures stand alone adequate, as the ultimate source of Wesley's belief and teaching. Oxford scholar that he was, he trusted only one Book as utterly reliable in the great issues of life. Though he read ten languages and published over four hundred pieces himself, these were only to understand better the one book. How could any doubt surround Wesley's view of the Scripture?[100]

After reading Wesley's works I must echo Dr. Dayton's conclusion. If anyone would question Wesley's commitment to the authority of Scripture, in all matters of faith and practice, I would suggest even a cursory review of Wesley's writings would remove this doubt.

---

[100] Wilbur Dayton, "The Bible in the Wesleyan Tradition," *Asbury Theological Journal 40* (1983) 28–29.

5

John Wesley and Biblical Instruction

Perhaps the best way to discern John Wesley's view of the Bible is to review the manner in which he used the Scripture in his everyday life and ministry. In chapter four I endeavored to show the lengths to which Wesley went to ensure that his preaching and teaching were biblical. In this chapter I want to go one step further, and thoroughly, yet concisely, review the manner in which Wesley used the Bible in different areas of instruction. The areas to be considered will include his use of the Bible in preaching, instruction to the church, his letters and hymns, his translation of the Greek New Testament, his *Explanatory Notes*, and his practice of bibliomancy. Finally, I believe it is important to stress that while Wesley claimed to be a "Man of One Book," a better name might be a "Man of a Thousand and One Books." After considering in depth Wesley's use of the Bible in all forms of instruction, I will briefly note his commitment to all forms of literature.

In this chapter it will become clear that the Bible was truly Wesley's second language. Wesley knew the Scripture so by heart that even his natural speech was biblical.[1] Not only in his preaching and teaching, but also his letters, hymns, and essays are woven and filled with biblical texts and paraphrases. The profound impact of Scripture upon Wesley's thought will be clearly evidenced as it is shown how impregnated all of his works are with the Scripture.

Wesley's Use of the Bible in Preaching

If one word was to be used to describe the thrust of John Wesley's ministry, that word might be "preacher." It is difficult to number the sermons John Wesley preached during the half century of his itinerant ministry. In 1765

---

[1] Albert Outler. *The Works of John Wesley. Vol. 1* (Nashville, Tenn.: Abingdon Press, 1984) 69.

Wesley stated he preached "about 800 sermons a year."[2] It is thought he must have preached three or four times a day during the last fifty years of his life. If this is true, as seems to be reflected in his *Journal* and sermon registers, than the numbers are monumental, numbering no fewer than 52,400 sermons.[3]

William C. Pellowe makes vast claims for Wesley the preacher stating that judging by results, the greatest preacher since the days of Jesus and of Paul, was John Wesley. His sermons reformed more lives, lifted more nations, produced more preachers, missionaries and Christian workers, released more social regenerative energies, and gave rise to more separate denominations than the sermons of any man that used the area of preaching as his instrument of productive action.[4] Considering Wesley's use of Scripture should also allow us to examine Pellowe's claim.

Wesley's extensive use of Scripture in his ministry is nowhere more thoroughly illustrated than in his sermons. The Bible, the whole Bible and nothing but the Bible, was the theme of John Wesley's preaching.[5] As Wesley's confidence and dependence upon the authority of Scripture was clearly evidenced in the last chapter, it should come as no surprise that his message was entirely and exclusively derived from the Bible.

To understand Wesley's dependence upon the Bible in his preaching we must note once again his belief that the Bible was from God and that the ultimate purpose of preaching was soteriological. For Wesley, the message that he was declaring was not a human theory, but a divine revelation. His message was not from below, but from above. It did not represent the latest theological invention, but the everlasting and unalterable truth of God. Wesley's message was taken straight from the authoritative record of salvation history to be found in the pages of Holy Writ.[6] As stated by Dr. L. M. Starkey, "His constant reference to the authority of the Bible reflects his conviction that the book literally was given by God to men and contains all those things necessary for the salvation of all mankind."[7] Rev. James Stewart states, "The first axiom of effective evangelism is that the evangelist

---

[2] *Journals* 5:116

[3] William Arnett, "John Wesley-The Man of One Book" (Ph.D. diss., Drew University, 1954).

[4] Ibid.

[5] Franz Hildebrandt, *The Works of John Wesley. Vol. 7.* (Nashville, Tenn.: Abingdon Press, 1983) 3.

[6] A. Skevington Wood. *The Burning Heart.* (Grand Rapids, Mich.: Wm B Eerdmanns Pub. Co., 1967) 209

[7] Ibid., 218.

must be sure of his message."[8] Wesley certainly had the clear conviction that the Bible was revealed truth with the power to save. For Wesley the Word of God was the "power of God unto salvation," and he demonstrated this view of Scripture more clearly in his ministry than in any affirmation.

Wesley's use of Scripture had one ultimate center and that was soteriological. All else was subservient to this. Wesley preached his first sermon one week after his ordination. His text was Matthew 6:33 "Seek ye first the Kingdom of God and His righteousness and all these things shall be added unto you." Sixty-five years later his last sermon, eight days before his death, was still soteriological. He preached upon Isaiah 55:6 "Seek ye the Lord while He may be found, call upon Him while He is near." Wesley's message never changed. For him the primary purpose of Scripture, with preaching as the mode of expression, was bearing the message of redemption.[9]

This high conception of the preacher's calling and the strict focus of his task is clearly summarized in Wesley's letter to a lay preacher, Christopher Hopper written from Bristol in 1755 :

> You have one business on earth-to save souls. Give yourself wholly to this.
> Fulfill the work of a preacher, and of an assistant as you never did before. Be another Thomas Walsh. Pursue the whole of scriptural Christianity.[10]

Recognizing both the source and the purpose of Scripture, it is understandable that Wesley would emphasize the importance of a minister having a clear knowledge of Scripture. A quotation from his essay, an "Address to Clergy" (1756), clearly expresses this necessity :

> Let us each seriously examine himself. Have I. 1) Such a knowledge of Scripture as becomes him who undertakes so to explain it to others, that it may be light in all their paths. Have I a full and clear view of the analogy of faith, which is the clue to guide me through the whole? Am I acquainted with the several parts of Scripture; with all parts of the Old Testament and the New? Upon the mention of any text, do I know the context and the parallel places? Have I that point at least of a good Divine, the being a good textuary? Do I know the grammatical construction of the four Gospels; of the Acts; of the Epistles; and am I a master of the spiritual sense

---

[8] Wilber Dayton, "The Bible in the Wesleyan Tradition," *Asbury Theological Journal* (1983) 22–28.

[9] Harold Kingdon, "John Wesley Bible Scholar Extraordinaire," *The Asbury Seminarian* (1985) 39–54.

[10] *Letters* 3:148.

(as well as the literal) of what I read? Do I understand the scope of each book, and how every part of it tends thereunto? Have I skill to draw the natural inferences, deducible from each text? Do I know the objections raised to them or from them by Jews, Deists, Papists, Arians, Socinians and all other sectaries who more or less corrupt or caponize the Word of God? Am I ready to give a satisfactory answer to each of these objections? And have I learned to apply every part of the sacred writings, as the various states of my hearers require?

2) Do I understand Greek and Hebrew? Otherwise, how can I undertake, (as every Minister does), not only to explain books which are written therein, but to defend them against all opponents? Am I not at the mercy of everyone who does understand, or even pretends to understand the original.[11]

In this quotation we begin to see Wesley's concern with biblical interpretation, which will be considered in detail in a later chapter. At this point, it is safe to say that Wesley would feel that one could not preach what one did not know. Therefore, a thorough knowledge of Scripture was required for all ministers who would preach or teach the gospel.

In an "Address to Clergy," we also see Wesley's concern that the Bible be preached accurately and without corruption. This message is even more clearly relayed in his sermon "On Corrupting the Word of God" (1727), based upon II Corinthians 2:17. In summarizing the key elements of this message, Wesley includes among the corrupters:

1). Those who introduce into it 'human mixtures' and blend with the oracles of God impure dreams, fit only for the mouth of the devil.

2). Those who mix it with false interpretation.

3). Those who do not add to it, but take from it, washing their hands of stubborn texts that will not lend to their purposes, or that plainly touch upon the reigning vices of the places where they live.

Those who do not corrupt the Word of God:

Preach it genuine and unmixed, unimpaired and in all its fullness. They speak with plainness and boldness and are not concerned to pollute their doctrine to reconcile it to the tastes of men. They will not, they dare not soften a threatening so as to prejudice its

---

[11] *Works* 10:490–491.

strength, neither represent sin in such mild colors as to impair its native blackness.[12]

As we recognize Wesley's concern with preaching the Bible accurately and without corruption, it stands to reason that Wesley would show complete dependence upon the Bible in his sermonizing. A glance at Wesley's sermon register from Jan 14, 1747 to December 25, 1761 clearly evidences the degree to which Wesley relied upon the Bible. In this section 1354 scriptural sources are noted, with 1088 from the New Testament and 266 from the Old Testament.[13]

Albert Outler gives an interesting summary of Wesley's use of the Bible in his preaching in the introduction of Vol. I in *The Works of John Wesley* (1984). According to the texts from which he preached, the Gospel of Matthew was his favorite book (1362 recorded usages), followed by Hebrews (965), John (870), Luke (853), and I Corinthians (779). His Old Testament favorites were Isaiah (668), Psalms (624), and Jeremiah (208). His favorite New Testament text was Mark 1:15 (190 usages), and his favorite Old Testament text was Isaiah 55:7 (112 usages). There were six Old Testament books from which he did not preach (Ezra, Nehemiah, The Song of Solomon, Obadiah, Nahum and Zephaniah). He cited the Apocrypha, but never took an apocryphal text for a sermon.[14] This summary obviously does not include all texts from which Wesley preached as it does not approach 52,400 sermons, but it does show his predilection for certain texts.

The most fascinating aspect of Wesley's use of the Bible in his preaching is the manner in which he wove Scripture into the text of his sermons. Passage after passage is used with ease, skill and freedom in setting forth a given idea. Indeed many paragraphs in Wesley' sermons are wholly composed of Scripture connected by a few words of his own writings.[15] W. E. Sangster rightly observes:

> Some of his pages are little more than a catena of quotations. He seems to have lived in the Scripture so long that Bible phrasing has become second nature to him, and he swims from one citation to another with effortless ease.[16]

---

[12] Albert Outler. *The Works of John Wesley. Vol. 4.* (Nashville, Tenn., Abingdon Press, 1987) 247.
[13] Samuel Rogal, "Scriptural Quotations in Wesley's Earnest Appeal," *Research Studies* (1979) 181–188.
[14] Albert Outler. *The Works of John Wesley. Vol. 1.* (Nashville, Tenn.: Abingdon Press, 1984) 70.
[15] William Pellowe, "John Wesley's Use of the Bible," *Methodist Review* (1923) 363.
[16] W. E. Sangster. *The Path to Perfection.* (Nashville, Tenn.: Abingdon Press, 1943) 36.

John Wesley and Biblical Instruction

Any number of Wesley's sermons could be considered as examples of this infusion of Scripture, but I will limit myself to two examples. One perfect example is the sermon "Scriptural Christianity" (1744).[17] Dr. William Arnett states that there are 176 scriptural passages woven into the first three sections of the sermon.[18] E. H. Sugden writes concerning this sermon:

> There is hardly a sentence which is not directly derived from the Scripture, but the arrangement is so skillful that the impression is not a pistachio of texts, but of a full flood of impassioned eloquence.[19]

One representative section from this message which evidences how impregnated the sermon is in Scripture, comes from the third section:

> Suppose now the fullness of time be come (Ephesians 1:10 or Galatians 4:4), and the prophecies to be accomplished—what a prospect is this! All is 'peace, quietness and assurance forever' (Isaiah 32:17). Here is no din of arms, no 'confused noise' (Isaiah 9:5), 'no garments rolled in blood' (Isaiah 9:5). 'Destructions are come to a perpetual end' (Psalms 9:6): 'wars ceased from the earth' (Psalm 46:9). Neither is there any intestine jar remaining: no 'brother rising up against brother;' (Matthew 10:21), no 'country or city divided against itself' (Matthew 12:25), and tearing out its own bowels. Civil discord is at an end for evermore and none is left to destroy or hurt his neighbor (Isaiah 11:9). Here is no oppression to 'make (even) the wise man mad' (Ecclesiastes 7:7); no extortion to 'grind the face of the poor' (Isaiah 3:15); no robbing or wrong: rapine or injustice; for all are 'content with such things as they possess' (Hebrews 13:5). Thus, 'righteousness and peace have kissed each other' (Psalm 85:10); they have 'taken root and filled the land' (Jeremiah 12:2), righteousness flourishing out of the earth, and 'peace looks down from heaven' (Psalm 85:11).[20]

Once again Dr. Arnett observes there are fourteen scriptural passages here, skillfully woven together. In fact of the 166 words in this section, 82 are from the Bible.[21]

---

[17] Albert Outler. *The Works of John Wesley. Vol. 1.* (Nashville, Tenn.: Abingdon Press, 1984) 159–180.

[18] William Arnett, "John Wesley-The Man of One Book" (Ph.D. diss., Drew University, 1954).

[19] Sermons 1:91.

[20] Albert Outler. *The Works of John Wesley. Vol.1.* (Nashville, Tenn.: Abingdon Press, 1984) 170–71.

[21] William Arnett, "John Wesley-The Man of One Book" (Ph. D. diss., Drew University, 1954).

Consider one other example of this scriptural saturation by observing over a dozen scriptural references in the following two paragraphs from "Salvation by Faith" (1738):

> 3. First, from the guilt of all past sin. For whereas 'all the world is guilty before God' (Romans 3:19); insomuch that should he 'be extreme to mark what is done amiss, there is none that could abide it' (Psalm 130:3); and whereas 'by the law is only the knowledge of sin,' but no deliverance from it, so that by 'fulfilling the deeds of the law no flesh can be justified in His sight;' 'now the righteousness of God which is by faith of Jesus Christ is manifested unto all that believe.' Now they are 'justified freely by His grace through the redemption that is in Christ Jesus. Him God hath set forth to be a propitiation through faith in His blood, to declare his righteousness for the remission of sins that are past' (Romans 3:20–25). Now hath Christ 'taken away the curse of the law being made a curse for us' (Galatians 3:13). He hath 'blotted out the handwriting that was against us, taking it out of the way, nailing it to His cross' (Colossians 2:14). 'There is therefore no condemnation now to them which believe in Christ Jesus' (Romans 8:1).
>
> 4. And being saved from guilt they are saved from fear. Not indeed from filial fear of offending, but from all servile fear from that 'fear which hath torment' (John 4:18, from fear of punishment, from fear of the wrath of God whom they no longer regard as severe master, but as indulgent Father. 'They have not received again the spirit of bondage, but the Spirit of adoption whereby they cry, Abba Father: the Spirit itself also bearing witness with their spirit that they are the children of God' (Romans 8:15–16). They are also saved from the fear though not of the possibility of falling away (II Thessalonians 2:13), from the grace of God and coming short of the great and precious promises (Hebrews 4:1). They are 'sealed with the Holy Spirit of Promise which is the earnest of their inheritance' (Ephesians 1:13). Thus have they 'peace with God through our Lord Jesus Christ. . . . They rejoice in hope of the glory of God. . . . and the love of God is shed abroad in their hearts through the Holy Ghost which is given unto them' (Roman 5:1–5). And hereby they are persuaded though perhaps not all times, nor with the same fullness of persuasion, 'that neither death nor life, nor things present, nor things to come, nor height nor depth, nor any other creature shall be able to separate them from the love of God which is in Christ Jesus our Lord'(Romans 8:38–39).[22]

---

[22] Albert Outler. *The Works of John Wesley. Vol. 1.* (Nashville, Tenn.: Abingdon Press, 1984) 122–23.

In considering this passage, we note, of the 425 words recorded, 307 are quotes or paraphrases of the Scripture. This is not an isolated incident. The next paragraph in this sermon is almost totally made up of quotations from I John, and the pattern is consistent, not isolated in Wesley's messages.

To summarize this section, it is clear that Wesley would have described his call and mission much as in his letter to Christopher Hopper. His call and duty was to fulfill the work of a preacher, to save souls, to preach the Gospel. As has been shown, for Wesley there was only one way to preach, and that was to preach the Bible, to "pursue scriptural Christianity."[23]

Wesley's Use of the Bible in Instruction

Certainly Wesley's preaching was instructive on most occasions. However, there were many other types of instruction beyond preaching for Wesley, and the Bible was just as critical in other forms. Some examples to consider are the organization and rules of the class meeting and band societies; Wesley's instructions to preachers; addressing social ills, and doctrinal correction.

Wesley considered the Bible to be the guide to church organization. Concerning the development of the Methodist Discipline Wesley said in his sermon "On God's Vineyard" (1787) "It is entirely founded on common sense, particularly applying to the general rules of Scripture."[24] As Wesley began the long hard process of organizing the Methodist movement, the Bible was the foundation and the emphasis of the organization, and the bulwark against which criticism was cast. Consider for example his quotation in "A People Called Methodists" (1749), concerning the rise of the class meeting:

> One and another came to us, asking what they should do, being distressed on every side, as everyone strove to weaken, and none to strengthen their hands in God. We advised them, 'Strengthen you one another.' Talk together as often as you can. And pray earnestly with and for one another, that you may endure to the end and be saved. Against this advice we presumed there could be no objection, as being grounded on the plainest reason, and so many Scriptures, both of the Old Testament and the New that it would be tedious to recite them.[25]

---

[23] *Letters* 3:148.

[24] Albert Outler. *The Works of John Wesley. Vol. 3.* (Nashville, Tenn.: Abingdon Press, 1986) 511.

[25] Rupert Davies. *The Works of John Wesley. Vol. 9.* (Nashville, Tenn.: Abingdon Press, 1989) 256.

When some objected there were no Scriptures for classes Wesley replied:

> I answer, (1) There is no Scripture against it. You cannot show one text which forbids them. (2) There is much Scripture for it, even all those texts which enjoin, the substance of those various duties, whereof this is only an indifferent circumstance, to be determined by reason and experience. (3) You seem not to have observed that the Scripture, in most points, gives only general rules, and leaves the particular circumstances to be adjusted by the common sense of mankind.[26]

When some said, there was no scriptural warrant to divide the bands into groups of married and unmarried men and women Wesley stated:

> I reply as before, there are also prudential helps grounded on reason and experience, in order to apply the general rules given in Scripture according to particular circumstances.[27]

Wesley, we see, took the general rules of Scripture to establish his classes and bands. Consider Wesley's own statement in the "General Rules of the United Societies" (1743):

> These are the General Rules of our societies all of which are taught of God to observe, even in His written Word, the only rule and sufficient rule, both of our faith and practice.[28]

In fact, the very test for membership in the societies was a scriptural one. In Wesley's "Plain Account of the Methodists" (1749) we see for each candidate there was only one requirement:

> 8. There is one only condition previously required in those who desire admission into the society, 'a desire to flee from the wrath to come, to be saved from their sins.'[29]

As we see there were no theological tests, no distinct opinion had to be held. Any mode of baptism was allowed. Only one condition was required, a real desire to save their souls.[30]

---

[26] Ibid., 263.
[27] Ibid., 268.
[28] Ibid., 73.
[29] Ibid., 256.
[30] Ibid., 256.

John Wesley and Biblical Instruction

When we consider the establishment of the bands, we can clearly see the importance of the Bible for instruction and devotion. Note these directions given to the Band Societies on December 25, 1744:

> III. Constantly to attend on all the ordinances of God in particular:
>
> 1. To be at church and at the Lord's table every week, and at every public meeting of the Bands.
>
> 2. To attend the ministry of the word every morning, unless distance, business or sickness prevent.
>
> 3. To use private prayer every day, and family prayer, if you are at the head of the family.
>
> 4. To read the Scriptures, and meditate therein, at every vacant hour, And,
>
> 5. To observe, as a day of fasting or abstinence, all Fridays in the year.[31]

Consider one other example as Wesley once again comments on the Means of Grace in his "Minutes of Several Conversations" (1744–1789):

> (2.) Searching the Scriptures by; (i.) Reading; Constantly, some part of everyday; regularly, all the Bible in order; carefully, with the Notes; seriously, with prayer before and after; fruitfully, immediately practicing what you learn there? (ii.) Meditating: At set times? By any rule? (iii.) Hearing: Every morning? carefully; with prayer before, at, after; immediately putting in practice? Have you a New Testament always about you?[32]

Another clear indication of the value Wesley placed on Scripture comes in the instruction and demands placed upon Methodist preachers. Wesley declared that one cannot be a "good Divine" without being a "good textuary." A minister of the Word ought to "know the literal meaning of every word, verse and chapter" . . . He also demanded that his preachers should have a knowledge of the original language.[33]

Another fashion in which Wesley used Scripture for instruction was in combating social ills. One clear, and perhaps the most well known ex-

---

[31] *Works* 8:273–74.
[32] Ibid., 8:323.
[33] Ibid., 10:482–83.

ample of this use of the Scripture, comes from his famous letter to William Wilberforce concerning the abolition of slavery written only days before Wesley's death:

> Unless the Divine power has raised you up to be as *Athanasius contra mundum,* I see not how you can go through your glorious enterprise, in opposing that execrable villainy, which is the scandal of religion, of England, and of human nature. Unless God has raised you up for this very thing, you will be worn out by the opposition of men and devils. But, 'If God be for you who can stand against you' (Romans 8:31)? Are all them stronger than God? Oh, 'Be not weary in well doing' (Galatians 6:9). Go on in the name of God and the power of his might, till even American slavery (the vilest that ever saw the sun) shall vanish away before it.[34]

One final example of John Wesley's use of the Bible for instruction is seen in the area of doctrinal correction. It was clearly shown in chapter three that Wesley used the Bible for the foundation of all doctrine. He also made the Bible the basis of any attempt at doctrinal correction. Wesley used Scripture to combat fanaticism of all kinds whenever they threatened the Methodist movement. He appealed again and again to Scripture as the criterion to judge the profession of those who meant well, but whose statements might have gone beyond the realm of Scripture or reason. To illustrate this point let us consider two examples; the issue of stillness, and that of Christian perfection.

Though, as has been noted, Wesley was certainly influenced in his life by mysticism, he later had to speak out against the efforts on occasion to misinterpret Scripture and throw away reason. For example, in a letter to Freeborn Garretson (1789), concerning Garretson's usage of the term "finding freedom to do this or that," Wesley states:

> If I have plain scripture or plain reason for doing a thing well. These are my rules and my only rules. I regard not whether I had freedom or no. This is an unscriptural expression and a very fallacious rule. I wish to be in every point, great and small, a scriptural, rational, Christian.[35]

Another phase of mystical fanaticism that endangered the Methodist movement was that of the Moravian "stillness," a beautiful, dreamy, but wholly impractical mysticism of German Quietism as interpreted by

---

[34] Ibid., 13:153.
[35] *Letters* 8:112.

Phillip Molther and Peter Bohler.[36] It was a part of stillness to refrain from the reading of Scripture, attending church, taking the sacraments, private prayers, or doing temporal good.[37] According to these men, those who did not have "true faith," should remain still and not use any means of grace until they were given faith.[38]

Wesley's challenge to the Moravians was based upon his understanding of the authority of Scripture. His attempts at correction were carefully constructed on a scriptural basis. Beginning with II Timothy 3:16 "All Scripture is inspired of God," he explained the ordinance as a means of grace.[39]

Concerning the assertion that there was but one commandment in the New Testament, "to believe," and that no duty lies upon us, and a believer is not obliged to do anything, Wesley wrote in his *Journal* in 1740 appealing to Scripture "How gross, palpable a contradiction is this to the whole tenor of the New Testament."[40] Wesley's appeal to Scripture led to a clean break with the English Moravian Church and an entire part of his *Journal* is dedicated to the details.[41]

Another doctrine that was liable to produce a fanaticism that Wesley would have to deal with was perfection. There were many who, in the flush of enthusiasm, professed to being entirely free from sin and indeed claimed they could not sin. Wesley appealed to the Bible to refute these exaggerated claims.[42] Wesley wrote his *Plain Account of Christian Perfection* to help deal with these problems. This doctrinal treatise was grounded in Scripture with 195 quotations from the Bible.[43] In dealing with complaints and misunderstandings about the doctrine Wesley constantly appealed to the Bible. Wesley stated, "How shall we avoid setting perfection too high or too low? By keeping to the Bible and setting it just as high as Scripture does."[44] When some challenged that this was Mr. Wesley's doctrine he replied:

---

[36] William Pellowe, "John Wesley's Use of the Bible," *Methodist Review* (1923) 368.

[37] Richard Heitzenrater and Reginald Ward, *The Works of John Wesley. Vol.19.* (Nashville, Tenn.: Abingdon Press, 1990) 131–32.

[38] Allen Coppedge. *John Wesley in Theological Debate.* (Wilmore, Ky.: Wesley Heritage Press, 1987) 59.

[39] Ibid., 59.

[40] Richard Heitzenrater and Reginald Ward. *The Works of John Wesley. Vol. 19.* (Nashville, Tenn.: Abingdon Press, 1990)) 155.

[41] Ibid., 119–20.

[42] William Pellowe, "John Wesley's Use of Scripture", *Methodist Review* (1923) 366.

[43] W. E. Sangster. *The Path to Perfection.* (Nashville, Tenn.: Abingdon Press, 1943) 36.

[44] John Wesley. *A Plain Account of Christian Perfection.* (Kansas City, Mo.: Beacon Hill

'This is Mr. Wesley's doctrine!' He preaches perfection! He does; yet this is not his doctrine, any more than it is yours, or anyone's else, that is a minister of Christ. For it is His doctrine, peculiarly, emphatically His; it is the doctrine of Jesus Christ. Those are His words, not mine: 'Ye shall therefore be perfect as your Father who is in heaven is perfect' (Matthew 5:48). . . . I tell you as plain as I can speak where and when I found this. I found it in the oracles of God, in the Old and New Testament.[45]

In his "Farther Thoughts on Christian Perfection" (1761) he challenged them to beware of enthusiasm and:

Try all things by the written Word, and let all bow down before it. You are in danger of enthusiasm every hour if you depart ever so little from the Scripture, yea, or from the plain literal meaning of any text, taken in connection with context.[46]

When some claimed to have the testimony from the Spirit that they would never sin Wesley declared:

We know not what God may vouchsafe to some particular persons; but we do not find any general state described in Scripture from which a man cannot draw back to sin. . . . Although, therefore, God may give such a witness to some particular persons, yet it is not to be expected by Christians in general, there being no Scripture whereon to ground such an expectation.[47]

In instructing critics, Wesley was content to say:

And what is there here which any man of understanding, who believes the Bible can object to? What can he deny, without flatly contradicting the Scripture? What retrench, without taking from the Word of God?[48]

In conclusion, it is clear that Wesley believed the Bible to speak practically to all areas of the life of the church. It was by the Bible Wesley sought to establish members of the society on a solid theological foundation. The Bible was the tool to correct false doctrine. In teaching, as with preaching, Wesley clearly recognized Scripture as the ultimate authority in all matters of faith and practice.

Press, 1971) 55.

[45] Ibid., 117.

[46] Ibid., 97.

[47] Ibid., 88.

[48] Ibid., 14.

Wesley's Use of the Bible in His Letters

A tremendous resource for learning Wesley's views on almost any subject is the thousands of letters which have been collected. John Telford's collection *The Letters of the Rev. John Wesley A.M.* (1931), contains over 2600 letters. More letters are available in the now being published by Abingdon Press. In these letters Wesley wrote on almost every *The Works of John Wesley* subject whether physical, social, spiritual, moral, political, or economic. He also spoke to men and women of every social rank, with a particular interest in his letters for all his lay preachers.

One of the most obvious characteristics of Wesley's letter writing is the constant use of Scripture. Long sections of his letters are little more than the stringing together of scriptural phrases.[49] As we have seen in his preaching, Wesley's constant use of the Bible had so been woven into the very texture of his mind that it automatically found its way into all manner of speaking and writing. This is not surprising when we remember what Wesley expressed in a letter to John Newton in 1766:

> My answer was: 'The Bible is my standard language as well as sentiment. I endeavor not only to think, but to speak as the oracles of God'. . . Therefore I keep to my old way and speak neither better nor worse than the Bible.[50]

Dr. William Arnett in his dissertation entitled *A Man of One Book* (1954), shows how closely Wesley abided by his expressed desire in his letters. Dr. Arnett's research revealed that in the eight volume set of letters collected by Telford, Wesley used approximately 2543 quotations.[51]

For a more specific example, consider that this letter written to Samuel Bridburn in 1775, consists of a quotation from the Psalms, "Trust in the Lord and do good, so shalt thou dwell in the land, and verily thou shalt be fed."[52]

Two lengthy letters are excellent examples of Wesley blending the Scriptures with his own thoughts. The first letter is to the members of the society at Leominster in 1746 who were disturbed by Calvinistic teaching. In this eleven line letter there are ten scriptural allusions.[53]

---

[49] Frank Baker. *The Works of John Wesley. Vol. 25.* (Nashville, Tenn.: Abingdon Press, 1980) 131.
[50] *Letters* 5:8.
[51] William Arnett, "John Wesley-A Man of One Book," (Ph.D. diss., Drew University, 1954).
[52] *Letters* 6:177.
[53] William Arnett, "John Wesley-A Man of One Book," (Ph.D. diss., Drew University, 1954).

> My dear Brethren, as many of you as have set your hands to the plough, see that you go on and look not back (Luke 9:62). The prize (Philippians 3:14) and the crown (II Timothy 4:8) are before you, and in due time you shall reap, if you faint not (Galatians 6:9). Meantime, fight the good fight of faith (I Timothy 6:12) enduring the cross and despising the shame (Hebrews 12:2). Beware that none of you return evil for evil or railing for railing, but contrariwise blessing (I Peter 3:9). Show forth out of a loving heart your good conversation with meekness and wisdom (James 3:13). Avoid all disputes as you would avoid fire; so shall you continue kindly affectioned toward one another (Romans 12:10). The God of peace be with you (Romans 15:33)—I am.[54]

A final example would be Wesley's letter to Alexander Knox in 1778 where he blends scriptural allusions into the text :

> My Dear Alleck- You have long been under that temptation of despising the day of small things, although indeed they are not small things which God has done for you already. That you are still lukewarm is most certain; you have need to stir up the gift of God that is in you; and you have need to praise Him that His hand is still upon you for good, preserving you from presumptuous sins. You ought to be sensible of this, and to be thankful for it, which you may be without 'applauding yourself.' That you have no 'right to expect the continuance of your health,' is undoubtedly true; that is, you cannot claim it from God's justice; you do not merit it at His hands. But is this the measure whereby he deals with His poor creatures? Does He give us no more blessing than we deserve? Does He treat us in all things according to His justice? Not so; but mercy rejoices over judgment! Therefore, expect from Him, not what you deserve, but what you want, health of soul and health of body: ask and you shall receive; seek, and you shall find; not for your worthiness, but because 'worthy is the Lamb.' The peace of God be with all your spirits.[55]

Wesley's Use of the Bible in His Hymns

It should come as no surprise that the Wesley hymns are heavily influenced by Scripture, when we recognize that the hymns, as well as the sermons and *Notes*, were the standard books of Wesley's doctrine. Only the sermons and *Notes* were "official documents," but it is highly doubtful whether without

---

[54] *Letters* 2:84

[55] *Letters* 6:317–18.

the hymns there would have been a Methodist Revival, for Methodism was "born in a song."⁵⁶

The hymnbook was to be used as a primer of theology, and a manual for both public worship and private devotion. The collection was devoted "to directions for making our calling and election sure, for perfecting holiness in the fear of God and the whole accent lies on scriptural Christianity."⁵⁷

The bulk of the hymns in the collection were Charles', rather than John's. Wesley comments in the preface to the hymnal that "but a small part of these hymns are of my composing."⁵⁸ However, it must be recognized that it was John who chose the hymns to be included, without consulting his brother. It was John who decided which verses to include or omit, and at times he took the liberty to alter or revise his brother's verses. Again, the reason for this manipulation was to form "a little body of experimental and practical divinity." He felt the hymnbook would be unique in furnishing "a distinct and full account of scriptural Christianity."⁵⁹

Recognizing Wesley's purpose for the hymns, it is understandable that we often find allusions to the Scriptures in almost every line of some hymns. Franz Hildebrandt in *The Works of John Wesley Vol. 7* (1983), states it would be almost impossible to cite every conceivable passage of Holy Scripture that might consciously or unconsciously have been in the mind of men so steeped in the Scripture. Hildebrandt further maintains that even in some of the lesser hymns there are scriptural allusions in 50% of the lines.⁶⁰

At this point let me include two examples of the use of scriptural allusions in the Wesley hymns. First consider one of Charles' hymns, remembering that John chose the hymns as well as altering and revising them:

318

O thou who camest from above (John 3:31)
Thy pure celestial fire t'impart (I Kings 18:38, Luke 12:49)
Kindle a flame of sacred love (I Chronicles 21:26)
On the mean altar of my heart (Leviticus 9:24, I Chronicles 21:26)

There let it for thy glory burn (II Chronicles 4:15, 8:19)
With inextinguishable blaze (Leviticus 6:13)

---

⁵⁶ Franz Hildebrandt. *The Works of John Wesley. Vol. 7.* (Nashville, Tenn.: Abingdon Press, 1983) 1.

⁵⁷ Ibid., 3.

⁵⁸ Ibid., 55.

⁵⁹ Ibid., 54.

⁶⁰ Ibid., 730.

And trembling to its source return (Job 5:7, Ecclesiastes 2:7)
In humble love and fervent praise (James 4:6, 10).

Jesu, confirm my heart's desire (Acts 14:22, Romans 10:1)
To work, and speak, and think for thee;
Still let me guard the holy fire, (Leviticus 6:13, I Thessalonians 5:19)
And still stir up thy gift in me; (II Timothy 1:6)

Ready for all thy perfect will (Romans 12:2, Titus 3:1)
My acts of faith and love repeat (I Thessalonians 1:3)
Till death thy endless mercies seal (Ephesians 4:30)
And make the sacrifice complete. (Romans 12:1, Philippians 2:17)

In choosing one of John's hymns it must be recognized that in several of the early volumes, hymns appeared under the names of both brothers making it difficult to identify the authorship of many classic hymns of Methodism. According to Samuel Bradburn, John and Charles agreed that they would not distinguish between each other's work, and that agreement continued until Charles Wesley's marriage, when it was necessary to identify his literary property in connection with his wife's marriage settlement.[61]

In recent years attempts have been made to draw up a list of criteria to distinguish Charles' hymns from John's. Henry Bett was the first, listing fifteen features which characterized John's poetry.[62] Not all agree with Bett's criteria, but Dr. Hildebrandt, bearing these criteria in mind, lists nine hymns that Wesley may have authored. I will list one example:

341

1 Come, Holy Ghost, all-quick'ning fire,
   Come, and my hallowed heart inspire,
       Sprinkled with atoning blood (I Peter 1:2)
   Now to my soul thyself reveal,
   Thy mighty working let me feel, (Colossians 1:29)
       And know that I am born of God. (I John 3:9)

Thy witness with my spirit bear (Romans 8:16)
That God, my God inhabits there,
    Thou with the Father and the Son

---

[61] Ibid., 734.
[62] Ibid., 735.

Eternal light's coeval beam;
Be Christ in me, and I in Him (Galatians 2:20)
    Till perfect we are made in one (John 17:23)

2 When wilt thou my whole heart subdue?
Come, Lord, and form my soul anew,
    Emptied of pride, and wrath, and hell;
Less than the least of all thy store (Genesis 32:10)
Of mercies, I myself abhor; (Ephesians 3:8)
    All, all my vileness may I feel.

Humble, and teachable, and mild,
O may I, as a little child, (Matthew 18:3-4)
    My lowly Master's steps pursue!
Be anger to my soul unknown;
Hate, envy, jealousy, be gone!
    In love create thou all things new. (II Corinthians 5:17)

3 Let earth no more my heart divide;
With Christ may I be crucified, (Galatians 2:20)
    To thee with my whole soul aspire;
Dead to the world and all its toys,
Its idle pomp, and fading joys,
    Be thou alone my one desire.

Be thou my joy; be thou my dread;
In battle cover thou my head, (Psalm 140:7)
    Nor earth nor hell I then shall fear;
I then shall turn my steady face; (Luke 9:51)
Want, pain defy, enjoy disgrace,
    Glory in dissolution near.

4 My will be swallowed up in thee;
Light in thy light still may I see, (Psalms 36:9)
    Beholding thee with open face: (II Corinthians 3:18)
Called the full power of faith to prove,
Let all my hallowed heart be love,
    And all my spotless life be praise.

> Come, Holy Ghost, all-quick'ning fire,
> My consecrated heart inspire,
> > Sprinkled with the atoning blood; (I Peter 1:2)
> Still to my soul thyself reveal,
> Thy mighty working may I feel, (Colossians 1:29)
> > And know that I am one with God!

Wesley and the Greek New Testament

Another clear example of the importance of Scripture to Wesley can be seen in his new translation of the New Testament in 1755. It appears that Wesley for many years had wished to produce a new and understandable translation of the New Testament. Wesley's primary desire was not for scholarship, but for a New Testament the people could understand. He realized that if converts to the Wesleyan Revival were to be retained they had to establish a knowledge of scriptural truth. Wesley followed Luther and the Reformation, and broke from the current position of the Church of England, which at that time did not consider Bible study a daily necessity for laymen.[63]

There had been at least seven widely accepted versions of the New Testament since the Reformation, but Wesley detected many inaccuracies and he recognized changes in the English language. He saw the need for a book of Scriptures translated "chiefly for plain unlettered men who understand only their mother tongue and yet reverence and love the Word of God and have a desire to save souls".[64] As Wesley states in his *Explanatory Notes On the New Testament* (1948), men need the Word of God in a language which:

> . . . studiously avoided not only all curious and critical inquiries, and all use of the learned languages, but all such methods of reasoning and modes of expression as people in common life are unacquainted with.[65]

Wesley delayed his translation primarily because of his own sense of inability. It was not until he was struck with a serious illness and believed he was going to die that he began a self examination:

---

[63] John Wesley. *John Wesley's New Testament.* (Philadelphia, Pa.: John C. Winston Co., 1953) 11.

[64] Ibid., 9.

[65] John Wesley. *Explanatory Notes Upon the New Testament.* (London, England: Epworth Press, 1948) 10.

> In my present state what can I do? I cannot travel. I cannot preach, but blessed be God I can still read and write and think, and I will do what little I can in this way because I can do nothing else. O that it may be to His glory.[66]

The result was the translation of the New Testament for the ordinary reader.

Wesley's New Testament was not just a paraphrase of either the King James Version, or earlier versions. It was a fresh, independent translation based on a superior knowledge of Greek and a first hand acquaintance with the conversational language of the marketplace, as well as the drawing room and the cloister. He minutely studied every word of the New Testament in the original Greek and produced a translation with over twelve thousand changes in words, sentence structure, and chapter division from earlier translations.[67]

It is not my purpose to examine the rationale of Wesley's changes, but a validation of his scholarship may be seen when it is noted that over three fourths of Wesley's modifications have been accepted into the Revised Version and other modern translations.[68] According to Dr, Ralph Earle, John Wesley's New Testament agrees with the Revised Standard Version in over 6500 instances. This would suggest his translation lies about halfway between The King James Version and the best modern translations.[69]

Clearly Wesley believed that one of the greatest contributions he could make to his Methodist preachers and laymen was to give them a clearer and more accurate translation of the New Testament. His success in doing this should certainly mark him as not only the founder of a great religious movement, but as one of the great religious scholars of the eighteenth century. At the very least it once again shows his whole hearted devotion to Scripture.

Wesley and His Explanatory Notes

Two of Wesley's more well known publications were his *Explanatory Notes Upon the Old Testament*, and his *Explanatory Notes Upon the New Testament*. These publications should be considered not only as an example of his use of Scripture, but as explanations of his views of Scripture. I have al-

---

[66] Ibid., 9.
[67] Ibid., 10.
[68] Jon Scroggins, "John Wesley Biblical Scholar," *Journal of Bible and Religion* (1960) 28:61–67.
[69] Ralph Earle, "John Wesley's New Testament," *The Asbury Seminarian* (1960) 14:61–67.

ready used quotations from both *Works* when commenting upon Wesley's views of inspiration, authority, interpretation and infallibility of Scripture. There is, however, one question that must be asked. When making these comments upon Scripture, was Wesley expressing his own views, or merely echoing the ideas of others? A study of the *Explanatory Notes* reveals that Wesley was greatly dependent upon men like Matthew Poole, Matthew Henry, and Albrecht Bengel. Just how dependent Wesley was will be shown in the following paragraphs.

In this section I will outline the background of the writing of both the *Old and New Testament Works*, beginning with the New Testament since it was published first. After outlining the development of these publications, I wish to consider a number of passages where Wesley makes clear his view of Scripture and compares them with Matthew Poole and Henry in the Old Testament sections, and Bengel in the New Testament. This should reveal how original or unoriginal Wesley's statements were. If we discover that Wesley basically copied the statements from other authors, it does not necessarily imply that Wesley did not believe what he said. In all likelihood we must assume he was merely affirming their statements. This would, however, remove any claim of originality.

Explanatory Notes Upon the New Testament

In his *Journal* Wesley notes that he began the *Explanatory Notes On the New Testament* on January 6, 1754:

> Fri. 4–I began drinking the water at the Hot Well, having a lodging at a small distance from it; and on Sunday the 6th I began writing *Notes Upon the New Testament*—a work which I should scarce ever have attempted had I not been so ill as not to be able to travel or preach, and yet so well as to be able to read and write.[70]

Wesley finished the work on September 23, 1755:

> Tues. 23–We walked up to Glastonbury Tower, which a gentleman is now repairing. It is the steeple of a church, the foundation of which is still discernible. On the west side of the tower there are niches for images, one of which, as big as the life, is still entire. The hill on which it stands is extremely steep, and of an uncommon height; so that it commands the country on all sides, as well as the Bristol Channel. I was weary enough when we came to Bristol, but

---

[70] *Journals* 4:91.

> I preached till all my complaints were gone, and I had now a little leisure to sit still, and finish the *Notes on the New Testament*.[71]

Wesley had desired for some time to publish such a work, but as was described earlier on page 187 in speaking of his translation of his Greek New Testament, it was only his illness that slowed him down enough to concentrate on these works. He makes his desire, his "call," clear in the preface:

> 1. For many years I have had a desire of setting down, and laying together, what has occurred to my mind, either in reading, thinking, or conversation, which might assist serious persons, who have not the advantage of learning, in understanding the New Testament. But I have been continually deterred from attempting anything of this kind by a deep sense of my own inability; of my want, not only of learning for such a work, but much more of experience and wisdom. This has often occasioned my laying aside the thought. And when, by much importunity, I have been prevailed upon to resume it, still I determined to delay it as long as possible, that (if it should please God) I might finish my work and my life together.
>
> 2. But having lately had a loud call from God to arise and go hence, I am convinced that, if I attempt anything of this kind at all, I must not delay any longer. My day is far spent, and, even in a natural way, the shadows of the evening come on apace; and I am rather induced to do what little I can in this way because I can do nothing else, being prevented by my present weakness from either traveling or preaching. But, blessed be God, I can still read and write and think. Oh that it may be to His glory![72]

In his preface Wesley also makes clear his purpose in publishing the *Explanatory Notes*, as well as the sources he used in the preparation:

> 3. It will be easily discerned, even from what I have said already, and much more from the notes themselves, that they were not principally designed for men of learning, who are provided with many other helps; and much less for men of long and deep experience in the ways and Word of God. I desire to sit at their feet, and to learn of them. But I write chiefly for plain, unlettered men, who understand only their mother-tongue, and yet reverence and love the Word of God, and have a desire to save their souls.

---

[71] Ibid., 137.

[72] John Wesley. *Explanatory Notes Upon the New Testament*. (London, England: Epworth Press, 1948) 5.

> 4. In order to assist these in such a measure as I am able, I design, first, to set down the text itself, for the most part, in the common English translation, which is, in general, so far as I can judge, abundantly the best I have seen. Yet I do not say it is incapable of being brought, in several places, nearer to the original. Neither will I affirm that the Greek copies from which this translation was made are always the most correct; and therefore I shall take the liberty, as occasion may require, to make here and there a small alteration.
>
> 6. I have endeavored to make the notes as short as possible, that the comment may not obscure or swallow up the text; and as plain as possible, in pursuance of my main design, to assist the unlearned reader. For this reason I have studiously avoided, not only all curious and critical inquiries, and all use of the learned languages, but all such methods of reasoning and modes of expression as people in common life are unacquainted with. For the same reason as I rather endeavour to obviate than to propose and answer objections, so I purposely decline going deep into many difficulties, lest I should leave the ordinary reader behind me.[73]

The primary source for the *Notes,* outside of the Scriptures themselves, was the *Gnomon Novi Testamenti* of Albrecht Bengel:

> 7. I once designed to write down barely what occurred to my own mind, consulting none but the inspired writers. But no sooner was I acquainted with that great light of the Christian world (lately gone to his reward) Bengelius than I entirely changed my design, being thoroughly convinced it might be of more service to the cause of religion, were I barely to translate his *Gnomon Novi Testamenti,* than to write many volumes upon it. Many of his excellent notes I have therefore translated; many more I have abridged, omitting that part which was purely critical, and giving the substance to the rest. Those various readings, likewise, which he has showed to have a vast majority of ancient copies and translations on their side, I have without scruple incorporated with the text; which, after his manner, I have divided all along (though not omitting the common division into chapters and verses, which is of use on various accounts) according to the matter it contains, making a larger or smaller pause, just as the sense requires. And even this is such a help, in many places, as one who has not tried it can scarcely conceive.[74]

---

[73] Ibid., 6–7.

[74] Ibid., 7–8.

How indebted was Wesley to Bengel? William Arnett in his unpublished dissertation *John Wesley—The Man of One Book*, gave a comparison made by John Simon comparing Wesley's *Notes* with Bengel's *Gnomon*. He concludes that any one who made such as examination, "will accept the statement that they are little more than abridged from Bengel."[75]

Simon goes on to state that all the *Notes* could be divided into three groups :

1. Notes taken from *Gnomon*.

2. Notes written by Wesley.

3. Composite notes-taken from Bengel but extended or corrected by Wesley.

He concluded that the first group is most prominent, but it was from the second and third group that the doctrines that came to prominence in the Methodist Revival received their fullest exposition.[76]

Although Bengel certainly had the greatest impact, Wesley also acknowledged other writers:

> 8. I am likewise indebted for some useful observations to Dr. Heylyn's *Theological Lectures*; and for many more to Dr. Guyse, and to *The Family Expositor* of the late pious and learned Dr. Doddridge. It was a doubt with me, for some time, whether I should not subjoin to every note I received from them the name of the author from whom it was taken, especially considering I had transcribed some, and abridged many more, almost in the words of the author. But upon further consideration I resolved to name none, that nothing might divert the mind of the reader from keeping close to the point in view, and receiving what was spoke, only according to its own intrinsic value.[77]

It becomes clear from reading his preface that Wesley did not intend to write a new commentary on the New Testament made up of his views. Instead he "borrowed" from the scholars he respected to publish a helpful commentary for the less learned. However, I still believe that it would be interesting to examine the passages in the *Explanatory Notes Upon the New Testament* that best express his views upon Scripture, and compare them with Bengel's original writings.

---

[75] William Arnett, "John Wesley-A Man of One Book", (Ph.D. diss., Drew University, 1954).

[76] Ibid.

[77] John Wesley. *Explanatory Notes Upon the New Testament.* (London, England: Epworth Press, 1948) 8.

We do not need to search very far to find the obvious comparisons between Bengel and Wesley. Compare, for example, a portion of Bengel's introduction with Wesley's preface:

Bengel:

The Word of the Living God, which had governed the primitive patriarchs, was committed to writing, in the age of Moses, who was followed by the other prophets. Subsequently, those things which the Son of God preached, and the Paraclete spoke through the apostles, were written down by the apostles and evangelists. These writings, taken together, are termed 'Holy Scriptures,' and bearing this title, they are themselves their own best eulogy. For it is because they contain God's words and are the Lord's Book, that they are called, 'Holy Scripture . . .'

They are the fountains of wisdom; which is preferred by those who have tasted it to all the compositions of other men, however holy, experienced devout or wise.[78]

Wesley:

10. Concerning the Scriptures in general, it may be observed, the Word of the living God, which directed the first patriarchs also, was, in the time of Moses, committed to writing. To these were added, in several succeeding generations, the inspired writings of the other prophets. Afterwards, what the Son of God preached, and the Holy Ghost spake by the apostles, the apostles and the evangelists wrote. This is what we now style the Holy Scripture: this is that 'Word of God which remaineth forever'; of which though heaven and earth pass away, one jot and tittle shall not pass away?' The Scripture, therefore, of the Old and New Testament is a most solid and precious system of divine truth. Every part thereof is worthy of God; and all together are one entire body, wherein is no defect, no excess. It is the fountain of heavenly wisdom, which they who are able to the taste prefer to all writings of men, however wise of learned or holy.[79]

It is clear that in this general statement on the inspiration and authority of Scripture Wesley merely paraphrased Bengel. Further examples

---

[78] John Albrecht Bengel. *New Testament Word Studies Vols. 1–2*. (Philadelphia, Pa.: Kregel Publications, 1971) xii.

[79] John Wesley. *Explanatory Notes Upon the New Testament*. (London, England: Epworth Press, 1948) 8–9.

will show again Wesley's dependence upon Bengel. For example concerning Galatians 3:8—"And the Scripture, foreseeing that God would justify the Gentiles by faith, declared before the glad tidings to Abraham," Bengel comments:

> Foreseeing implies divine foreknowledge, more ancient than the law. The great excellence of sacred Scripture is, that all that can be controverted is foreseen and decided in it, even in the most appropriate language . . . God foreknew that he would act thus with the Gentiles; God therefore already dealt similarly with Abraham; God also caused it to be written; and that too when it was still future.[80]

Wesley:

> 'And the Scripture'—That is, the Holy Spirit, who gave the Scripture. 'Foreseeing that God would justify the Gentiles'—So great is the excellency and fullness of the Scripture, that all the things which can never be controverted are therein both foreseen and determined.[81]

Bengel commenting on II Timothy 3:16:

> It was divinely inspired, not merely while it was written, God breathing through the writers, but also while it is being read. God breathing through Scripture, and the Scripture breathing into him. Hence, 'it is profitable for doctrine. . . .'[82]

Wesley:

> The Spirit of God not only once inspired those who wrote it, but continually inspires, supernaturally assists those who read it with earnest prayer; Hence, it is so profitable for doctrine. . . . [83]

Bengel commenting on I Corinthians 7:25:

> For, the apostles wrote nothing, not given by inspiration; but they sometimes had a special revelation and command. The rest they derived from the habitual faith, which had arisen in them from

---

[80] John Albrecht Bengel. *New Testament Word Studies Vols. 1–2* (Philadelphia, Pa.: Kregel Publications, 1971) 353.

[81] John Wesley. *Explanatory Notes Upon the New Testament.* (London, England: Epworth Press.: 1948) 687.

[82] John Albrecht Bengel. *New Testament Word Studies Vols. 1–2.* (Philadelphia, Pa.: Kregel Publications, 1971) 560.

[83] John Wesley. *Explanatory Notes Upon the New Testament.* (London, England: Epworth Press, 1948) 794 .

experience of the Lord's mercy; as in this verse; and also from the treasury of the Spirit of God.[84]

Wesley:

> 'I have no commandment from the Lord.' By a particular revelation. Nor was it necessary I should; for the apostles wrote nothing which was not divinely inspired; but with this difference—sometimes they had a particular revelation, and a special commandment; and at other times they wrote from the divine light which abode with them, the standing treasure of the Spirit of God.[85]

In comparing these passages it becomes clear that Wesley merely paraphrased Bengel. The substance of each section was clearly Bengel's, while Wesley clarified or shortened as he saw fit. Again, it should be noted that because Wesley quoted from Bengel this should not lead us to believe the statements do not reflect Wesley's own views. As Wesley notes in his preface, it is because he is in such close agreement with Bengel that he chose to adopt the *Gnomon* for his New Testament works.

Explanatory Notes Upon the Old Testament

Wesley followed his *Explanatory Notes Upon the New Testament* with his *Explanatory Notes Upon the Old Testament*. This second publication was never as popular as the first. As with the first publication Wesley was reluctant to begin this second work:

> 1. About ten years ago I was prevailed upon to publish *Explanatory Notes Upon the New Testament*. When that work was begun, and indeed when it was finished, I had no design to attempt anything farther of the kind. Nay I had a full determination, Not to do it, being thoroughly fatigued with the immense labour (had it been only this; tho this indeed was a small part of it,) of writing twice over a Quarto book containing seven or eight hundred pages.

> 2. But this was scarce published before I was importuned to write *Explanatory Notes Upon the Old Testament*. This importunity I have withstood for many years. Over and above the deep conviction I had, of my insufficiency for such a work, of my want of learning, of understanding, of spiritual experience, for an undertaking more difficult by many degrees, then even writing on the New Testament,

---

[84] John Albrecht Bengel. *New Testament Word Studies Vols. 1–2* (Philadelphia, Pa.: Kregel Publications, 1971) 203.

[85] John Wesley. *Explanatory Notes Upon the New Testament*. (London, England: 1948) 605.

> I objected. That there were many passages in the Old, which I did not understand myself, and consequently could not explain to others, either to their satisfaction or my own. Above all, I objected the want of time: Not only as I have a thousand other employments, but as my Day is near spent, as I am declined into the vale of years. And to this day it appears as a dream, a thing, a thing almost incredible, that I should be entering upon a work of this kind, when I am entering my sixty-third year of my age.[86]

As with the *New Testament Notes*, Wesley would not attempt to write all the commentary himself. Instead he chose two different authors to abridge for his *Old Testament Notes*. The first author he chose was Matthew Henry:

> 3. Indeed these considerations, the last particular, still appear of such weight, that I cannot entertain a thought of composing a body of Notes on the whole Old Testament. All the question remaining was, 'Is there existant any Exposition which is worthy of abridging?' Abundantly less time will suffice for this and less abilities of every kind. In considering this question, I soon turned my thought on the well known Mr. Henry. He is allowed by all competent judges, to have been a person of strong understanding, of various learnings, of solid piety, and much experience in the ways of God. And his exposition is generally clear and intelligible, the thoughts being expressed in plain words: it is also found, agreeable to the tenor of Scripture, and to the analogy of faith.[87]

For those who wondered why another commentary was necessary as long as Matthew Henry's was available, Wesley replied that his commentary was sufficient for those who believed in Unconditional Predestination. However, not all believed this, and not all could afford to purchase it or find the time to read it.[88]

Wesley makes clear it is not his intention to merely abridge Henry's work, but also to make alterations and additions:

> 13. I do not therefore intend the following Notes for a bare abridgment of Mr. Henry's exposition. Far from it: I not only omit much more than nineteen parts of it out of twenty of what he has written, but make many alterations and many additions, well nigh from the

---

[86] John Wesley. *Explanatory Notes Upon the Old Testament.* (Salem, Ohio.: Schmul Publishers, 1975) iii.

[87] Ibid., iv.

[88] Ibid., iv.

beginning to the end. In particular, I everywhere omit the far greater part of his inferences from and improvement of the chapter.[89]

Wesley also chose to use Matthew Poole's *Annotations upon the Bible*. According to William Arnett, Poole (1624–79), was a non-conformist who wrote a massive five volume publication in Latin, *Synopsis Criticorum Biblicorum*, intended primarily for scholars.

Wesley comments on his use of Matthew Poole in his preface:

> Nay, from the time that I had more maturely considered Mr. Poole's annotations on the Bible, (which was soon after I had gone through Genesis) I have extracted far more from him than from Mr. Henry: it having been my constant method, after reading the text, first to read and weigh what Mr. Poole observed upon every verse, and afterwards to consult Mr. Henry's exposition of the whole paragraph. In consequence of this, instead of short additions from Mr. Poole to supply what was wanting in Mr. Henry, (which was my first design) I now only make extracts from Mr. Henry, to supply so far as they are capable, what was wanting in Mr. Poole.[90]

Luke Tyerman explains the difficulty Wesley faced in completing this work, when faced with all the problems of his continuing ministry:

> His societies were now so numerous and important, that it was a gigantic task to visit them, and regulate their multifarious affairs once a year. In addition, he was bringing out his *Notes on the Old Testament*, a work in itself, quite sufficient for the time and energies of any ordinary man; and further, he had to enforce and to defend his doctrines of Christian perfection, a doctrine imperfectly understood, and bitterly assailed.[91]

A letter written "To Subscribers to 'Notes Upon the Old Testament," (1766) reveals Wesley's difficulties. Note the similar themes to his preface:

> From the time that I published the *Notes on the New Testament* I was importuned to publish *Notes on the Old*. I long resisted that importunity; but at length yielded and began the work, supposing that it need not be above twice as long as the former, otherwise all the importunity in the world would not have prevailed on me to undertake it. But I had not gone through the Book of Exodus before I began to find my mistake. I perceived the work would be

---

[89] Ibid., vii.

[90] Ibid., viii.

[91] Luke Tyerman. *The Life and Times of the Reverend John Wesley*. (New York, N.Y.: Harper Bros., 1870) 2:593.

considerable longer than I expected if I designed to make it intelligible to common reader, and therefore immediately consulted with my friends what was best to be done.

Here was a difficulty on each hand. If I had went on as I begun, and explained every text so as to be understood by every reader, then the work would swell to 100, perhaps 110 or 112 numbers. This, it was easily foreseen, many would complain of, especially those who did not observe that it was not possible to make the notes shorter without making them almost useless. On the other hand, if I left many texts unexplained, they would have reason to complain. This was judged the greater evil of the two: so that every one to whom I spoke earnestly desired me to go on as I had begun and not to cramp the work. Several of them added that, even if the work should swell to 120 numbers, it would be far better than by labouring to shorten notes to make them unintelligible to ordinary readers.

In the meantime I myself have far the worst of it: the great burden falls upon me—a burden which, if I had seen before, all the world would not have persuaded me to take up. I am employed day and night, and must go on, whether I will or no, lest the printer should stand still. All my time is swallowed up, and I can hardly catch a few hours to answer the letters that are sent me.[92]

The *Notes* were finally finished in 1765. Tyerman records an advertisement from Lloyd's Evening Post, June 5, 1765:

> On Thursday the 1st of August will be published, price, 6 d., Number 1. of *Explanatory Notes Upon the Old Testament*, by John Wesley M.A., late fellow of Lincoln College, Oxford. Conditions,1. That this work be printed in quarto, on a superfine paper. 2. That it will be comprised in about 60 numbers (as near as can be computed) making two handsome volumes. 3. That each number will contain three sheets of letterpress, printed on a new type. 4. That the first number will be considered as a specimen, and, if not approved of, the money paid for it shall be returned. 5. That the work will be delivered weekly to the subscribers, without interruption, after the publication of the first number. 6. That the whole will be published in an elegant manner, no way inferior to the very best work of the kind offered to the public. Bristol: Printed by William Pine. Sold by J. Fletcher & Co., in St. Paul Churchyard, London; and by the Booksellers of Great Britain and Ireland.[93]

---

[92] *Letters* 5:13.

[93] Luke Tyerman. *The Life and Times of the Reverend John Wesley.* (New York, N.Y.: Harper Bros., 1870) 2:552–53.

As with the *Explanatory Notes Upon the New Testament,* I propose to compare sections from Wesley's *Notes,* concerning his views on Scripture, with Matthew Henry and Matthew Poole's views, to discover just how accurate Wesley was in proclaiming he was not just abridging their work.

One interesting comparison is portions of Matthew Poole's preface with Wesley's "A Clear and Concise Demonstration of the Divine Impartation of the Holy Scriptures," and his comments on the Song of Solomon, in his *Explanatory Notes*. Poole comments on the books of the Old and New Testament:

> . . . every reasonable man finds them of so venerable antiquity, and discerneth in them such stamps of divinity in their majesty of style, the printing of the matter, the sublimeness and spirituality of the propositions contained in them, the self-denial of the penmen, the heavenliness of the scope and end of those sacred writings, the harmony of the parts, the seal of the miracles, and principally in the mighty power and efficacy of them upon the souls and consciences of multitudes, both for conviction, and for support and consolation, that he easily concludes, this is the voice of God, and not of man . . .[94]

Wesley in his "Clear and Concise Demonstration," advocates similar views:

> There are four grand and powerful arguments which strongly induce us to believe that the Bible must be from God; viz., miracles, prophecies, the goodness of the doctrine and the moral character of the penmen. All the miracles flow from the divine power; all prophecies from divine understanding; the goodness of the doctrine, from divine goodness; and the character of the penmen, from divine holiness.[95]

Wesley's comments upon the Song of Solomon again show Poole's influence:

> That this book was of divine inspiration is so clear, that as the Jewish writers note, none ever questioned it, although some doubted of some other of Solomon's writings. And the same arguments which prove the divinity of other books, are found here, such as the quality of the penman, who was confessedly a man inspired by God; the excellency and usefulness of the matter; the sacred and sublime

---

[94] Matthew Poole. *Commentary on the Bible.* (London, England: The Banner of Trust, 1962) 1:iii.
[95] *Works* 11:484.

majesty of the style, and the singular efficacy of it upon the hearts of sober and serious persons.[96]

In comparing these comments with Poole's we discover this is a direct quotation, with Wesley merely omitting these comments: . . . who read it with due preparation; and those other characters which are commonly known, and therefore it is needless here to enumerate.[97]

In considering Isaiah 59:21, Wesley comments that the Word of God has been uttered by the virtues of God's Spirit:

> . . . My covenant-what I have promised to them that turn from their iniquity. 'My Words'—which thou has uttered by virtue of My Spirit. 'Of Thy seed'—a promise of the perpetual preference of His Word and Spirit with the prophets, apostles; and teachers of the church to all ages.[98]

Compare to Poole:

> . . . or rather, he seems to promise the perpetual presence of His Word and Spirit with the prophets, apostles, and ministers, and teachers of the church to all succeeding ages thereof, and may have a special reference to the gospel, or new covenant in Christ.[99]

Another interesting passage to consider is Deuteronomy 17:18–20. Speaking on this passage, which commands the King to write out a copy of the Law, Wesley directly quotes the comments of Poole for vss. 18 and 20. Poole intimates that the Scripture:

> . . . diligently read and studied, are a powerful and probable means to keep him humble, because they show him that, though a king, he is subject to a higher monarch.[100]

Wesley then turns to Matthew Henry for his comments on vs. 19, concerning the importance of not only having a Bible but using it:

---

[96] John Wesley. *Explanatory Notes Upon the Old Testament.* (Salem, Ohio.: Schmul Publishers, 1975) 3:925.

[97] Matthew Poole. *Commentary on the Bible.* (London, England: The Banner of Trust, 1962) 2:308.

[98] John Wesley. *Explanatory Notes Upon the Old Testament.* (Salem, Ohio.: Schmul Publishers, 1975) 3:1203.

[99] Matthew Poole. *Commentary on the Bible.* (London, England: The Banner of Trust, 1962) 2:468.

[100] Ibid. 1:370.

Matthew Henry:

> Having a Bible by him in his own writings, he must not think it enough to keep it in his cabinet, but he must read therein all the days of his life, vs. 19. It is not enough to have Bibles, but we must use them, use them daily, as the duty and necessity of every day requires: our souls must have their constant meals of that manna; and, if well digested, it will be true nourishment, and strength to them.[101]

Wesley:

> Tis not enough to have Bibles, but we must use them, yes, use them daily. Our souls must have constant meals of that manna, which if well digested, will afford them true nourishment and strength.[102]

Another example of Wesley's dependence on Matthew Henry, in referring to Scripture, is Deuteronomy 11:19.

Henry:

> Let us all be directed by these three rules here given:

> 1. Let our hearts be filled with the Word of God: Lay up these words in your heart and in your soul. The heart must be the treasury or storehouse, in which the Word of God must be laid up, to be based upon all occasions. We cannot expect good practices in the conversation, unless there be good thoughts, good affections, and good principles, in the heart.[103]

Wesley:

> Lay up-Let us all observe these three rules, 1. Let our hearts be filled with the Word of God. Lay up these words in your hearts, as in a store-house, to be used upon all occasions.[104]

As we have seen Wesley had a high view of the Bible and regarded the Scriptures as the divinely inspired Oracles of God. On several occasions he referred to the human authors as inspired men, and at times refers directly

---

[101] Matthew Henry. *Matthew Henry's Commentary on the Whole Bible.* (New York, N.Y.: Fleming H. Revell Company, nd.) 258.

[102] John Wesley. *Explanatory Notes Upon the Old Testament.* (Salem, Ohio.: Schmul Publishers, 1975) 1:638.

[103] Matthew Henry. *Matthew Henry's Commentary on the Whole Bible.* (New York, N.Y.: Fleming H. Revell Company, nd) 250.

[104] John Wesley. *Explanatory Notes Upon the Old Testament.* (Salem, Ohio.: Schmul Publishers, 1975) 1:620.

to the Holy Spirit as the author of particular passages of Scripture. In commenting on Genesis 2:8–15, he directly quotes from Matthew Henry:

> The inspired penman in this history writing for the Jews first, and calculating his narratives from the infant state of the church, describes things by their outward sensible appearances, and leaves us, by further discoveries of the divine light, to be led into the understanding of the mysteries couched under them.[105]

In commenting on Genesis 5:6–19 Wesley states, "We have here all that the Holy Ghost thought fit to leave upon record concerning five of the patriarchs before the flood . . ."[106] In this long commentary Wesley mainly summarizes Matthew Henry's notes on this passage. He leaves out some small sections that he may have considered less important. For example he excluded Henry's comments on the listing of ages:

> When we are informed how old they were when they brought forth a son, and how many years they afterward lived, a very little skill in arithmetic will enable a man to tell how long they lived at all; yet the Holy Ghost sets down the sum total, for the sake of those that have not even so much skill as this.[107]

Again, speaking of the genealogies in Genesis 11:10, Wesley exactly quotes Matthew Henry:

> Observe here, 1. That nothing is left upon record concerning those of this line, but their names and ages; the Holy Ghost seeming to hasten through them to the story of Abraham.[108]

Conclusion

It is evident in comparing both the *Explanatory Notes Upon the Old Testament,* and the *Explanatory Notes Upon the New Testament* with Bengel, Henry, and Poole, that Wesley was not particularly interested in originality. Instead, he found men whom he respected, and as he suggested, merely summarized and edited. This is also true concerning the passages where he commented on Scripture. This should not lead one to ignore Wesley's com-

---

[105] Ibid., 1:11.

[106] Ibid., 1:26.

[107] Matthew Henry. *Matthew Henry's Commentary on the Whole Bible.* (New York, N.Y.: Fleming H. Revell Company, nd.) 21.

[108] John Wesley. *Explanatory Notes Upon the Old Testament.* (Salem, Ohio.: Schmul Publishers, 1975) 1:50.

ments in his *Notes;* instead we must recognize that in quoting these men he was acknowledging their veracity, and stating his own opinions.

Wesley and Bibliomancy

A final and rather unusual use of the Bible by Wesley is a usage called bibliomancy, which is a kind of magic lottery from which to draw instructions about conduct. At times, when Wesley was in doubt, he would take the Bible in hand; offer a prayer for it to open to the right place; allow it to fall open and take that passage which his eye first fell upon as a message from God informing him what to do.[109]

For Wesley, it seemed reasonable to believe that a God who was as interested in earthly affairs as the Bible indicated, would not be unready to offer guidance to Christians who sought it by faith. This direction took different forms such as the casting of lots (sortilege), and bibliomancy.[110]

Wesley informs of this confidence in his *Journal* in 1738:

> Hereby I am come to know assuredly that if 'in all our ways we acknowledge' God, He will, where reason fails, 'direct our paths' by lot or by the other means which he knoweth.[111]

This unusual custom Wesley seems to have derived from the Moravians, specifically the Herrnhut Brethren. He mentions learning from them to use the biblical lot when faced with difficult decisions in his *Journal* of February 3, 1738.[112] Wesley defended himself on the grounds that this method is not forbidden in Scripture, and the practice was employed only after he exhausted all other means of reaching a decision.

For this study I am more interested in his use of bibliomancy than his use of lots, however, we see both usages occur on different occasions in Wesley's decision making processes. In fact, the most remembered use of this mystical form of securing wisdom from God may be Wesley's casting of lots concerning his proposed marriage in Georgia. According to Wesley's own words:

> Having both of us sought God by deep consideration, fasting and prayer, in the afternoon we conferred together, but could not come to any decision. We both apprehended Mr. Ingham's objection to

---

[109] William Pellowe, "John Wesley's Use of the Bible," *Methodist Review* (1923)369.

[110] Stanley Ayling. *John Wesley.* (Nashville, Tenn.: Abingdon Press, 1979) 107.

[111] Richard Heitzenrater and Reginald Ward. *The Works of John Wesley. Vol. 18.* (Nashville, Tenn.: Abingdon Press, 1988) 479–80.

[112] Ibid., 221–222.

be the strongest.... At length we agreed to appeal to the Searcher of Hearts. I accordingly made three lots.[113]

The result of the lot casting was that Wesley was to "think of her no more" and he was able to say cheerfully, "Thy will be done."

Wesley used the casting of lots clearly believing it was based upon Scripture. At the same time, he tried to guard against using the text of the Bible mechanically like an oracle, and he always endeavored to do justice to the context of the Scripture.[114]

The most remarkable use of bibliomancy by Wesley can be seen in its use to determine whether he would leave the promising work in London to join Whitefield in Bristol in open air preaching. This was truly a critical turning point in Wesley's religious career, and it was determined to a large extent by bibliomancy. Wesley was reluctant to leave, but George Whitefield and his friend Seward entreated him to come without delay. Wesley was in a quandary and began to open the Bible and consider the first text to meet his eye. All the verses seemed to indicate disaster. Wesley in 1739 in his *Journal* wrote of his dilemma:

> So that I had no thought of leaving London when I received (after several others) a letter from Mr. Whitefield, and another from Mr. Seward entreating me in the most pressing manner to come to Bristol without delay. This I was not at all forward to do, and perhaps a little less inclined to do it (though I trust I do not count my life dear unto myself, so I may finish the course with joy), because of the remarkable Scriptures which offered as often as we inquired touching the consequences of this removal, though whether this was permitted only for the trial of our faith, God knoweth, and the events will show.[115]

Finally on March 28, 1739 Wesley wrote:

> My journey was proposed to our society in Fetter Lane. But my brother Charles would scarce bear the mention of it; till, appealing to the oracles of God, he received those words as spoken unto himself and answered not again: 'Son of man, behold, I take from thee the desire of thine eyes with a stroke; yet shalt thou not mourn or weep, neither shall thy tears run down.' Our other brethren, however, continuing the dispute without any probability of their

---

[113] Ibid., 479–80.

[114] Ibid., 221–22.

[115] Richard Heitzenrater and Reginald Ward. *The Works of John Wesley. Vol. 19* (Nashville, Tenn.: Abingdon Press, 1990) 37.

coming to one conclusion, we at length all agreed to decide it by lot. And by this it was determined I should go. Several afterwards desiring we might open the Bible concerning the issue of this, we did so on the several portions of scripture which I shall set down without reflection upon them.[116]

So we find at this most crucial time in Wesley's ministry the use of both lots and bibliomancy in discovering the will of God. There would continue to be times in the future where he would be 'crying out to God, I took up the Bible which opened to these words,'[117] or in 1741 "I besought God to show me where this would end and opened my Bible on these words."[118]

I believe it is important in recognizing Wesley's use of bibliomancy to keep in mind that this was only used after much prayer and fasting, as a last resort. It is Sugden's opinion that due to the silence about these two practices in his sermons we can safely conjecture that he had come by this time (1750) to see the superstitious and enthusiastic character of such methods of ascertaining the will of God.[119]

In whatever manner we view these two usages, it still points out the fact that for all regulating principles in his life the Scripture was to be the guide and the authority.[120]

Wesley: A Man of One Thousand and One Books

Though Wesley fiercely proclaimed himself a "Man of One Book," and we have clearly seen that the Bible was the centerpiece of all his instruction, it would be inaccurate to conclude that he had no interest in other writings. Wesley himself was a voluminous author and editor with over 400 publications to his credit.[121]

Wesley did not neglect other writings as of no importance. He had a strong belief in the study of logic to develop the faculty of thought and the field of medicine, history and literature in order to become a more efficient servant of God by better understanding the human situation and the power of experience.[122]

---

[116] Ibid., 38.

[117] Ibid., 16.

[118] Ibid., 191.

[119] *Sermons* 1:97.

[120] William Arnett, "John Wesley-A Man of One Book" (Ph.D. diss., Drew University, 1954).

[121] Ibid.

[122] Colin Williams. *John Wesley's Theology Today.* (Nashville, Tenn.: Abingdon Press, 1960) 24.

Wesley felt that reading the Bible and nothing else would certainly lead to decline and make preaching superfluous. He opposed any high sounding claims about studying only the Bible as rank enthusiasm. If anyone had no taste for reading, he would be better off to return to his trade. In his "Minutes of Several Conversations" (1744-89) he writes:

> (1). Read the most useful books, and that regularly and constantly. Steadily spend all the morning in this employ, or, at least, five hours in four and twenty. 'But I read only the Bible.' Then you ought to teach others to read only the Bible, and, by parity of reason, to hear only the Bible: But if so, you need to preach no more. Just so said George Bell. And what is the fruit? Why, now he neither reads the Bible, nor anything else. This is rank enthusiasm. If you need no book but the Bible, you are got above St. Paul. He wanted others too. 'Bring me the books,' says he, 'but especially the parchments' (those wrote on parchment) (II Timothy 4:13). 'But I have no taste for reading.' Contract a taste for it by use, or return to your trade.[123]

To avoid his preachers not reading widely, Wesley set up the Christian Library. He had two desires: first, that they would acquire a tolerable general knowledge of the basic ancient writings used in the English schools of that period. Also, he hoped that their knowledge of Christian literature would embrace a wide ecumenical selection to introduce them in an unprejudiced way to the value of Roman Catholic, Presbyterian and Pietistic books. At their conferences the preachers were given a list of books which included classical writers, humanists, French Catholics, German Pietists, other authors, and of course tracts he had written.[124]

In summary, John Wesley may have styled himself a "Bible Bigot" and rightly so, but in point of fact there were few in his day who were his superiors in general scholarship and knowledge. He studied, read, and wrote voluminously and encouraged his preachers to do likewise. The fact remains, however, that in all aspects of his instruction the one book he exalted was the Bible. A letter to Richard Thompson in 1755 summarizes Wesley's thoughts concerning not only his written tracts, but all manner of his instructions:

> If you have observed anything in any of the tracts I have published which you think are not agreeable to Scripture or reason, you will oblige me by pointing it out and by communicating to me any re-

---

[123] *Works* 8:315.

[124] Martin Schmidt. *John Wesley a Theological Biography Vol. 2.* (Nashville, Tenn.: Abingdon Press, 1973) 110.

marks you have occasionally made. I seek two things in the world, truth and love.[125]

---

[125] Frank Baker. *The Works of John Wesley. Vol. 26.* (Oxford, England: Oxford University Press, 1982) 567.

Section II

John Wesley's View of Inspiration and Infallibility

6

John Wesley and the Inspiration of Scripture

WE BELIEVE indeed that:

> "all Scripture is given by inspiration of God"(II Timothy 3:16), and herein we are distinguished from Jews, Turks, and infidels. We believe this written Word of God to be the only and the sufficient rule both of Christian faith and practice; and herein we are fundamentally distinguished from those of the Romish Church.[1]

According to Dr. George Turner, for Wesley the belief that the Bible was the revelation of God was one of the two most fundamental convictions in Wesley's outlook. In rare moments of agnosticism there were two convictions which remained. There is a God and God has revealed himself in a book.[2]

As will be revealed in later chapters, Wesley had great respect for reason and the natural faculties of man. However, true spiritual knowledge of God could not come by natural faculties alone. Instead this required revelation came from God, and God had revealed himself in a book:

> God himself has condescended to teach the way: for this very end He came from heaven. He hath written it down in a book. Oh give me that book! At any price give me the Book of God. I have it. Here is knowledge enough for me. Let me be *homo unius libr.*[3]

Wesley's view of the inspiration of Scripture was in line with the classic views of Augustine and the Reformers, but out of line with the rationalists of his day. However, even when dealing with deists or other destructive

---

[1] Rupert Davies. *The Works of John Wesley. Vol. 9* (Nashville, Tenn.: Abingdon Press, 1989) 33–34.

[2] George Allen Turner. *Inspiration and Interpretation.* (Grand Rapids, Mich.: Wm B. Eerdmanns Pub Co., 1957) 160.

[3] Albert Outler. *The Works of John Wesley. Vol. 1.* (Nashville, Tenn.: Abingdon Press, 1984) 105.

critics he did not feel the need to establish the authority of the Bible. He might appeal to reason and conscience, but to those who would not accept the Scriptures, no defense was needed. For Wesley, as for a majority of Jews and Christians of that day, the Bible was the inspired Word of God for man mediated through human instruments.[4]

On many occasions in sermons, his *Journal*, letters, and *Notes* Wesley proclaimed the Bible to be the inspired Word of God. Consider a few of these proclamations. First, Wesley's comments on II Timothy 3:16 from his *Explanatory Notes Upon the New Testament*:

> All Scripture is inspired by God—The Spirit of God not only once inspired those who wrote it, but continually inspires, supernaturally assists those that read it with earnest prayer. Hence it is so profitable for doctrine, for instruction of the ignorant, for the reproof or conviction of them that are in error or sin; for the correction or amendment of whatever is amiss, and for instructing or training up the children of God in all righteousness.[5]

Wesley expounds on this theme in a number of his sermons. In "The Witness of Our Own Spirit" (1746), he refers to the Word of God as, "the Christian rule of right and wrong," and than goes on to define it as:

> the writings of the Old and New Testament: all which the prophets and the 'holy men of old' wrote 'as they were moved by the Holy Ghost;' all that 'Scripture which was given by inspiration of God,' and which is indeed 'profitable for doctrine,' or 'teaching the whole will of God;' 'for reproof' of what is contrary thereto: 'for correction of error,' and 'for instruction (or training us up) in righteousness.'[6]

In his sermon "The Law Established Through Faith II" (1750), he writes:

> We know that 'all Scripture given by the inspiration of God is profitable' either 'for doctrine' or 'for reproof,' 'for correction' or 'for instruction in righteousness' and 'that the man of God,' in the process of the work of God in his soul, has need of every part thereof

---

[4] George Allen Turner. *Inspiration and Interpretation*. (Grand Rapids, Mich.: Wm B. Eerdmanns Pub Co., 1957) 161.

[5] John Wesley. *Explanatory Notes Upon the New Testament*. (London, England: Epworth Press, 1948) 227.

[6] Albert Outler. *The Works of John Wesley. Vol. 1*. (Nashville, Tenn.: Abingdon Press, 1984) 302–03.

that he 'may' at length 'be perfect, thoroughly furnished unto all good works.'[7]

One final quotation that clearly shows Wesley's view that the Scriptures are from God, comes from his forceful answer in his letter to John Smith in 1747:

> I am as fully convinced today that the Scriptures are of God as that the Sun shines. And this conviction (as every good gift) cometh from the Father of Lights. Yet I may doubt of it tomorrow. I may throw away a good gift of God. "But we were speaking, not of man's opinions, but of God's facts." We were speaking of both: of men's opinions or judgments, concerning God's facts. "But could he to whom Christ said, 'Thy sins are forgiven thee,' ever doubt or deny that Christ said so?" I question not but in the process of time he might, particularly if he drew back unto perdition. But however that may be, it is no 'blasphemous supposition,' but a plain, undeniable truth, that the god of this world can obliterate what the God of heaven has strongly imprinted upon the soul. Yea, and that he surely will, unless we stir up the gift of God which is in us, by earnestly and continually watching unto prayer.[8]

This quotation must be understood in light of an argument over the witness of the Spirit. The fact that a person might doubt today that he is a Christian does not destroy the fact he did not know it before. Wesley is saying "Just because I doubt tomorrow that the Scriptures are from God does not change the fact that they are from God." A person could doubt regardless of how certain he had been, but that does not change the truth of the matter.

Even if one accepts the fact that Wesley believed the Bible to be the inspired Word of God, there remain certain questions that should be asked. First, what proof did Wesley have to convince him of the divine inspiration of Scripture? Second, what exactly did Wesley mean when he claimed that all Scripture was given by inspiration? Did Wesley believe in a specific mode of inspiration and did he view all Scripture as equally inspired?

---

[7] Ibid., 2:37
[8] Frank Baker. *The Works of John Wesley. Vol.26.* (Oxford, England: Oxford University Press, 1982) 249.

Proofs of Inspiration for Wesley

The place to begin in considering why Wesley believed the Bible to be from God is his essay "A Clear and Concise Demonstration of the Divine Impartation of the Holy Scriptures":

> There are four grand and powerful arguments which strongly induce us to believe that the Bible must be from God; viz., miracles, prophecies, the goodness of the doctrine, and the moral character of the penmen. All miracles flow from divine power; all the prophecies, from divine understanding; the goodness of the doctrine from divine goodness; and the character of the penmen, from divine holiness.
>
> Thus Christianity is built upon four grand pillars; viz., the power, understanding, goodness, and holiness of God. Divine power is the source of all miracles, divine understanding of all the prophecies, divine goodness, of the doctrine; and divine holiness, of the moral character of the penmen.
>
> I beg leave to propose a short, clear, and strong argument to prove the divine inspiration of the Holy Scriptures.
>
> The Bible must be the invention of good men or angels; bad men or devils, or of God.
>
> 1. It could not be the invention of good men or angels: for they neither would nor could make a book, and tell lies all the time that they were writing it saying, 'Thus sayeth the Lord,' when it was their own invention.
>
> 2. It could not be the invention of bad men or devils; for they would not make a book which commands all duty, forbids all sin and condemns their soul to hell for all eternity.
>
> 3. Therefore, I draw the conclusion, that the Bible must be given by divine inspiration.[9]

In considering this essay it is clear that Wesley felt that believing in divine inspiration was logical, as is evidenced by the closing points. He also lists four "proofs" of divine inspiration in the first paragraph namely: miracles, prophecies, the goodness of the doctrine and the moral character of the penmen. In others of his writings he expanded upon these points in proving divine inspiration.

For example, Wesley felt fulfilled prophecy was one evidence that Scripture was divinely inspired. In his *Journal* of 1738 he comments on the

---

[9] *Works* 11:484.

words of one Christian David, whose teachings Wesley encountered on his journey to Hernhutt:

> Are the New Testament prophecies fulfilled? This I next set myself to examine. I read them carefully over and could not but see every event answered the prediction, so that the more I compared one with the other, the more fully I was convinced that 'all Scripture was given by inspiration of God.'[10]

In regarding the Scriptures as the divinely inspired Oracles of God Wesley on several occasions referred to the human authors as inspired men of great moral character. Note once again his comments upon the Song of Solomon in his *Explanatory Notes Upon the Old Testament*:

> That this book was of divine inspiration is so clear, that as the Jewish writers note, none ever questioned it, though some doubted of some other of Solomon's writings. And the same arguments which prove the divinity of other books, are found here, such as the quality of the penman, who was confessedly a man inspired of God; the excellency and usefulness of the matter; the sacred and sublime majesty of the style; and the singular efficacy of it upon the hearts of sober and serious persons.[11]

In this quotation Wesley also touched upon another proof of divine inspiration of Scripture, the goodness of the doctrine. He describes the "excellency and usefulness," the "sacred sublime majesty," the "efficacy of the Scripture" as proof of divine inspiration. All these qualities made the Scriptures unique from other writings in Wesley's eyes and were further proof of their divine origin.

One further quotation will summarize Wesley's clear belief in the divine origin and inspiration of Scripture based upon the proofs just considered. In Wesley's *A Compendium of Natural Philosophy* (1784) he considers the question of whether revelation is divine and whether Scripture is of divine authority. To consider these questions he maintains that:

> First, that, as God has made men the immediate instruments of all revelation, so evangelical faith must be partly founded on human testimony. By men were both the Old and New Testament written: and if we consider them abstracted from their divine authority, they must be allowed to be of equal credibility at least with all other

---

[10] Reginald Ward. *The Works of John Wesley. Vol. 18.* (Nashville, Tenn.: Abingdon Press, 1988) 273–74.

[11] John Wesley. *Explanatory Notes Upon the Old Testament.* (Salem, Ohio.: Schmul Publishers, 1975) 3:1925.

ancient writings. Though we should suppose them to be upon the foot of mere human testimony, yet would our knowledge of them be, at least, of equal certainty with that founded upon profane history. Now if to this human we add such divine testimony as cannot be pretended for any other writings in the world, as the miracles of Christ and His apostles: the concurrent completion of all prophecies from the beginning of the World in Him alone; the Scripture being the only Book in the world that gives us any account of the whole series of God's dispensations toward man, from the creation four thousand years, the great exaltation of natural religion visible in every part of it, and lastly the providential care so manifest in every age, for transmitting down several books, written at such great distances of time from one another, and all of them from us, there being at this day so void of any material error, that in the infinite various readings which have been carefully collected, there cannot be found one contrariety in any fundamental point of faith or practice, if these things I say are considered, they give the Scripture such a certainty as no writing merely human can have, and are the greatest evidences for the truth of them which are capable of receiving with a continual daily reception of miracles.[12]

Clearly for Wesley, belief that the Scripture was divinely inspired was not based merely upon faith. He felt that proof such as miracles, fulfilled prophecies, the clear superiority of the biblical writers, the providential transmission and the interconnection of the Old and New Testaments, would lead a logical person to believe the Bible was divinely inspired. In considering Wesley's statements, all might not agree with his conclusions, but none should question his belief in the divine inspiration and thus the divine authority of Scripture.

Wesley's View of Divine Inspiration

In considering the question "What exactly did Wesley mean when he said the Scriptures were divinely inspired" one might begin the answer by stating that John Wesley did not appear to hold to any special theory of inspiration. He committed his connection to no special theory. It is interesting to note in his *Fifty-Three Standard Sermons*, that there is not a single sermon devoted to explaining what the Bible is, its inspiration, or how to interpret

---

[12] Robert Burtner and Robert Chiles. *A Compend of Wesley's Theology.* (Nashville, Tenn.: Abingdon Press, 1954) 23–24.

it.[13] However in reading Wesley one can still draw some legitimate conclusions.

For Wesley the Bible was inspired in the fullest sense. This meant that the Scriptures were the very words of God given to man. The Bible came to us in "words taught by the Spirit" (I Corinthians 2:13). In his *Explanatory Notes Upon the New Testament* Wesley comments upon this Scripture passage saying, "Such are all the Words of Scripture. How high a regard we ought then to retain for them."[14] He would go on later in this work to comment on Galatians 3:8 maintaining:

> That is, the Holy Spirit, who gave the Scripture. So great is the excellency and fullness of the Scripture, that all the things which can ever be controverted are therein both foreseen and determined.[15]

Wesley often referred to the biblical passages as being the words of the Spirit Himself as can be seen in his sermon "The Means of Grace" where he states "the Holy Spirit expressly declares."[16] Wesley felt free to make these statements believing, as earlier noted in his comments upon II Timothy 3:16, that the "Spirit of God not only once inspired those who wrote it, but continually inspires, supernaturally assists those that read it with earnest prayer."[17]

For Wesley there was a divine interconnectedness of Scripture that could be a result only of divine revelation given to inspired writers in the fullest sense. Note his remarks in his sermon "On Divine Providence" (1786):

> It is the beautiful remark of a fine writer, 'Those who object to the Old Testament, in particular that it is not a connected history of nations, but only a congeries of broken unconnected events, do not observe the nature and design of these writings. They do not see that Scripture is the history of God.' Those who bear this upon their minds will easily perceive that the inspired writers never lose sight of it, but preserve one unbroken connected chain from the beginning to the end. All over that wonderful Book, as 'life and

---

[13] William Pellowe, "John Wesley's Use of the Bible," *Methodist Review* (1923) 359.

[14] John Wesley. *Explanatory Notes Upon the New Testament*. (London, England: Epworth Press, 1948) 591.

[15] Ibid.s, 667.

[16] Albert Outler. *The Works of John Wesley. Vol. 1.* (Nashville, Tenn.: Abingdon Press, 1984) 388.

[17] John Wesley. *Explanatory Notes Upon the New Testament*. (London, England: Epworth Press, 1948) 794.

immortality' (immortal life), is gradually 'brought to light,' so is 'Immanuel, God with us,' and His kingdom ruling over all.[18]

Stating that Wesley believed the Bible to be "fully" inspired is not to imply that he lost sight of the fact that revelation was given through human agents. Wesley did not have a mechanical dictation approach to inspiration. In commenting upon Acts 15:7 in his *Explanatory Notes Upon the New Testament* Wesley notes:

> For how really soever they were inspired, we need not suppose their inspiration was always so instantaneous and express as to supersede any deliberation in their own minds, or any consultation with each other.[19]

Later in the *Explanatory Notes Upon the New Testament* Wesley comments upon Hebrews 2:7, showing he did not believe in mechanical dictation but realized that the Scriptural writers accepted tradition and quoted Scripture without exactness. Here he states that the apostles:

> ... constantly cited the Septaguint translation, very frequently without variation. It was not their business, in writing to the Jews, who at that time had it in high esteem, to amend or alter this, which would of consequence have occasioned disputes without end.[20]

Wesley understood that inspiration of Scripture required accommodating the truth of God to the limitation of the human mind. Bernard Ramm states "To be meaningful the revelation had to come in human language, in human thought forms and referring to objective experience."[21] Wesley points out this same necessity in his *Explanatory Notes Upon the New Testament* when he states "It is necessary that the Scripture should let itself down to the language of man."[22]

Wesley expounds upon this concept further when he states:

> As God has made men the immediate instruments of all his revelations, so he hath condescended to make use of human language as

---

[18] Albert Outler. *The Works of John Wesley. Vol. 2.* (Nashville, Tenn.: Abingdon Press, 1985) 536.

[19] John Wesley. *Explanatory Notes Upon the New Testament.* (London, England: Epworth Press, 1948) 453.

[20] Ibid., 814.

[21] Larry Shelton, "John Wesley's Approach to Scripture in Historical Perspective," *Wesleyan Theological Journal 16* (1981) 37.

[22] John Wesley. *Explanatory Notes Upon the New Testament.* (London, England: Epworth Press, 1948) 542.

John Wesley and the Inspiration of Scripture

well as our natural ideas and conceptions for the clear and easy representation of the supernatural, and otherwise incomprehensible.[23]

Another point to consider, is that although Wesley felt the Scripture to be fully inspired, he did not maintain all Scripture was of equal value. In his sermon "Charity" (1784) he remarks:

> We know, 'All Scripture is given by inspiration of God,' and is therefore true and right concerning all things. But we know likewise, that there are some Scriptures which more immediately commend themselves to every man's conscience.[24]

Again in his sermon on "Of Hell" (1782) he writes:

> 1. Every truth which is revealed in the Oracles of God is undoubtedly of great importance. Yet it may be allowed that some of those which are revealed therein are of greater importance than others as being more immediately conducive to the grand end of all, the eternal salvation of men.[25]

From these statements we can see that Wesley had a high estimate of the inspiration of the Word of God, but he did not believe that this made all Scripture of equal value.

In conclusion it is clear that Wesley believed the Scriptures to be the divinely inspired Word of God. He would presumably have felt little sympathy for those who felt otherwise, in that even the "devils" believed in the inspiration of the Bible. In his sermon "The Marks of the New Birth" (1748) he states:

> To say this were to say (which who could bear) that the devils were born of God. For they have their faith. They trembling believe both that Jesus is the Christ and that all Scripture, having been given by inspiration of God, is true as God is true.[26]

There is certainly room for discussion on how Wesley conceived the method of divine inspiration, for it seems to have been his desire to accept the Bible as the one source of divine revelation without raising questions about the method. As will be shown in later chapters the question for Wesley was not "How were the divine words put into the writer's minds

---

[23] Robert Burtner and Robert Chiles. *A Compend of Wesley's Theology.* (Nashville, Tenn.: Abingdon Press, 1954) 24.

[24] Albert Outler. *The Works of John Wesley. Vol. 3.* (Nashville, Tenn.: Abingdon Press, 1986) 292.

[25] Ibid., 3:31.

[26] Ibid., 1:418.

and mouths, but, what does the word mean, when interpreted by the best rules of interpretation?"[27]

Thus, while some may argue about the mode of inspiration that Wesley advocated, there should be no debate on what he took to be the effect of inspiration. The Bible was God's divinely inspired Word to man, altogether true and worthy of God. There was a divine interconnectedness that joined the Old and New Testament giving the history of God's dealing with his creation. This divine revelation was given to inspired men who answered the impressions upon their minds in language which was exact to the highest degree. For Wesley, the Bible was divine, fully inspired, given through the instrumentation of men, forever true, eternally valid. As was noted earlier Wesley summarizes his views quite clearly in his preface to *The Explanatory Notes Upon the New Testament:*

> Concerning the Scriptures in general, it may be observed the Word of the living God, which directed the first patriarchs also, was in the time of Moses committed to writing. To this were added, in several succeeding generations, the inspired writing of the other prophets. Afterwards, what the Son of God preached and the Holy Ghost spake by the apostles, the apostles and evangelists wrote. This is what we now style the Holy Scripture: this is that 'Word of God which remaineth forever;' of which, though 'heaven and earth pass away, one jot or tittle shall not pass away.' The Scripture, therefore, of the Old and New Testament is a most solid and precious system of divine truth. Every part thereof is worthy of God; and all together are one entire body, wherein is no defect, no excess. It is the fountain of heavenly wisdom, which they who are able to taste prefer to all writings of men, however wise or learned or holy.
>
> An exact knowledge of the truth was accompanied, in the inspired writers, with an exactly regular series of arguments, a precise expression of their meaning and a genuine vigour of suitable affections. The chain of argument in each book is briefly exhibited in the table prefixed to it, which contains also the sum thereof, and may be of more use than prefixing the argument to each chapter: the division of the New Testament into chapters having been made in the dark ages, and very incorrectly, often separating things that are closely joined and joining those that are entirely distinct from each other. In the language of the sacred writings we may observe the utmost depth, together with the utmost ease. All the elegancies of human composures sink into nothing before it: God speaks not as man but as God. His thoughts are very deep and thence His words are of inexhaustible virtue. And the language of his messengers also,

---

[27] William Pellowe, "John Wesley's Use of the Bible," *Methodist Review.* (1923) 360.

is exact in the highest degree: for the words which were given them accurately answered the impression made upon their minds; and hence Luther says, 'Divinity is nothing but a grammar of the language of the Holy Ghost.'[28]

---

[28] John Wesley. *Explanatory Notes Upon the New Testament*. (London, England: Epworth Press, 1948) 8–9.

7

John Wesley and the Infallibility of Scripture

> 'All Scripture is given by inspiration of God,' (consequently all scripture is infallibly true), 'and is profitable for doctrine, for reproof, for correction, for instruction in righteousness,' to the end, 'that the man of God may be perfect, thoroughly furnished unto all good works.'[1]

UPON READING this quotation from Wesley's sermon "Means of Grace" (1746) one might be moved to say, why continue? Surely Wesley's view on infallibility is clearly stated. It appears, based on his own words, for Wesley all Scripture was infallibly true. This issue however, is not that cut or dried. Considering the fact that the infallibility of Scripture is very controversial, even among evangelical elements in today's church, it should come as no surprise that the question of Wesley's view on the infallibility of the Bible is a controversial issue as well.

At this point it might be well to remind the reader that the purpose of this chapter is not to determine whether the original autographs were infallibly true as given by God. The purpose, as has been the case in all chapters, is to determine Wesley's views upon the Bible. In this chapter the question will be asked, "Did Wesley consider the Bible to be infallible?" The next important question then becomes, "if Wesley did hold this view, what exactly did he mean by the term infallibility?" If Wesley believed in infallibility did he mean by this the inerrancy of the original autographs, or was his view of infallibility more limited or accommodating to the idea of error in the Scriptures?

---

[1] Albert Outler. *The Works of John Wesley. Vol. 1* (Nashville, Tenn.: Abingdon Press, 1984) 388.

In an attempt to answer these questions, I will provide quotations showing Wesley's views concerning the infallibility of Scripture. Then, I will attempt to interpret Wesley in light of his eighteenth century context.

Wesley's Views upon Infallibility

On occasion in his writings Wesley designated the Scriptures as being infallible. As noted above in his sermon "The Means of Grace" (1746) he states "that all Scripture is infallibly true."[2] On another occasion in his sermon "The Cause and Cure of Earthquakes" (1750) he challenges the reader to, "Prove thine ownself by the infallible Word of God."[3] It appears that Wesley was quite willing to acknowledge human fallibility, but he would not accept the same imperfections in the Word of God. For example in his letter to Mr. Downes in 1759 he states:

> I beg you would please, (1) to explain this, and (2) to prove that we ever yet (whoever taught us) 'set up for infallible interpreters of Scripture.' So far from it that we have over and over declared, in print as well as in public preaching: 'We are no more to expect any living man to be infallible, than to be omniscient.'[4]

Again, commenting on his own human limitations in his *Explanatory Notes Upon the New Testament* he states, "I cannot flatter myself so far (to use the words of one of the above named writers) as to imagine that I have fallen into no mistakes in a work of so great difficulty."[5]

So we see Wesley admitted to and accepted human limitations in the ability to interpret and communicate the Bible. Would he accept the same limitations, mistakes and defects in the Bible itself? In 1776 Wesley spoke in his *Journal* of a tract entitled "Internal Evidence of the Christian Religion" (1776) wondering if the author was a deist, Christian or an atheist:

> If he is a Christian, he betrays his own cause by averring that 'all Scripture is not given by inspiration of God, but writers of it were sometimes left to themselves, and consequently made some mistakes.' Nay, if there be any mistakes in the Bible, there may as well be a thousand. If there is one falsehood in that book it did not come from the God of truth.[6]

---

[2] Ibid., 388.

[3] *Works* 7:399.

[4] Rupert Davies. *The Works of John Wesley. Vol. 9*. (Nashville, Tenn.: Abingdon Press, 1989) 353.

[5] John Wesley. *Explanatory Notes Upon the New Testament*. (London, England: Epworth Press, 1948) 8.

[6] Reginald Ward and Richard Heitzenrater. *The Works of John Wesley. Vol. 23*. (Nashville,

In a letter to the Bishop of Gloucester in 1762 he states:

> But how did he inspire the Scripture? He so directed the writer that 'no considerable error, should fall upon them?' Nay, will not allowing there is any error in Scripture shake the authority of the whole?[7]

Finally, in his *Explanatory Notes Upon the New Testament* he states that:

> The Scripture, therefore, of the Old and New Testament is a most solid and precious system of divine truth. Every part thereof is worthy of God and altogether are one entire body wherein is no defect, no excess. It is the fountain of heavenly wisdom, which they who are able to taste prefer to all writings of men, however wise or learned or holy.[8]

This belief that the Bible was without defect or error is not difficult to understand when one remembers Wesley's view of the inspiration and authority of the Bible. As was mentioned in the last chapter, Wesley did not seem to believe in a mechanical dictation theory, but he did believe that inspiration went beyond general content and concepts to the actual vocabulary of Scripture. Remember for Wesley, as we saw in his quotation of Luther in his *Explanatory Notes Upon the New Testament,* Scripture was the "grammar of the Holy Ghost."[9] and later "nothing written therein could be rejected."[10] He believed that one could not "lay aside these expressions seeing they are the Words of God and not of man."[11] With this high view of Scripture it is not difficult to see why Wesley believed, "If there is one falsehood in that Book it did not come from the God of truth."[12]

Interestingly enough, in spite of these strong statements, Wesley did not ignore the fact that there might be problem passages in the Bible. For example, in his *Explanatory Notes Upon the New Testament*, consider his comments upon problems in the genealogy of Jesus:

Tenn.: Abingdon Press, 1993) 25.

[7] *Letters* 4:369.

[8] John Wesley. *Explanatory Notes Upon the New Testament.* (London, England: Epworth Press, 1948) 9.

[9] Ibid., 9.

[10] Ibid., 350.

[11] Albert Outler. *The Works of John Wesley. Vol. 2.* (Nashville, Tenn.: Abingdon Press, 1985) 100.

[12] Reginald Ward and Richard Heitzenrater. *The Works of John Wesley. Vol. 23.* (Nashville, Tenn.: Abingdon Press, 1995) 25.

> If there were any difficulties in this genealogy, or that given by St. Luke which could not easily be removed, they would rather affect upon the Jewish tables, than the credit of the evangelists; for they act only as historians, setting down these genealogies as they stood in those public and allowed records. Therefore they were to take them as they found them. Nor was it needful they should correct the mistakes, if there were any. For these accounts sufficiently answer the end for which they were recited. They unquestionably prove the grand point of view that Jesus was of the family from which the promised Seed was to come. And they had more weight with the Jews for this purpose than if alterations had been made by inspiration itself. For such alterations would have occasioned endless disputes between them and the disciples of our Lord.[13]

Thus Wesley recognized the possibility of mistakes in Scripture, but he would affirm that the mistakes were in the Jewish records not by the inspired writers. Wesley believed that Matthew and Luke were inspired of God to report the traditional genealogical tables of the Jews.[14] Certainly there would be limitations in scientific, historical knowledge, or genealogical records, but those would not affect the inspiration or infallibility of Scripture. The authors accurately recorded what God inspired them to write, enabling Wesley to state that the Scriptures were without defect, falsehood or error.

Interpreting Wesley's Views on Infallibility

After considering Wesley's words it might be asked, "What are we trying to interpret?" "Certainly his views are clearly outlined in his writings." Wesley clearly believed in the absolute authority and total reliability of the Bible. The Scriptures stood alone and adequate as the ultimate source of Wesley's beliefs and teaching. As Dr. Wilber Dayton states," "Nothing would have been more repugnant to original Methodism than to cast doubt on the Word of God, the very source of life."[15]

However, there are those who would allege that Wesley's statements should not be taken at face value, and one should be careful not to read incorrect views into his statements on infallibility. In fact, there are scholars

---

[13] John Wesley. *Explanatory Notes Upon the New Testament*. (London, England: Epworth Press, 1948) 15.

[14] Daryl McCarthy, "Early Wesleyan Views of Scripture," *Wesleyan Theological Society 16*. (1981) 98.

[15] Wilber Dayton. "John Wesley and Infallibility," in *Inerrancy and the Church*. (Chicago, Ill.: Moody Press, 1984) 223.

who would insist that Wesley could not have meant that the Scriptures were totally without errors in the original autographs for that "inerrantist" view did not exist in Wesley's time.

Jack Rogers and Donald McKim in their book *The Authority and Interpretation of the Bible* claim the idea of inerrancy was spawned by "ailing evangelicals" particularly of the Princeton School. The problem was traced to Francis Turretin, a Genevan theologian of the 17th century, who dared to assert that the authority of Scripture was based on its form of inerrant words. Inspired men thought God's words after Him and transmitted them in writing.[16] This view was revived in the late nineteenth century at Princeton Seminary by Charles Hodge and B. B. Warfield.[17] Hodge, in his *Systematic Theology Vol. I* states, "The infallibility and divine authority of the Scriptures are due to the fact that they are the Word of God; and they are the Word of God because they were given by inspiration of the Holy Ghost."[18] The Princeton theologians did not believe that they had constructed the biblical doctrine of inspiration, but they argued that it had been taught in the Scriptures and believed in the church from apostolic times to the present.

Benjamin Warfield states:

> The church has always believed her Scriptures to be the book of God, of which God was in such a sense the author that every one of its affirmations of whatever kind is to be esteemed as the utterance of God, of infallible truth and authority.[19]

According to Ernest Sandeen in his book *The Roots of Fundamentalism*, the Princeton theologians had three main emphases:

1. The inspiration of the Scriptures extends to the words.

2. The Scriptures taught their own inerrancy, meaning the Bible is free of error, contradiction, paradoxes and inconsistencies. Warfield makes the strongest statement when he says, "A proved error in Scripture contradicts not only our doctrine, but the Scripture claims and therefore, its inspiration in making these claims."

---

[16] Ibid., 225.

[17] Larry Shelton., "John Wesley's Approach to Scripture in Historical Perspective," *Wesleyan Theological Journal 16* (1981) 38.

[18] Charles Hodge. *Systematic Theology Vol. I*. (New York, N.Y.: 1874) 153.

[19] Ernest Sandeen. *The Roots of Fundamentalism*. (Chicago, Ill.: University of Chicago Press, 1970) 123.

3. Princeton theologians emphasized the inspiration of the original autographs. Verbal and inerrant inspiration was not claimed for the Bible as we now have it, but for books of the Bible as they came from the hands of the original authors. To prove the Bible in error required finding the original manuscripts.[20]

Though there is certainly similarity in language between these views and certain statements of Wesley, it seems unfair to force a nineteenth century view upon an eighteenth century evangelist. They instead maintain that Wesley was strongly influenced by Patristic and Reformation sources that accepted the fact that God accommodated Himself to human frailty and error. Rogers and McKim feel that the "central church tradition is much richer and more flexible" than the strict inerrant viewpoint.[21] Instead of basing biblical authority on the assumption of the infallibility of the external text of the autographs, they would look to the inner spiritual content.[22]

This viewpoint need not maintain that the Scriptures are therefore unreliable. Clearly Wesley did not believe that to be the case. However, some might maintain there could be errors on non-faith, non-practical issues in the original manuscripts. It could be that one of the significant aspects of the Holy Spirit's inspiration would be to guard the writers against error in doctrinal or practical matters. At the same time the Bible might contain errors in non-essential areas such as science, mathematics, geography, etc.

Did Wesley accept this view of non-essential errors in Scripture? Dr. Kenneth Grider attests that Wesley's statements about infallibility, or no mistakes in Scripture, did not include unimportant issues. He refers to the before mentioned genealogical passage from Matthew 1 as an example. Dr. Grider concludes, that this section in Wesley's *Explanatory Notes Upon the New Testament* shows Wesley's willingness to accept unimportant errors. Therefore, when Wesley speaks of the Bible being "infallibly true" he must be referring to consequential matters. Daryl McCarthy, however, concludes that in all of his writings Wesley never once gave the slightest indication of a dichotomy between the inerrancy of "spiritual matters" and the errancy of historical and other "non-spiritual" matters.[23]

---

[20] Ibid., 124–30.

[21] Wilber Dayton. "John Wesley and Infallibility," in *Inerrancy and the Church*. Chicago, Ill.: Moody Press, 1984) 226.

[22] Larry Shelton, "John Wesley's Approach to Scripture in Historical Perspective," *Wesleyan Theological Journal 16* (1981) 38.

[23] John Hannah. *Inerrancy and the Church*. (Chicago, Ill.: Moody Press, 1984) 231.

What exactly did Wesley mean when he said that the Bible was infallibly true and without mistake or falsehood? It is true it would be wrong to place twentieth century views of infallibility upon Wesley. At the same time it should not be necessary to have to prove that eighteenth century John Wesley did not borrow his views of Scripture from nineteenth century Princeton scholars. Instead, one should consider the climate in which Wesley developed his own views, and then allow him to speak for himself.

As was clearly documented in chapter one, Wesley was nurtured in a tradition that held a high view of Scripture. In fact, Dr. Harold Lindsell in his book *The Battle for the Bible* maintains from a historical perspective that "it can be said that for two thousand years the Christian Church has agreed that the Bible is completely trustworthy; it is infallible or inerrant."[24] Dr. Lindsell notes that the early church faced numerous controversies such as Christology, particularly the Arian controversy. The doctrine of anthropology vexed the church, for example with Pelagius. All sorts of heretical, reforming, and reactionary groups arose including the Ebionites, Gnostics, Manicheans, Montanists, Novationists, Donatists and others. However, in spite of all this the issue of biblical inerrancy never was a real issue in the church until the nineteenth and twentieth centuries. The early church faced numerous controversies, none of which had to do with the question of the infallibility of Scripture.[25]

Dr. Lindsell in his book devotes chapter three to quotations from the early church fathers, through the Reformation, to the time of Wesley in an attempt to show that the infallibility of the Scripture was the prevailing view in the church until the last century.

H. D. McDonald in his book *Theories of Revelation* seems to support this viewpoint when he concludes that prior to 1860 the idea of the infallibility or inerrancy of the Scripture was the prevailing view. Apart from the Quakers, the doctrine of inerrancy and literal inspiration of the Bible was almost everywhere held in its strictest form.[26]

A survey of biblical infallibility in the history of the church is far beyond the scope of this study. It is interesting to note, however, that even some scholars who do not share the view of the infallibility of Scripture have had to admit that this was a well established tradition of the church down through the centuries. For example, Dr. Kirsop Lake, an eminent

---

[24] Harold Lindsell. *The Battle for the Bible*. (Grand Rapid, Mich.: Zondervan Publishers, 1976) 19.

[25] Ibid., 42.

[26] Skevington Wood. *The Burning Heart*. (Grand Rapids, Mich.: Wm B. Eerdmanns Pub. Co., 1967) 246.

New Testament scholar from the early part of this century, concludes that at times even educated people, who have little knowledge of historical theology, conclude that fundamentalism is something new. In reality it is the uneducated survival of a view once held universally by the church. Even in the Eighteenth Century there would have been few who did not hold to the infallible inspiration of Scripture. According to Dr. Lake the fundamentalists might be wrong, but they were not the ones who had departed from church tradition. No, "The Bible and the *corpus theologicum* of the church is on the fundamentalist side."[27]

A similar view is expressed by Oxford church historian C. J. Cadoux in his book *The Case For Evangelical Modernism* who concludes that the inerrancy of Scripture was accepted by Christianity with practical unanimity from the second to the nineteenth century. The fact that inerrancy was not incorporated into a creed was not due to the fact that it was not believed, but because no one challenged it.[28]

This analysis is particularly interesting when we realize that Dr. Cadoux did not share the belief in infallibility, but felt that this viewpoint should be abandoned. However, he does contend that the central tradition of the church was its confidence in an inerrant Bible as the fully reliable Word of God.[29]

The *New Catholic Encyclopedia* expresses a similar view:

> The inerrancy of Scripture has been the constant teaching of the Fathers, the theologians, and recent Popes in their encyclicals on Biblical studies (Leo XIII, Ench. Bibl. 124–31; Benedict XV, Ench. Bibl. 453–61; Pius XII, Ench. Bibl. 560). It is nonetheless obvious that many biblical statements are simply not true when judged according to modern knowledge of science and history.[30]

Finally, George Barry from his book *The Inspiration and Authority of Holy Scriptures, A Study in the Literature of the First Five Centuries* concludes that the lack of feeling the necessity to formulate a definite doctrine of inspiration for fifteen centuries, shows the universal belief that the Scripture was God's handiwork. Modern scholars might view this as a mechanical and erroneous view of inspiration that was accepted and taught by the church of the first five centuries. The Scripture was regarded as writing

---

[27] Kirsop Lake. *The Religion of Yesterday and Tomorrow.* (Boston, Mass.: Houghton Press, 1926) 61.

[28] John Hannah. *Inerrancy and the Church.* (Chicago, Ill.: Moody Press, 1984) 232–33.

[29] Ibid., 233.

[30] *New Catholic Encyclopedia Vol. 2.* (New York, N.Y.: McGraw Publishers, 1967)

of the Holy Spirit. The writers were used by Him as a workman uses his tools; in a word, the Books, the actual words, rather than the writers were inspired.[31] Again, it is interesting to note that Barry did not believe in infallibility or inerrancy, but felt it truly was the predominant view.

If this was a study on the whole issue of the "infallible Bible," many scholars of opposing views could be quoted. For example Jack Rogers in his *Confession of a Conservative Evangelical* studied the writings of the seven Englishmen and four Scotsmen on the committee that wrote the article of faith on Scripture for the Westminster Confession. In his opinion, "Not one of them in his writings taught that Scripture is inerrant on matters such as science and history."[32]

Which view is more historically accurate? Did the idea of scriptural infallibility, meaning in this sense inerrancy in the original autographs, not arise until the seventeenth century in the mind of Francis Turretin? Or in fact, was infallibility the prevailing view of the Christian Church from the second to the nineteenth century? Was it the rise of theological liberalism and historical criticism that placed the view of scriptural infallibility in doubt? Again, the correctness or incorrectness of this view is not the issue at this point. However, it is important to attempt to determine the prevailing mind set of the age in which Wesley lived and was trained. This must be taken into consideration in any interpretation of his views.

To draw any accurate conclusion concerning Wesley's understanding of infallibility it is obvious that merely quoting his words may not give a final answer. As Dr. Frank Spina noted at a Wesleyan Theological Society meeting in Nov.,1994:

> Those holding inerrancy have little trouble citing statements indicating Wesley's support. Likewise, those believing inerrancy cannot be squared with Wesley note that he used the critical methods available to him and generally treated Scripture more flexibly than an inerrancy position would permit.[33]

To avoid merely proof testing Wesley's quotations they must be placed accurately within the age that he lived. If we place his statements within his historical period and consider closely the standards upon which he based

---

[31] George Barry. *The Inspiration and Authority of the Holy Scriptures, A Study of the Literature of the First Five Centuries*. 10.

[32] J. Kenneth Grider, "Wesleyanism and the Inerrancy Issue," *Wesleyan Theological Society* 19 (1984) 74.

[33] Frank Spina, "More Criticism, More History, More Bible—Wesleyan Faith Seeking Understanding," *Wesleyan Theological Society* (1994) 6.

his ministry, I believe that it might be possible to draw conclusions on whether Wesley believed in a fully infallible Bible.

It should be recognized that great changes were taking place in the world and the church in the 17th and 18th century. Note that Barry commented on the first fifteen centuries of the church. Did something happen to change the prevailing view of the church on the Scriptures, after this period. If we assume Paul More in his book *Anglicanism* is correct when he says, "All branches in the church in the 17th century held the Bible to be infallibly true, inspired by God," we still should look carefully at what was going on in Wesley's day.[34]

Wesley's comments in both essays and sermons must be understood in light of his opposition to the rationalistic deism of the Age of Enlightenment. Even if H. D. McDonald that prior to 1860 the idea of infallibility or inerrancy of the Scripture was the prevailing view,"[35] it is also true by the 18th century, the Christian who wished to remain faithful to both his church and his Bible, found his faith under attack by contemporary social and intellectual forces. Ernest Sandeen in his book *The Roots of Fundamentalism* comments concerning this period that Protestants based their beliefs on revelation and miracles in an age which doubted the value and possibility of both. The Bible, filled with miracles, was under attack. For many empirical investigation and reason were surer grounds for knowledge than revelation. The Bible lost influence with the rise of science, not always because of direct attacks, but because of satire such as Voltaire, and the biblical criticism of men like Thomas Paine.[36]

The struggle over the authority of Scripture could probably be traced back to the Renaissance with the desire of men to liberate their minds from authority and tradition. This mind set was sure to have an impact on the view of Scripture as "supernaturally guaranteed revelation beyond the scope of rational inquiry."[37] By the 17th century esteem for Scripture was less reverent, for some persons, than had been the case in the past.

Two philosophers who were examples of the growing rationalism and declining authority of Scripture in the 17th century were Thomas Hobbes

---

[34] Paul More and Frank Cross. *Anglicanism*. (London, England: SPCK Press, 1957) XXIX.

[35] A Skevington Wood. *The Burning Heart*. (Grand Rapids, Mich.: Wm B. Eerdmanns Pub Co., 1967)

[36] Ernest Sandeen. *The Roots of Fundamentalism*. (Chicago, Ill.: University of Chicago Press, 1970) 104.

[37] S. L. Greenslade. *The Cambridge History of the Bible*. (Cambridge, England: Cambridge at the University Press, 1963) 238.

and Benedict Spinoza. Hobbes in his book *Leviathan* anticipates the modern theory, in indicating the Bible was not the revelation of God, but the record of that revelation:

> ... to say that God hath spoken to him in the Holy Scripture is not to say that God hath spoken to him immediately, but by the mediation of the prophets, or of the apostles, or of the church, in such a manner as he speaks to all other Christian men.[38]

Benedict Spinoza felt the need to examine Scripture:

> ... afresh in a careful, impartial and unfettered spirit, making no assumptions concerning it ... Hence we must not suppose that everything is prophecy or revelation which is described in Scripture as told by God to anyone.[39]

Spinoza believed that at any point where a divine decree seemed irrational, it should not be charged to God. According to Robert Grant in his book *A Short History of the Interpretation of the Bible*, "The result of his investigation shows the complete rationality of the biblical revelation."[40]

Spinoza himself has this to say:

> I found nothing taught expressly by Scripture which does not agree with our understanding or which is repugnant thereto, ... I became thoroughly convinced that the Bible leaves reason absolutely free, that it has nothing in common with philosophy, in fact that revelation and philosophy stand on totally different footings.[41]

The divorce of theology from philosophy results in the abandonment of traditional theology by modern man. Only the irrational man finds Scripture authoritative. The Bible is to be studied only for its historical interest. For Spinoza, the real importance of the biblical narratives was not the events narrated, but the separate religious lessons they convey. Having used historical context and linguistics to set the historical sense, then seek for the ultimate meaning of Scripture, the universal truth.[42] Spinoza states:

> The meaning of Scripture should be gathered from its own history, and not from the history of nature in general which is the basis of

---

[38] Robert Grant. *A Short History of the Interpretation of the Bible*. (New York, N.Y.; Macmillan Company, 1972) 145.

[39] Ibid., 147.

[40] Ibid., 147.

[41] Ibid., 148.

[42] Hans Frei. *The Eclipse of the Biblical Narrative*. (New Haven, Conn.: Yale University Press, 1974) 43–46.

philosophy. The ultimate purpose of this study is the discovery of 'universal truths, expressly taught.'[43]

It must be recognized, by Wesley's day in the eighteenth century, rationalism had achieved great popularity. Men like Pierre Bayle (1647–1707), and John Locke (1632–1704) laid the foundation for rationalistic criticism of Scripture in the eighteenth century.[44] Rationalism in the eighteenth century was not a system of beliefs antagonistic to Christianity, but an attitude of mind which assumed that in all matters reason was supreme.

Bayle in his writings made revelation appear so unreasonable that the deists of the first half of the eighteenth century had more than enough ammunition to attack the traditional approach. Locke in his book *The Reasonableness of Christianity* tried to show that reason and revelation were not opposed.[45]

Of course, deists and churchmen agreed that reason is important, but how important is it? Must the Bible be proved to be true to have credibility? The deists began a series of arguments about the credibility of divine revelation dealing with two major issues:

> 1. The rationality and credibility of the idea of historic revelation . . .
>
> 2. Granting the rationality or possibility of revelation, how likely is it that such a thing actually took place? . . . How authoritative are biblical accounts, especially of miracles, since the natural presuppositions of the scientific age was against them. Closely associated with the idea of miracles was the fulfillment of Old Testament Prophecy.[46]

In the first half of the eighteenth century pamphlets were published which expressed in popular form what the philosophers had been saying. Thomas Woolston's "Discourses on Miracles" was most influential. He was tried for blasphemy and fined one hundred pounds.[47] He maintained in his book that the miracles of the New Testament were so fantastic that no rea-

---

[43] Robert Grant. *A Short History of the Interpretation of the Bible.* (New York, N.Y.: MacMillan Company, 1972) 149.

[44] S. L. Greenslade. *The Cambridge History of the Bible.* (Cambridge, England: Cambridge at the University Press, 1963) 240.

[45] Ibid., 241.

[46] Hans Frei. *The Eclipse of the Biblical Narrative.*(New Haven, Conn.: Yale University press, 1974) 53.

[47] Robert Grant. *A Short History of the Interpretation of the Bible.* (New York, N.Y. MacMillan Company, 1972) 151.

sonable person could believe them possible. The only truth in the miracles were spiritual truths.[48]

Some other authors in the deistic controversy were men like John Toland, who wrote in his book *Christianity Not Mysterious* that mystery was contrary to reason, so anything incomprehensible or absurd in the Bible should be removed.[49] Matthew Tindale in *Christianity as Old as Creation*, stated that true Christianity is surely, essentially reasonable. The Gospel and natural law are one and the same, and any suggestions of a special revelation through the Bible is superfluous.[50] This cause was also championed by men like William Whiston in his Unitarian work *Primitive Christianity Revived*. As a result of this work Whiston broke with the Religious Societies because of their pre-critical faith in the infallibility of the Bible which carried with it an indiscriminate treatment of the Old and New Testaments as the literal Word of God.[51]

On the side of orthodoxy were men like Berkeley and Butler, supported by Addison, Pope and Swift. These men were more than equal to the task of debating intellectually with the deists over the authority of Scripture. In must be remembered that the two sides still had much in common. The deists believed in a God not all that different from the God proclaimed from most pulpits.

Though the orthodox writers may have won the day in the pamphlet war, this conflict still would leave the traditional view of the Bible in a weakened position. *The Cambridge History of the Bible* summarizes this period stating that making the Scriptures the small change of pamphleteers unseated the Bible from the pedestal on which it had been placed in the 17th century. The reverence and exaltation of infallible authority that had surrounded the Bible was soon tarnished in the rough and tumble of debate.[52]

Wesley lived, and ministered, in a age of controversy. In considering how this controversy affected Wesley's views of Scripture two observations can be made. First, Wesley reacted against any view that would downgrade the authority of Scripture. Wesley would certainly have felt that the deists fit into this category. For Wesley, Scriptural Christianity was an indictment

---

[48] S. L. Greenslade. *The Cambridge History of the Bible*. (Cambridge, England: Cambridge at the University Press, 1963) 246.

[49] Ibid., 241.

[50] Ibid., 248.

[51] Martin Schmidt. *John Wesley a Theological Biography Vol. 2*. (Nashville, Tenn.: 1972) 191.

[52] S. L. Greenslade. *The Cambridge History of the Bible*. (Cambridge, England: Cambridge at the University Press, 1963) 243.

of the present age.[53] By word and deed Wesley made it clear he would have no part of a system that might cast doubt or lead to unbelief in the Scripture. He went to the Word of God to be judged, not to judge it. The simple reason was that there was no single authority equal to that of Scripture "The church in all cases is to be judged by Scripture, not Scripture by the Church."[54]

A second interesting factor to note, is how little interest Wesley seemed to have in debating these issues. Wesley not only seemed little influenced by the controversy, but he had more important tasks on which to concentrate his time. Wesley, Whitefield, and their disciples had little interest in the questions of the deists or their orthodox opponents. They were interested in revitalizing the church by the power of the Spirit, winning souls, and reforming godless contemporary society. Their preaching of a full-blooded salvation, with heaven and hell, grace and damnation, went hand in hand with a literal acceptance of the Scriptures as the very Word of God. With God working Pentecostal type miracles, who cared about academic arguments over the Bible which would not save the soul from sin?[55]

If one takes Wesley at face value and assumes that he meant what he said, then it is difficult to doubt that he believed in the infallibility of all Scripture. Remember, Wesley was not attempting to be either a professional theologian or a philosopher. He was an evangelist and desired "plain truth and plain words."[56]

It has been suggested by some, such as Dr. Grider who was mentioned earlier in this chapter, that Wesley's main concern was soteriological and that he was referring only to the saving message of Scripture when he said that Scripture could be fully trusted. Since the Bible is not a text book of history and science the assumption would be that inspiration does not cover statements of historical or scientific impact.

It is true, Wesley's primary concern was the message of salvation, but that does not necessarily imply that he saw other parts of the Bible as being less inspired or less true. As was noted in chapters three and four, Wesley believed that what the Bible said, God said. When the Bible spoke concerning a matter, God had spoken and God cannot err. Whether the passage was directly related to the central theme of salvation, or referred to more temporal affairs such as history and science, anything in scientific theory or

---

[53] Martin Schmidt. *John Wesley a Theological Biography. Vol. 2* (Nashville, Tenn.: 1972) 191.

[54] *Works,* 10:142.

[55] S. L. Greenslade. *The Cambridge History of the Bible.* (Cambridge, England: Cambridge at the University Press, 1963) 254.

[56] Albert Outler. *The Works of John Wesley. Vol. 1.* (Nashville, Tenn.: Abingdon Press, 1984) 104.

reason that contradicted Scripture was not received.[57] Wesley did not stop to differentiate between Scriptures as to their truthfulness. They were all from the God of truth. Wesley did not consider the Bible inspired to the extent that there were only minor errors of a non-important nature. Instead he concluded "Will not allowing there is any error in Scripture shake the authority of the whole,"[58] and "If there be any mistakes in the Bible; there may as well be a thousand. If there be one falsehood in that Book it did not come from the God of truth."[59]

The fact that Wesley held to the infallibility of the Scripture does not mean that he lacked confidence in the use of reason, the scientific method, or the values of research. As will be clearly shown in chapter nine, Wesley valued reason as a source of authority. As he states clearly in his sermon "The Case For Reason Impartially Considered" (1781):

> Is it not reason (assisted by the Holy Ghost) which enables us to understand what the Holy Scriptures declare concerning the being and attributes God? Concerning his eternity, and immensity, his power, wisdom, and holiness? It is by reason that God enables us in some measure to comprehend his method of dealing with the children of men; the nature of his various dispensations, of the Old and New Covenant, of the law and the gospel.[60]

In chapter nine I will show that Wesley emphasized experience and church tradition as sources of authority. However, for Wesley there was one higher, more reliable source of knowledge. In the matters where the Bible had spoken, God had spoken and He could not be wrong. Let reason, human experience, human wisdom do all that it could. Wesley states "Let reason do all that reason can. Employ it as far as it will go."[61] But reason, tradition and experience did not hold the central place. Scripture was the hub, the one infallible rule. As Dr. Wilber Dayton stated quite succinctly in his chapter "John Wesley and Infallibility":

> Whatever allowance others made for error in the Bible in matters of science and history, Wesley was not caught in that inconsistency. It would have violated the integrity of his whole ministry to publish

---

[57] Wilber Dayton, "The Bible in the Wesleyan Tradition," *Asbury Theological Journal 40* (1983) 22–28.

[58] *Letters*, 4:369.

[59] Reginald Ward and Richard Heitzenrater. *The Works of John Wesley. Vol. 23.* (Nashville, Tenn.: Abingdon Press, 1995) 25.

[60] Albert Outler. *The Works of John Wesley. Vol. 2.* (Nashville, Tenn.: Abingdon Press, 1985) 592.

[61] Ibid., 600.

a volume of "speculative science" that disagreed with his one valid authority, the Bible.[62]

Conclusion

The difficulty in defining John Wesley's view upon biblical infallibility results from trying to understand eighteenth century language and thought in that light of twentieth century concepts. Statements across time cannot always be taken at face value, if it can be clearly shown that the terms in the different eras were defined differently. As I have attempted to show there are scholars who feel that Wesley's use of the terminology such as "infallibility' and "without error or defect" should not be taken at face value. He could not have meant that the Bible was infallible in all aspects of the original autographs, for that view was a late arriving nineteenth century view. Other scholars have an opposing view that the infallibility of Scripture has in fact been the orthodox view of the church from the second century, and only in the nineteenth century did this view begin to erode. I am in no position to study the issue of infallibility throughout the centuries to discern which view is correct. However, I believe that the burden of proof must be upon those who insist that Wesley's words, and seeming intentions, should not be taken at face value. Those who insist that Wesley could not have meant what he said are the ones who must prove their case. I am not convinced this has been done. When one considers Wesley's own words, the world in which he lived and the climate in which he was raised, it seems more reasonable to assume that when he said that Scripture was infallible and without mistake or error he meant exactly what he said. One might disagree with his view, and many do, but this appears to be his view. I can only conclude with the Wesley scholar Dr. Frank Baker "Wesley was one with the Reformers in the tendency to substitute the infallible Bible for the infallible Church."[63]

---

[62] Wilber Dayton, "The Bible in the Wesleyan Tradition," *Asbury Theological Journal* (1983) 243.

[63] Frank Baker. *John Wesley and the Church of England*. (London, England: Epworth Press, 1970) 270.

Section III

John Wesley's View of Scriptural Interpretation

8

John Wesley's Rules of Scriptural Interpretation

Part 1

IN THE previous chapters it has been clearly shown that for John Wesley there was one fundamental authority, the Holy Scriptures. No matter what the issue or the problem, whether it was practical or doctrinal, Wesley referred all to the Bible. As he stated in a letter to William Dodd in 1756, "I search for truth, plain Bible truth, without any regard to the praise or dispraise of men."[1] Later he wrote again to Dodd, "But I try every Church and every doctrine by the Bible. This is the word by which we are to be judged in that day."[2] For Wesley the Bible "was" the answer to men's questions and needs and therefore it was imperative that the Bible be used. In his *Explanatory Notes Upon the Old Testament* Wesley comments upon Deuteronomy 17:19. Wesley writes:

> Tis not enough to have Bibles, but we must use them, yea, use them daily. Our souls must have constant meals of that manna, which if well digested will afford them true nourishment and strength.[3]

These are very high sounding words and seem very simplistic. All problems, issues and questions are to be referred to the Bible. In considering these statements the question may arise, "Was Wesley naive enough to believe that everyone would read the Bible and find answers in it the same way?" At times Wesley would contend with groups he felt were rejecting the clear teaching of Scripture. On those occasions it would be expected

---

[1] *Letters* 3:157.

[2] Ibid., 3:172.

[3] John Wesley. *Explanatory Notes Upon the New Testament.* (Salem, Ohio.: Schmul Publishers, 1975) 1:638.

that he would refer them back to what he understood the Bible to say. But what about the times Wesley had clear cut differences with religious groups who also based their views on the authority of Scripture? Many of Wesley's debates were not with those whom he felt were out and out pagans or heretics. On many occasions he disputed with mystics, Calvinists, members of the Church of England and Roman Catholics. In many cases any or all of these groups would refer back to the Bible for authority. Did Wesley make a distinction in these instances or did he blindly and narrowly hold to a simplistic "call back to the Bible," and ignore the interpretations of those who might disagree with him?

In reading Wesley, one soon discovers that he was not a naive biblicist. He realized that it was not always sufficient merely to refer men to the authority of the Bible. Disagreements would still arise. Therefore, if the Bible was to be used, it had to be interpreted.

For Wesley, there were a number of clear reasons why the Bible needed to be interpreted. He knew from the reading of Jerome, and others, that ancient manuscripts of the Bible were sometimes copied by heretics who mixed in their own ideas with the Scripture. This required study and interpretation.[4] Wesley also recognized that there were obscure and controversial passages that might be difficult to understand. He certainly knew that many passages had been interpreted by sincere Christians in different and conflicting ways. In a letter to Dr. Middleton in 1749 Wesley expressed that the clearness of the Scriptures "does not prove that they need not be explained, nor their completeness that they need not be enforced."[5]

Finally, Wesley knew that regardless of the purity of motive, error may creep into interpretation. He was quick to call for recognition that differences in interpretation were not necessarily proof that one was not a child of God. In his sermon "Christian Perfection" (1741) he states:

> 5. Nay with regard to the Holy Scriptures themselves, as careful as they are to avoid it, the best of men are liable to mistake and do mistake day by day; especially with respect to those parts thereof which less immediately relate to practice. Hence, even the children of God are not agreed as to the interpretation of many places in Holy Writ; nor is their difference of opinion any proof that they are not the children of God on either side. But it is a proof that we are no more to expect any living man to be infallible than to be omniscient.[6]

---

[4] Mack Stokes. *The Bible in the Wesleyan Heritage*. (Nashville, Tenn.: Abingdon Press, 1979) 23.

[5] *Letters*, 2:325.

[6] Albert Outler. *The Works of John Wesley. Vol. 2*. (Nashville, Tenn.: Abingdon Press, 1985) 102.

Wesley was quick to disclaim any infallibility in interpretation for himself, though his conscience was clear. In his introduction to *The Explanatory Notes Upon the New Testament*, Wesley states:

> I cannot flatter myself so far (to use the words of one of the above named writers), as to imagine that I have fallen into no mistakes in a work of so great difficulty. But my own conscience acquits me of having designedly misrepresented any single passage of Scripture, or having written one line with a purpose of inflaming the hearts of Christians against each other.[7]

When accused by Mr. Downes, in 1759, that the Methodists were "infallible interpreters of Scripture," Wesley replied, "So far from it that we have over and over declared, in print as well as public preaching: We are no more to expect any living man to be infallible than to be omniscient."[8] Wesley was always ready to be convinced of his own fallibility if it could be shown by Scripture. In a letter to Henry Venn in 1763 he states, "If any one will convince me of my errors, I will heartily thank him. I believe all the Bible as far as I understand it, and I am ready to be convinced."[9]

Thus we see that John Wesley clearly recognized the fallibility of men and the necessity of biblical interpretation. The question then becomes, what principles of interpretation did Wesley practice? In the next two chapters I will outline what I believe to be the main rules of interpretation that Wesley followed in his preaching and teaching. I believe it will be discovered, as stated by Larry Shelton in an article entitled "John Wesley's Approach to Scripture in Historical Thought," that "Wesley rests in the mainstream of orthodox hermeneutics reflecting the basic emphasis of the Fathers and Reformers."[10]

In studying Wesley's Works and reading other students of Wesley, a number of clear principles emerge in relation to his views upon biblical interpretation. The order in which the principles are outlined in the following chapters reflects my choice for consistency and order. It is not meant to suggest that this order represents Wesley's own prioritizing of these principles. I have chosen an order for this chapter and the next which has a sense

---

[7] John Wesley. *Explanatory Notes Upon the New Testament.* (London, England: Epworth Press, 1948) 8.

[8] Rupert Davies. *The Works of John Wesley. Vol. 9.* (Nashville, Tenn.: Abingdon Press, 1989) 353.

[9] *Letters* 4:216.

[10] Larry Shelton, "John Wesley's Approach to Scripture in Historical Perspective," *Wesleyan Theological Journal 16* (1981) 36.

of continuity and consistency. Regardless of order, each principle described clearly guided Wesley in his interpretation of the Holy Scriptures.

Interpretation Requires Inspiration

As we saw earlier in chapter six Wesley was convinced that the Bible was inspired by God. For Wesley, if the Bible was inspired by God it was consistent to suppose that the Spirit of God would supplement that revelation. Wesley had a firm conviction that the Holy Spirit had to illuminate God's Word and by regenerating grace restore the spiritual senses by which human beings could understand it.[11]

Wesley believed that Scripture could be understood only through the same Spirit by which it was given. Consider some select portions of a letter to the Bishop of Gloucester in 1762:

> We must apply to the 'Guide of Truth,' to prevent our being 'carried about with divers and strange doctrines.' Is He not then everywhere to illuminate the understanding, as well as to rectify the will? And indeed, do we not need the one as continually as the other?[12] I do firmly believe (and what serious man does not), we need the same Spirit to understand the Scripture which enabled the holy men of old to write it.[13] In reading God's Word, he profiteth most . . . who is most inspired with the Holy Ghost. Human and worldly wisdom is not needful to the understanding of the Scripture, but the revelation of the Holy Ghost who inspireth the true meaning unto them who with humility and diligence search for it.[14]

For Wesley the reading of Scripture was based upon a two-fold inspiration. Note his thoughts in his *Explanatory Notes Upon the New Testament* commenting on II Timothy 3:16, "The Spirit of God not only once inspired those who wrote it, but continually inspires, and supernaturally assists those that read it with earnest prayer."[15]

In a similar vein in his book the *Christian's Pattern,* Wesley gives an extract from *The Imitation of Christ* by Thomas A Kempis giving this guideline upon reading the Holy Scripture, "Truth not eloquence is to be sought

---

[11] Timothy Smith, "John Wesley and the Wholeness of Scripture," *Interpretation: A Journal of Bible and Theology* (1985) 262.

[12] Gerald Cragg. *The Works of John Wesley. Vol. 11.* (Nashville, Tenn.: Abingdon Press, 1989) 504.

[13] Ibid., 509.

[14] Ibid., 524.

[15] John Wesley. *Explanatory Notes Upon the New Testament.* (London, England: Epworth Press, 1948) 794.

for in the Holy Scripture. All Scripture is to be read in the same Spirit wherewith it was written."[16]

Another example of this philosophy can be seen in the abridgment Wesley made of the homilies of Thomas Cranmer, late Archbishop of Canterbury. In his abridgment entitled *The Doctrine of Salvation, Faith, and Good Works Extracted from the Homilies of the Church of England,* Wesley clearly accepted Cranmer's views concerning the necessity of divine inspiration in biblical interpretation:

> He that desires more perfectly to understand these great doctrines of Christianity ought diligently to read the Holy Scriptures, especially St. Paul's Epistles to the Romans and the Galatians. And whosoever giveth his mind to the Holy Scripture with diligent study and burning desire, it cannot be that he should be left without help. For either God will send him some a godly doctor to teach him or God himself from above will give light unto (his) mind and teach (him) those things which are necessary for (him). Man's human and worldly wisdom or science is not necessary to the understanding of Scripture, but the revelation of the Holy Ghost, who inspireth the true meaning unto them that with humility and diligence search for it.[17]

So we see that for Wesley the ministry of the Holy Spirit was necessary, "to enlighten the understanding and to rectify the will."[18] Wesley's concept of the sufficiency of the Scriptures was closely connected to his understanding of the ministry of the Spirit in interpreting and applying the truth to the humble hearted Christian. We see in a letter to Mr. Potter in 1758:

> Else, be the Scriptures ever so complete, they will not save your soul. How, then, can you imagine that it is unnecessary and the (inspiration of the Spirit) is unnecessary and that 'the supposed need of it is injurious to the written Word.'[19]

Wesley was so convinced of the necessity of the inspiration of the Holy Spirit for interpretation he not only desired it for himself, but exhorted his preachers, in the same letter, to desire, 'God's holy inspiration'

---

[16] John Wesley. *The Christian Pattern.* (Salem, Ohio.: Schmul Press, 1975) 15.
[17] Albert Outler. *John Wesley.* (Oxford, England: Oxford University Press, 1964) 123.
[18] *Letters* 4:43.
[19] Ibid., 43.

both in order' to think the things that be good,' and also 'perfectly to love Him and worthily to magnify His holy name.'[20]

To receive the inspiration of the Holy Spirit in biblical interpretation required dedication of the individual in meditation and prayer. Wesley also realized that the dependence on inward inspiration could be abused and he warned against taking it to extremes in a letter to Mr. T. H. in 1760:

> 'If every man be furnished with an inward light as a private guide and director must it not supersede the necessity of revelation?' This affects the Quakers, not the Methodists who allow no inward light but what is subservient to the written Word and to be judged thereby . . .[21]

In chapter nine I will show as confident as Wesley was that divine guidance was needed in biblical interpretation, that did not eliminate the need for reason, experience or tradition. Divine guidance was merely one rule of interpretation, to be used complimentarily with the other rules which will be discussed. However, according to Dr. George Turner, "No one more painstakingly, or more daringly, brought to bear upon his interpretation of Scripture, the criterion of the Spirit's work in men's hearts."[22]

Scripture Should Be Interpreted Literally

Wesley delineates this principle quite clearly when he states in a letter to Samuel Furley in 1755:

> The general rule of interpreting Scripture is this: the literal sense of every text is to be taken if it be not contrary to some other texts. But in that case, the obscure text is to be interpreted by those which speak more plainly.[23]

This is but one of many examples in sermons, letters, and essays where Wesley advocates interpreting the Scriptures literally whenever possible. He exhibits the desire quite clearly in the preface to Explanatory Notes upon the Old Testament, when he writes that his desire is to:

> Give the direct, literal meaning of every verse of every sentence, and as far as I am able of every word of the oracles of God . . . It is not

---

[20] Ibid., 44.

[21] *Works* 13:391–92

[22] John Walvoord. *Inspiration and Interpretation*. (Grand Rapids, Mich.: Wm B. Eerdmanns Pub. Co., 1957) 175.

[23] Frank Baker. *The Works of John Wesley. Vol. 26.* (Oxford, England: Oxford University Press, 1982) 557.

my design to write a book, which a man may read apart from the Bible, but barely to assist those who fear God in hearing and reading the Bible itself, by showing the natural sense of every part in as few and plain words as I can.[24]

It was clearly Wesley's desire that interpreters of the Bible would emphasize the plain, natural meaning of Scripture. For example, in his sermon "The Witness of the Spirit II" (1767), Wesley responded to the question, "Is this the direct testimony of the Spirit?" His reply: "I believe there is, because that is the plain natural meaning of the text. The Spirit itself beareth witness with our spirit, that we are the children of God."[25]

In fact Wesley was so convinced of the literalness of Scripture that he believed that without this view some Scriptures had no meaning at all. In a letter to Mary Bishop in 1776 he states, "Either that text in Ezekiel 33:8 means literally, or it has no meaning at all . . . But the most decisive of all proofs is the Scripture."[26]

The fact that Wesley clearly advocated interpreting Scripture literally did not mean that he did not recognize that the Bible contained figurative language and symbolic passages. His desire was that the minister first search for the literal meaning of a passage as a necessary foundation. From there the minister could search for the spiritual meaning, the application. This basically was the same method followed by Luther and the Reformers who refused to base doctrine on the allegorical sense and emphasized the plain rules of grammar and syntax giving the meaning of any statement without recourse to esoteric spiritualizations.[27]

As I pointed out in chapter five in quoting from Wesley's "Address to the Clergy," (1756) Wesley desired the minister to have a knowledge of history, ancient customs, chronology, geography, science, art, logic, metaphysics and geometry. He also spoke of several gifts a clergyman should have, but all of these were needed because they were essential to a full understanding of the literal sense of the Scriptures.[28]

Recognizing Wesley's emphasis on the literalness of Scripture, the question then becomes, what exactly does it mean to interpret the Scripture literally? For Wesley this meant to accept the plain, natural meaning of a

---

[24] John Wesley. *Explanatory Notes Upon the Old Testament*. (Salem, Ohio.: Schmul Publishers, 1975) viii.

[25] Albert Outler. *The Works of John Wesley. Vol. 1.* (Nashville, Tenn.: Abingdon Press, 1984) 288.

[26] *Letters* 6:245.

[27] Larry Shelton, "John Wesley's Approach to Scripture in Historical Perspective," *Wesleyan Theological Journal 16* (1981) 42.

[28] James Clemons, "John Wesley—Biblical Literalist?" *Religion in Life* (1977) 336.

passage unless it led to absurdity, was contradictory to other Scripture passages, was contrary to reason, or ignored the context. In his sermons and letters Wesley spoke clearly to the literal interpretation of Scripture unless literalness was disqualified by one of the preceding circumstances. Consider the following examples of Wesley calling for literal interpretation, while recognizing possible exceptions.

Wesley believed the Bible should be interpreted literally unless that interpretation led to absurdity. For example in his sermon "Of the Church" (1785), Wesley states:

> Some indeed have been inclined to interpret this in a figurative sense, as if it referred to the Baptism of the Holy Ghost which the apostles received at the Day of Pentecost, and which in a lower degree is given to all believers. But, it is a stated rule in interpreting Scripture never to depart from the plain, literal sense unless, it implies an absurdity.[29]

Again in the sermon "A Call to Backsliders" (1778), Wesley makes the same point, as well as raising the issue of contradicting other Scripture:

> It is true some are of the opinion that these words 'it is impossible' are not to be taken literally as denoting an absolute impossibility, but only a very great difficulty. But it does not appear that we have any sufficient reason to depart from the literal meaning, as it neither implies any absurdity, nor contradicts any other Scripture.[30]

Wesley commented also in a letter to Lady Cox in 1738 on the literalness of Scripture, unless it contradicts some other Scripture:

> To anyone who asketh me concerning myself or these whom I rejoice to call my brethren, what our principles are, I answer clearly, We have no principles but those revealed in the Word of God. In the interpretation whereof we always judge the most literal sense to be the best, unless where the literal sense of one contradicts some other Scripture.[31]

Closely connected to the issue of absurdity in interpretation was the importance of not interpreting Scripture contrary to reason. I will consider the issue of reason in interpretation in the next chapter, but note in the

---

[29] Albert Outler. *The Works of John Wesley.* Vol. 3. (Nashville, Tenn.: Abingdon Press, 1986) 49–50.

[30] Ibid., 215.

[31] Frank Baker. *The Works of John Wesley.* Vol. 25. (Oxford, England: Oxford University Press, 1980) 533.

sermon "The Love of God" (1733), Wesley calls for literal interpretation as long as it is not contrary to reason:

> Tis true, if the literal sense of these Scriptures were absurd, and apparently contradictory to reason, then we should be obliged not to interpret them according to the letter, but to look out for a looser meaning.[32]

Finally, in his *Plain Account of Christian Perfection*, Wesley emphasized the literal translation as long as an effort was made to consider the context:

> Try all things by the written word and let all bow down before it. You are in danger of enthusiasm every hour, if you depart ever so little from Scripture; yea, from the plain literal meaning of any text taken, in connection with the context.[33]

Clearly Wesley believed in interpreting the Bible literally and could be called a literalist if one takes into account the guidelines of reason, context and the analogy of faith (comparing Scripture with Scripture). James Clemons in his article "John Wesley-Biblical Literalist?" states that it is correct to call Wesley a biblical literalist if one realizes:

> 1. That his literalism was not based on a word, phrase, or verse apart from context.
>
> 2. That the literal meaning of a word might vary from one passage to another, even within the same epistle.
>
> 3. That the literal meaning, having been ascertained through diligent study of language, history and church tradition, was to be used in coming to the spiritual meaning, before proceeding to the moral application.
>
> 4. That the 'analogy of faith,' that is, what the church understood by certain basic doctrine, was an essential control for a literal interpretation.[34]

This section closes with Wesley applying this interpretive method to Scripture, speaking of God creating the Sabbath in his sermon "On the Sabbath" (1730):

---

[32] Albert Outler. *The Works of John Wesley. Vol.* (Nashville, Tenn.: Abingdon Press, 1987) 337.

[33] John Wesley. *A Plain Account of Christian Perfection.* (Kansas City, Mo.: Beacon Hill Press, 1971) 97.

[34] James Clemons, "John Wesley–Biblical Literalist?" *Religion in Life.* (1977) 340.

Indeed, so soon as it shall be proved that there is an absurdity in taking this in the plain literal sense, then we shall be forced to take it in a less plain, in a figurative sense, and to say, 'Though this is related as done at creation, it was not done till the giving of manna in the time of Moses, four or five and twenty hundred years after creation.' But till this absurdity be shown, we have no pretence for giving up the letter. We have no pretence to interpret Scripture figuratively, but when an absurdity follows a proper interpretation.[35]

Whatever one may think of Wesley's dating of creation, his attempt to interpret the Bible literally, whenever possible, is clear.

Scripture Should Be Interpreted according to Context

On a number of occasions in his writings Wesley emphasized the importance of examining not only the text, but the context in interpretation. In his long letter to Dr. Warburton, the Bishop of Gloucester, in 1762 Wesley contends:

> My objections to this account are, first it contradicts St. Paul, and secondly it contradicts itself. First, it contradicts St. Paul. It fixes a meaning upon his words foreign both to text and context.[36]

In his sermon "On Corrupting the Word of God" (1727), Wesley issues several warnings about ignoring the narrow context, being the immediate preceding and following passages, as well as giving advice about the correct manner to interpret Scripture:

> . . . a second method of corrupting it-by mixing it with false interpretations. And this is done, sometimes, by repeating the words wrong: and sometimes by repeating them right, but putting a wrong sense upon them, one that is either strained and unnatural, or foreign to the writer's intention in the place from whence they are taken—perhaps contrary either to his intention in that very place, or to what he says in some other part of his writings. And this is easily effected: any passage is easily perverted by being recited single, without any of the preceding or following verses. By this means it may seem to have one sense, when it will be plain by observing what goes before and what follows after that it is really has the direct contrary . . .[37]

---

[35] Albert Outler. *The Works of John Wesley. Vol. 4.* (Nashville, Tenn.: Abingdon Press, 1987) 272–73.

[36] *Letters* 4:347.

[37] Albert Outler. *The Works of John Wesley. Vol. 4* (Nashville, Tenn.: Abingdon Press, 1987) 247.

Later in this sermon Wesley contends that the Scripture should be:

> (2) explained in the most natural obvious way, by what precedes and what follows the place in question, and commented on by the most sure way, the least liable to mistake or corruption, the producing of those parallel places that express the same thing the more plainly.[38]

As was seen earlier in the quotation from "A Plain Account of Christian Perfection," Wesley was convinced that the best way to avoid error was to:

> Try all things by the written Word of God and let all bow down before it. You are in danger of enthusiasm every hour if you depart even so little from Scripture, yea from the plain, literal meaning of any text taken in connection with context.[39]

While recognizing Wesley's clear statements concerning the importance of context, it must be mentioned that in practice he was pre-dominantly a textual or topical preacher, not an expository preacher. His series of messages "Upon Our Lord's Sermon on the Mount I-XIII" (1748–50), would probably be the closest to an expository series. Here Wesley took pains to look at the original setting and the original sense of words and clauses. These sermons include solid exposition, exegesis, textual criticism and historical backgrounds.[40]

Wesley seems to have practiced the topical-textual approach for two primary reasons. First, as I will discuss in the next point, Wesley was more concerned about interpreting a verse by the general tenor of Scripture as a whole rather than by its immediate context.[41] With his view of revelation Wesley viewed the Bible, both Old and New Testaments, as a whole, and the various texts were viewed as a part of a single theology. Therefore, as we will see, Wesley was more concerned with interpreting "Scripture by Scripture" according to the "analogy of faith." So, although Wesley rarely ignored the immediate context, he seldom gave special attention to it. Any sermon could cover the whole range of relevant biblical theology.[42]

---

[38] Ibid., 247–49.

[39] John Wesley. *A Plain Account of Christian Perfection*. (Kansas City, Mo.: Beacon Hill Press, 1971) 97.

[40] John Walvoord. *Inspiration and Interpretation*. (Grand Rapids, Mich.: Wm B. Eerdmanns Pub. Co., 1957) 166.

[41] Ibid., 170–71.

[42] Wayne McCowen and James Massey. *Interpreting God's Word for Today: An Inquiry Into Hermeneutics From a Biblical, Theological Perspective*. (Anderson, Ind.: Warner Press, Inc., 1982) 5.

Also, to understand Wesley's interpretive practices we must remember his primary purpose in teaching or preaching the Scriptures. Wesley was more often concerned with being an evangelist in his preaching, than in being an exegete. His every use of the Bible was subordinate to making the Word of God available to the common people. Often a chosen passage only served as a spring board for a discourse on practical theology.[43]

Wesley was more interested in the people he was preaching to than the people who were originally addressed in the Scripture. Outside of some exceptions mentioned earlier, Wesley seldom took the time to elucidate the historical setting, or the original interests of the writer, but pressed the text to its immediate objective, the spiritual quickening of the readers. His main concern was the relevance of the passage to the hearers, and their proper response to the Word of God. The sermon was not to inform, but to convert. It seems at times, the tools of the scholar were subordinated to the note of evangelistic urgency, which may account for the ring of authenticity in his messages.[44]

Finally, we should remember that Wesley often used Scripture for an apologetic purpose. He was very concerned about establishing sound doctrine as he disputed theological positions such as Christian perfection, original sin, and predestination. At times Wesley approached the Scripture more theologically than exegetically, and cited proof texts rather then a survey of the general teaching of a book. This was a common practice among Protestants in the eighteenth century. The Scriptures were surveyed deductively or topically. A proposition was made and texts were cited in defense of it. A good example would be his *Plain Account of Christian Perfection*, According to W. E. Sangster, Wesley uses 195 quotations in support of this doctrine with 172 from the New Testament and 23 from the Old Testament (1943, 168). With his view of the entirety of revelation Wesley might interpret a passage as a whole without limiting himself to a literal-historical interpretation.[45]

This use of proof texting might be questioned in the light of modern hermeneutical principles, and this issue will be discussed in more detail in chapter nine. At this point let me once again quote Wesley from his *Explanatory Notes Upon the New Testament* where he states:

---

[43] Ibid., 752.

[44] John Walvord. *Inspiration and Interpretation.* (Grand Rapids, Mich.: Wm B. Eerdmanns Pub. Co., 1957) 167.

[45] Ibid., 168.

> But my own conscience acquits me of having designedly misinterpreted any single passage or having written one line with the purpose of inflaming the hearts of Christians against each other.[46]

Wesley's good intentions would not necessarily deliver him from error if he ignored good hermeneutical principles, but we will discover that he did not seek to distort Scripture to support Methodist doctrine. He was willing to distinguish between sound doctrine and opinions. He was honest and used good judgment, and though at times he may have slighted the immediate context, he was careful to attempt to interpret a particular verse according to the general theme of Scripture.

Interpret Scripture according to Scripture

In his sermon "The New Creation" (1785), Wesley makes the following comments:

> It must be allowed that after all the researches we can make, still our knowledge of the great truth which is delivered to us in these words is exceedingly short and imperfect. As this is a point of mere revelation, beyond the reach of all our natural faculties, we cannot penetrate far into it, nor form any adequate conception of it. But it may be an encouragement to those who have in any degree tasted of the powers of the world to come to go as far as we can go, interpreting Scripture by Scripture, according to the analogy of faith.[47]

In this phrase "Interpreting Scripture by Scripture according to the analogy of faith" we have two closely connected parts of one key interpretive principle. Interpreting Scripture by Scripture probably needs no explanation, though I will amplify and expand on Wesley's understanding of this concept. The phrase "analogy of faith" may be less clearly understood, but it is closely connected and must be defined.

By the analogy of faith Wesley meant the interpreting of Scripture by Scripture, with special reference to its doctrinal teaching. Because of his understanding of revelation, Wesley approached the Bible as a whole, the various texts as part of a single theology.[48] The Scripture as a message of God for man, was not a group of unrelated statements. He had a feel

---

[46] John Wesley. *Explanatory Notes Upon the New Testament.* (London, England, Epworth Press, 1948) 8.

[47] Albert Outler. *The Works of John Wesley. Vol. 2.* (Nashville, Tenn.: Abingdon Press, 1985) 501.

[48] Wayne McCowen and James Massey. *Interpreting God's Word for Today: An Inquiry Into Hermeneutics From a Biblical, Theological Perspective.* (Anderson, Ind.: Warner Press, Inc., 1982) 752.

for the wholeness of biblical theology which affected all efforts at biblical interpretation.

Any attempt at biblical interpretation therefore, must concentrate on the Holy Scriptures as a whole. This idea of the "whole Scriptures" or the "whole analogy of faith" is a favorite metaphor of Wesley's occurring over 15 times in his sermons.[49] Wesley challenged therefore that one is "not to build your faith on a single text of scripture and much less on a particular sense of it."[50] Instead in a letter to John Smith in 1745 Wesley states:

> As to the Word of God, you well observe, 'We are not to frame doctrines by the sound of particular texts, but the general tenor of Scripture, soberly studied and consistently interpreted.'[51]

For Wesley the Bible was equally inspired, though each passage might not be of equal importance. There is a message in every part of Holy Writ and it is always the same essence. There are grand truths that run throughout the Bible so individual passages cannot be interpreted in isolation. Scripture must be interpreted by Scripture, by the analogy of faith, so that the interconnectedness can be seen—"Causes of the Inefficacy of Christianity" (1789):

> How few know what Christianity means? How small a number will you find that have any conception of the analogy of faith, of the connected chain of Scripture truths and their relation to each another.[52]

In Wesley's *Explanatory Notes Upon the New Testament*, he comments upon Romans 12:6:

> ... 'let us prophesy according to the analogy of faith'—St. Peter expresses it as the oracles of God: according to that general tenor of them, according to the grand scheme of doctrine which is delivered therein, touching original sin, justification by faith, and present, inward salvation. There is a wonderful analogy between all these; and a close and intimate connection between the chief heads of that faith which 'was once delivered to the saints.' Every article therefore, concerning which there is any question, should be determined

---

[49] Albert Outler. *The Works of John Wesley. Vol. 1.* (Nashville, Tenn.: Abingdon Press, 1984) 182.
[50] *Letters* 5:328.
[51] Frank Baker. *The Works of John Wesley. Vol. 26.* (Nashville, Tenn.: Abingdon Press, 1982) 158.
[52] Albert Outler. *The Works of John Wesley. Vol. 4.* (Nashville, Tenn.: Abingdon Press, 1987) 89.

by this rule; every doubtful Scripture interpreted, according to the grand truths which run through the whole.[53]

Thus recognizing the connection between all Scripture, the Bible is to be read as a whole, with the expectation that the clearer texts will illuminate the obscurer ones. For Wesley, there was no authority above Scripture, from which a more definitive interpretation of revelation might be sought.[54] Clearly he agreed with his father's admonition "You ask me which is the best commentary on the Bible? I answer the Bible."[55] Therefore, Wesley could say in his tract "Popery Calmly Considered":

> And Scripture is the best expounder of Scripture. The best way therefore to understand it, is carefully to compare Scripture with Scripture, and thereby learn the true meaning of it.[56]

Also, along the same lines, in the "Address to Clergy" (1756), Wesley stressed the importance of . . . "a knowledge of all the Scriptures; seeing Scripture interprets Scripture one part fixing the sense of another."[57]

Again emphasizing the importance of "Scripture interpreting Scripture," Wesley states in his preface to the *Standard Sermons* in his own sermon preparation, "I then search after and consider parallel passages of Scripture, comparing spiritual things with spiritual."[58]

Again in his sermon "On Corrupting the Word of God" (1727), he states that the Bible must be:

> (2.) explained in the most natural, obvious way by what precedes and what follows the place in question; and commented on by the most sure way, the least liable to mistake or corruption, the producing of those parallel places that express the same thing more plainly.[59]

In closing this point consider several examples of Wesley's use of "Scripture interpreting Scripture by the analogy of faith," in a number

---

[53] John Wesley. *Explanatory Notes Upon the New Testament.* (London, England: Epworth Press, 1948) 569–70.

[54] Albert Outler. *The Works of John Wesley. Vol. 1.* (Nashville, Tenn.: Abingdon Press, 1984) 59–59.

[55] A. Skevington Wood. *The Burning Heart.* (Grand Rapids, Mich.: Wm B. Eerdmanns Pub. Co., 1967) 136.

[56] *Works* 10:142.

[57] *Works* 10:482.

[58] *Sermons* 1:32.

[59] Albert Outler. *The Works of John Wesley. Vol. 4.* (Nashville, Tenn.: Abingdon Press, 1987) 249.

of his sermons. Note the emphasis on the "whole scope and tenor of the Scripture" in contemplating every text and doctrine. In each instance Wesley is dealing with a somewhat controversial doctrine.

"On Sin In Believers" (1763):

> I cannot therefore, by any means receive this assertion, 'that there is no sin in a believer from the moment he is justified.' First, because it is contrary to the whole tenor of Scripture . . .[60]

"The End of Christ's Coming" (1781):

> And yet, if we believe the Bible, who can deny it? Who can doubt it? It runs through the Bible from the beginning to the end, in one connected chain. And the agreement of every part of it with every other is properly the analogy of faith.[61]

Finally, Wesley made some very strong statements about predestination. This, of course, was a very controversial topic which Wesley had to address, and did on a number of occasions. Wesley summarized his views very early in a letter to his mother in 1725, "This is the sum of what I believe concerning predestination, which I think is agreeable to the analogy of faith."[62]

In His sermon "Free Grace" (1739), Wesley shows why he cannot accept this doctrine, because it contradicts the general tenor of Scripture. Here Wesley clearly shows that one cannot interpret a text or texts of Scripture, if it contradicts other Scripture. This is a perfect example of Wesley "interpreting Scripture by Scripture by the analogy of faith":

> And as this doctrine manifestly and directly tends to overthrow the whole Christian revelation, so it does the same thing by plain consequence in making that revelation contradict itself. For it is grounded on such an interpretation of some texts (more or fewer it matters not), as flatly contradicts all other texts and indeed the whole scope and tenor of Scripture. They infer from this text . . . they contradict the whole oracles of God . . . this is flatly contrary to the whole tenor of Scripture . . . flatly contrary to this are all the Scriptures . . . Thus manifestly does this doctrine overthrow the whole Christian revelation, by making it contradict itself; by giving such an interpretation of some texts as flatly contradict all

---

[60] Ibid. 1:325.

[61] Ibid., 2:483.

[62] Frank Baker. *The Works of John Wesley. 25.* (Oxford, England: Oxford University Press, 1982) 180.

other texts, and indeed the whole scope and tenor of Scripture—an abundant proof that it is not of God.[63]

Interpretation Is Linked to Application

Previously it was noted that Wesley's preaching was often textual or topical. Sometimes the text was used as a pre-text or merely a jumping off point. This is more easily explained when it is remembered that Wesley's aim was always practical. He always spoke to the immediate situation. For Wesley, the proper interpretation of Scripture could not be isolated from present situations.

As an interpreter of the Bible Wesley's most characteristic role was that of a preacher, not an exegete, but an evangelist. While he did not totally ignore the historical context, he was much more concerned about present application. John Oswalt in his article "John Wesley's Use of the Old Testament in His Doctrinal Teaching" referred to Wesley using the Scripture at times in an "illustrative" manner. The biblical experience or statement was used to illustrate the present situation.[64] George Turner refers to this usage, showing how Wesley's use of Scripture at times resembles Peter's use of the Old Testament at Pentecost. This usage seems to indicate that the manner in which Scripture illuminates present experience seems more important than the historical situation.[65]

In light of Wesley's emphasis upon application in interpretation it should be recognized that his purpose was primarily evangelical. The Scripture was his guide and the medium was the sermon. Wesley's main desire was to deliver the truth of the gospel and to see a salvific result. As Wilber Mullen states, "His method of biblical interpretation might be summarized as soteriologically motivated and pragmatically implemented."[66]

Thus we see that Wesley was not only concerned that men study the Bible, but that they do something with what they learn. For this to be possible it was necessary that biblical interpretation be made practical and understandable for the masses of unlearned people. There was little room

---

[63] Albert Outler. *The Works of John Wesley. Vol. 3.* (Nashville, Tenn.: Abingdon Press, 1986) 552–554.

[64] John Oswalt, "John Wesley's Use of the Old Testament in Doctrinal Teachings," *Wesleyan Theological Journal 12* (1977) 42.

[65] John Walvoord. *Inspiration and Interpretation.* (Grand Rapids, Mich.: Wm B. Eerdmanns Pub. Co., 1957) 239.

[66] Wilber Mullen, "John Wesley's Method of Biblical Interpretation," *Religion in Life* (1978) 102.

in Wesley's mind for complicated hermeneutical theories. He desired plain truth for plain people as can be seen in the preface to his *Sermons* (1746):

> I design plain truth for plain people. Therefore of set purpose I abstain from all nice and philosophical speculations: from all perplexed and intricate reasonings, and as far as possible from even the show of learning, unless in sometimes citing the original Scriptures. I labour to avoid all words which are not easy to be understood, all which are not used in common life: and in particular those kinds of technical terms that so frequently occur in bodies of divinity, those modes of speaking which men of reading are intimately acquainted with, but which to common people are an unknown tongue.[67]

The desire that the study of the Bible be applicable insured that Wesley was much more concerned with the practical than the theoretical. He had little time or interest in dwelling on speculative theology. Wesley states this well in a letter to Christopher Hopper in 1788:

> What I said was that Bengelius had given it as his opinion, not that the world would then end, but that the Millennial reign of Christ would begin in the year 1836. I have no opinion at all upon that head. I can determine nothing about it. These calculations are far above, out of my sight. I have only one thing to do, save my own soul and those who hear me.[68]

E. H. Sugden summarizes not only Wesley's views, but also the views of early Methodists on this subject when he states:

> Methodism is the only branch of the Christian Church which bases its theology on preached sermons: hence the emphasis which it lays upon the practical doctrines of religion and the comparatively small importance which it attaches to the more speculative and theoretical aspects of divine truth.[69]

For Wesley, one read and interpreted the Bible for more than mere enlightenment or understanding. The Bible was to be interpreted so that it could be understood and applied to life. Thus he exhorts his readers in his *Explanatory Notes Upon the Old Testament*, "3. To read this with a single eye, to know the whole will of God, and a fixed resolution to do it."[70]

---

[67] Albert Outler. *The Works of John Wesley. Vol. 1.* (Nashville, Tenn.: Abingdon Press, 1984) 104.

[68] *Letters* 8:63.

[69] *Sermons* 1:29.

[70] John Wesley. *Explanatory Notes Upon the Old Testament.* (Salem, Ohio.: Schmul Publishers, 1975) ix.

Application was such an important part of Bible study for John Wesley I believe I can agree with Dr. Melvin Dieter's statement, "Wesley would simply say that any pattern of biblical interpretation which does not have the practical result as its immediate goal in this life is suspect."[71]

---

[71] Melvin Dieter, "Musings," *Wesleyan Theological Journal* 14 (1979) 1.

9

John Wesley's Rules of Scriptural Interpretation

Part 2

As has been clearly outlined in earlier chapters, Wesley's standard of judgment for any doctrine was the Scripture. When challenged for authority on any question, his first appeal was the Holy Bible. Note his letter to William Dodd in 1756:

> I therein build on no authority, ancient or modern, but the Scripture. If this supports any doctrine, it will stand; if not, the sooner it falls the better. Neither the doctrine in question nor any other is anything to me, unless it be the doctrine of Christ and His Apostles. I search for truth, plain Bible truth without any regard to the praise or dispraise of men.[1]

However, Wesley also knew that quoting Scripture rarely solved any controversial point. Far too often Wesley and his critics would come to an impasse merely citing proof texts, often using the same parts of Scripture. Wesley also recognized that "scarce ever was any heretical opinion either invented or revised but Scripture was quoted to defend it."[2] Therefore, some secondary authority was needed to help in the interpreting of the Bible.

Wesley's views in this area were greatly influenced by his growth and training in the Anglican tradition, as indicated in chapter one. Since the Edwardian Reformers, (Cranmer and Harpsfield in particular), the Church of England had been placed under the authority of Scripture. The primary source for discovering God's supreme law was the Bible, and where one spiritual passage was obscure or ambiguous, others would be consulted to

---

[1] *Letters* 3:157–58
[2] Albert Outler. *The Works of John Wesley. Vol. 4.* (Nashville, Tenn.: Abingdon Press, 1987) 247.

resolve difficulties, always reading Scripture in the plainest most obvious sense. As a secondary source of authority, never to be used as a substitute but always as a corrective, there was the appeal to Christian tradition, beginning with the Church Fathers and following down the unbroken tradition to the Church of England. Wesley felt that the Church of England was the nearest church to the Bible, and therefore able to offer authoritative interpretation. The recognition of the fundamental authority of the Scripture was not meant to preclude an appeal to the saintly Christians of other ages.[3]

At times even Scripture and tradition were not enough, and therefore God implanted within man reason, by which one could instinctively recognize divine law and make one's own valid interpretation of Scripture. For Wesley, reason was a gift of God, and though affected by the fall, it was still in operation. Because it was reflective of the image of God, all true religion would be reasonable in essence.[4] Thus, according to Anglican theology, the will of God could be discovered through the Bible, interpreted by reason, and the ancient church. Thomas Tenison, (Archbishop of Canterbury when John Wesley was born), defined Protestant theological methods as the "conjoint use of Scripture, tradition and reason." Even after Wesley, Francis Paget could claim quite plainly, "the distinctive strengths of Anglicanism rest on the equal loyalty to the unconflicting rights of reason, Scripture and tradition."[5] This was the tradition within which Wesley grew and took his stand.

Wesley however, did not limit himself to this triad, but went on to add another element, that being Christian experience. Wesley insisted on "heart religion" in the place of normal Christian orthodoxy. He found support for this in Cranmer's wry comments in *Homilies IV* about the devils who assent to every tenet of orthodoxy and yet they are still devils. Christian experience adds nothing to the substance of Christian truth. Its distinctive role is to energize the heart so as to enable the believer to speak and do the truth in love.[6] Thus we find what has come to be known as the Wesleyan Quadrilateral. Here we find four different elements of authority, but it is important to realize that these were not equal elements. Scripture was clearly the pre-eminent authority interacting with tradition, reason and Christian

---

[3] Frank Baker. *John Wesley and the Church of England*. (London, England: Epworth Press, 1970) 13.

[4] Allen Coppedge, "John Wesley and the Issue of Authority," *Wesleyan Theological Journal* 19 (1984) 627.

[5] Albert Outler. *The Works of John Wesley. Vol. 2.* (Nashville, Tenn.: Abingdon Press, 1985) 8.

[6] Ibid., 9–10.

experience in the interpretation of the Word of God. Colin Williams in his book *John Wesley's Theology Today* states "That Wesley continually subjected reason, tradition and experience to the written Word of God, even a casual reading of his works will reveal."[7] In the Wesleyan Quadrilateral reason, experience, and tradition are secondary means of evaluating truth. They are viewed as subordinate criteria and never of equal authority with the Scripture. However, there is clearly a place under the umbrella of the Word of God for the proper use of reason, scripture and tradition. Scripture is clearly unique and the final authority, but this in turn can be illuminated by the collective Christian wisdom of the ages. Bible interpretation can benefit from the discipline of critical reason, but always biblical revelation must be received in the heart by faith. Thus the stress on Christian experience gives biblical interpretation an existential force.[8]

In the remainder of this chapter I will discuss in more detail Wesley's use of reason, Christian tradition, and Christian experience in the interpretation of Scripture. In each instance the emphasis will be upon the importance Wesley placed upon these elements in biblical interpretation; the manner in which they were to be used; and the dangers to be avoided.

The Use of Reason in Interpreting Scripture

John Wesley knew it was not always enough merely to base one's assertions upon the authority of the Bible. Everyone who reads the Bible must interpret it. Wesley wished to make sure that the people called Methodists interpreted it as correctly as possible. Correct interpretation required the use of reason as Wesley declares in a letter to Dr. Rutherford in 1768:

> It is a fundamental principle with us (the Methodists), that to renounce reason is to renounce religion, that religion and reason go hand in hand, and that all irrational religion is false religion.[9]

The importance of reason was not that it provided another source of revelation. Man cannot fully know God through reason, but only through revelation which includes Scripture and the experience of the inward witness. However, the role of reason is essential. It is through reason that the rational comparison of Scripture and experience can be made. It is by our logical faculties that we are enabled to order the evidence of revelation, and

---

[7] Colin Williams. *John Wesley's Theology Today*. (Nashville, Tenn.: Abingdon Press, 1960) 23.

[8] Albert Outler. *The Works of John Wesley. Vol. 2.* (Nashville, Tenn.: Abingdon Press, 1985) 9–11.

[9] Rupert Davies. *The Works of John Wesley. Vol. 9.* (Nashville, Tenn.: Abingdon Press, 1989) 382.

along with tradition it provides us with the necessary weapons for guarding against the danger of unbridled interpretation of Scripture. Wesley was very concerned that the principle of "sola scriptura" might be manipulated in such a way to open up the faith to all manner of unchecked excesses, such as exhibited by the Mystics. Therefore he placed a strong emphasis upon the place of tradition and the place of reason in the structure of authority.[10]

The best route to understanding Wesley's view is by reading his sermon "The Case For Reason Impartially Considered" (1781). Here Wesley clearly shows that Scripture is foundational, but reason is essential for proper interpretation:

> The foundation of true religion stands upon the Oracles of God. It is built upon the prophets and the apostles, Jesus Christ himself being the chief cornerstone. Now of what excellent use is reason if we would either understand ourselves, or explain to others, those living oracles! And how is it possible without it to understand the essential truths contained therein? A beautiful summary of which we have in that which is called the Apostle's Creed. Is it not reason (assisted by the Holy Ghost), which enables us to understand what the Holy Scriptures declare concerning the being and attributes of God. Concerning His eternity and immensity, his power, wisdom and holiness? It is by reason that God enables us in some measure to comprehend his method of dealing with the children of men, the nature of his various dispensations, of the Old and New Covenant, of the law and the gospel. It is by this we understand (His Spirit opening and enlightening the eyes of our understanding), what that repentance is, not to be repented of; what is that faith whereby we are saved, what is the nature and condition of justification, what are the immediate and what the subsequent fruits of it. By reason we learn what is that new birth without which we cannot enter into the kingdom of heaven, and what that holiness is, without which no man shall see the Lord? By the due use of reason we come to know what are the tempers implied in inward holiness and what it is to be outwardly holy, holy in all manner of conversation-in other words, what is the mind that was 'in Christ,' and what it is to walk as Christ walked.[11]

---

[10] Wayne McCowen and James Massey. *Interpreting God's Word for Today: An Inquiry into Hermeneutics From a Biblical, Theological Perspective.* (Anderson, Ind.: Warner Press, 1982) 32.

[11] Albert Outler. *The Works of John Wesley. Vol. 2.* (Nashville, Tenn.: Abingdon Press, 1985) 592–93.

In this passage Wesley clearly shows how important reason is to the clear understanding of the Oracles of God. At the same time he interjects that reason is not enough in itself, but that our understanding and enlightenment must be assisted by the Holy Spirit. He emphasized that reason was only to be a "hand-maiden of faith, the servant of revelation."[12] Wesley was fully aware of the danger of the under or over use of reason pressed to extremes. Again we see in "The Case for Reason Impartially Considered":

> 4. They that are prejudiced against the Christian revelation, who do not receive the Scriptures as the Oracles of God almost universally run into this extreme. 5. Is there no medium between these extremes undervaluing or overvaluing reason?[13]

Reason, with the assistance of the Holy Spirit, helps the individual to understand the doctrines of Christianity, but it has severe limitations and cannot be trusted alone. Instead he goes on to advise:

> Let reason do all that reason can: employ it as far as it will go. But at the same time acknowledge it is utterly incapable of giving either faith, or hope or love: and consequently of producing either real virtue or substantial happiness. Expect these from a higher source, even from the Father of the spirits of all flesh.[14]

While Wesley recognized the inherent dangers of overvaluing reason, he also recognized that the use of reason was absolutely essential if doctrine was to avoid being swept away by an overemphasis on enthusiasm or impressions. Note the following warning from his sermon "The Nature of Enthusiasm" (1750):

> 38. Beware you do not fall into the second sort of enthusiasm fancying you have those gifts from God which you have not. Trust not in visions or dreams, in sudden impressions or strong impulses of any kind. Remember, it is not by these you are to know what is 'the will of God' on any particular occasion, but by applying the plain scriptural rule, with the help of experience and reason, and the ordinary assistance of the Spirit of God.[15]

Note a similar warning directed toward Count Zinzendorf and his followers who allowed mysticism at times to overwhelm reason. Wesley

---

[12] *Journals* 5:492.
[13] Albert Outler. *The Works of John Wesley. Vol. 2.* (Nashville, Tenn.: Abingdon Press, 1985) 588.
[14] Ibid., 600.
[15] Ibid., 59.

would not allow impressions to contradict Scripture and reason. In a letter to Elizabeth Ritchie in 1786 he states:

> Count Zinzendorf observes there are three different ways wherein it pleases God to lead His people: some are guided almost in every instance by apposite texts of Scripture; others see a clear and plain reason for everything they are to do; and yet others are led not so much by Scripture or reason as by particular impressions. I am very rarely led by impressions, but generally by reason and by Scripture.[16]

Clearly for Wesley, believers were to be guided and doctrine was to be understood by scripture and reason. Observe in his "The Principles of a Methodist Explained" (1746):

> If this can be proved by Scripture or reason to be enthusiastic or erroneous doctrine, we will then plead guilty to the indictment of 'teaching error and enthusiasm.'[17]

In "A Farther Appeal to Men of Reason and Religion Part III" (1745):

> What is it you would have us prove by miracles? That the doctrines we preach are true? This is not the way to prove that . . . We prove the doctrines we preach by Scripture and reason, and if need be, by antiquity.[18]

Wesley showed clearly that it was his desire to be led by Scripture and reason, and he exhorted his followers to be guided by them as well. In a letter to Dr. Lavington, the Bishop of Exeter in 1749 he writes:

> I am not above reason or Scripture. To either of these I am ready to submit. But I cannot receive scurrilous invective instead of Scripture, nor pay the same regard to low buffoonery as to clear and cogent reasons.[19]

In a letter to John Smith in 1745 he states, "I entirely agree with you that the children of light walk by the joint light of reason, Scripture, and the Holy Ghost."[20] He also issues a challenge in his "Thoughts On the Consecration of Churches" (1788):

---

[16] *Letters* 7:319.

[17] Rupert Davies. *The Works of John Wesley. Vol. 9.* (Nashville, Tenn.: Abingdon Press, 1989) 229.

[18] Gerald Cragg. *The Works of John Wesley. Vol. 11.* (Nashville, Tenn.: Abingdon Press, 1989) 310.

[19] Ibid., 370.

[20] *Letters* 3:158.

8. I take the whole of this practice to be mere relic of Romish superstition. And I wonder that any sensible Protestant should think it right to countenance it, much more that any reasonable man should plead the necessity of it! Surely it is high time now we should be guided not by custom, but by Scripture and reason.[21]

In summary, Wesley assumed that since God is rational, interpretation of Scripture should be rational, and therefore reason cannot be excluded from biblical interpretation. In summarizing Wesley's thoughts from his "Case For Reason Impartially Considered" (1781), reason is not to be discredited or despised. Reason is not to be driven from the temple of religion as if it had no place in the service of God. Religion is built on the Bible and reason. It is reason which enables men to understand the Bible, to grasp its statements of truth concerning God and his relation to the universe, and to comprehend his method of dealing with the children of men.[22]

The Use of Experience in Interpreting Scripture

Wesley gave a large place to experience, which in his mind, could authenticate a particular interpretation of Scripture. In fact, his theology has been called a "theology of experience" resting upon the two pillars of Scripture and experience. Dr. George Cell in his book, *The Re-discovery of John Wesley*, goes as far as to say:

> It is safe to say that no other teacher of the Christian Church and preacher of the Gospel ever laid upon experience so heavy a burden of responsibility for discerning and confirming the truth-values of the Christian faith. In respect to the primacy accorded to religious experience, the extent to which he made experiential thinking his principal method, and the results of his researches into the meaning of God in Christian experience, it can be said that Wesley started theology on the paths in which today's religious thought moves increasingly.[23]

The emphasis which Wesley placed upon experience in the Christian faith centered around his spiritual struggles. When presented with the necessity to interpret some portions of Scripture, Wesley wished to examine conduct, men's professions, the possibilities in living men, to see if the

---

[21] Rupert Davies. *The Works of John Wesley. Vol. 9.* (Nashville, Tenn.: Abingdon Press, 1989) 533.

[22] William Cannon. *The Theology of John Wesley.* (Nashville, Tenn.: Abingdon Press, 1946) 158–59.

[23] George Cell. *The Rediscovery of John Wesley.* (New York, N.Y.: University Press of America, 1935) 71–72.

interpretation was true to life.[24] A perfect example would be the instruction by Peter Bohler concerning justification by faith and the assurance of forgiveness of sin. After being shown that Scripture would bear such an interpretation, he still had the question, "are there any whose Christian experience can support such an interpretation?" Note Wesley's thoughts from his *Journal* in 1738:

> 12. When I met Peter Bohler again, he readily consented to put the dispute upon the issue which I desired, viz., Scripture and experience. I first consulted the Scripture. But when I set aside the glosses of men, and simply considered the Words of God, comparing them together and endeavoring to illustrate the obscure by the plainer passages, I found they all made against me and was forced to retreat to my last hold, that experience would never agree with the literal interpretation of those Scriptures. Nor could I therefore allow it to be the true till I found some living witnesses of it.[25]

After his own "heart warming experience" at Aldersgate Wesley was concerned that the mere acceptance of the authority of Scripture and tradition would lead to a formal religion such as he had experienced in the Church of England. After being raised himself to think of the Christian religion only in the terms of duty, he feared any kind of formal religion that would short circuit a living relation with God. He feared the formalism of the Church of England where so many had a proper understanding of Christianity, but had no vital experience in their lives. He certainly did not wish that to happen to the Methodists:

> I am not afraid that the people called Methodists should never cease to exist either in Europe or America. But I am afraid lest they should exist only as a dead sect, having the form of religion without the power. And this undoubtedly will be the case unless they hold fast to the doctrine, spirit, and discipline with which they first set out.[26]

For Wesley, the mere acceptance of the authority of Scripture and tradition was never adequate until it was seen that the authority was conferred upon them by the Holy Spirit. He wished for experience to drive men back to the Scripture, to see if they understood it. Wesley was convinced that experience, whether contemporary or ancient, could clarify and confirm

---

[24] William Pellowe, "John Wesley's Use of the Bible," *Methodist Review* 106 (1923) 353–374.
[25] Reginald Ward and Richard Heitzenrater. *The Works of John Wesley. Vol. 18.* (Nashville, Tenn.: Abingdon Press, 1988) 248.
[26] *Letters* 2:519.

Scripture, but it would never supersede it.[27] He would never have agreed that an appeal to experience is sufficient in itself. He would certainly have agreed with P. T. Forsyth that the Witness of the Spirit must not be divorced from the Witness of the Word.[28]

This is a very important point. For Wesley, experience was not to be the final test of truth. Christian experience added nothing to the substance of Christian truth. Its distinctive role was to energize the heart so as to enable the believer to speak and to do truth in love. Wesley feared any approach to doctrine which overlooked the necessity of personal experience, but he was equally concerned about the danger of relying upon experience as the ground of truth if it ignored the Scripture. This very possible danger will be discussed shortly.

In considering the relationship between Scripture, reason and experience the best term for experience might be "confirmatory." Isabel Rivers in her article "John Wesley and the Language of Scripture, Reason, and Experience" shows this connection quite clearly stating that Wesley's appeal to the three-fold authority of Scripture, reason, and experience as sources of religious truth, was intended as a kind of self-regulating check against the errors of both the moralist and the antinomians. Wesley believed that man cannot know God through reason, but only through revelation-Scripture-and experience-the inward witness. However the role of reason is essential because only through reason can man interpret Scripture. For Wesley, if a particular interpretation of Scripture is not borne out by the evidence of experience, then the interpretation must be wrong (this was an important argument in Wesley's doctrine of perfection). Conversely, if a particular experience does not follow a scriptural pattern (for example, if an individual's claim to be justified does not issue in the fruits of a holy life), then the experience is invalid.[29]

Clearly, the appeal to experience was not to be independent of other sources, nor was it to supersede the Bible as being primary. On the other hand, experience can confirm the Scripture at numerous points.[30] There is a natural affinity between the testimony of Scripture, the witness of the Spirit, and genuine Christian experience. The three should complement and explain each other. The experience of God which the individual has

---

[27] *Journals* 2:352.

[28] R. Benjamin Garrison, "Vital Interaction: Scripture and Experience, John Wesley's Doctrine of Authority," *Religion in Life* 25 (1956) 571.

[29] Isabel Rivers, "John Wesley and the Language of Scripture, Reason and Experience," *Prose Studies* 4 (1981) 253.

[30] William Arnett, "John Wesley-The Man of One Book" (Ph.D. diss., Drew University, 1954)

should be checked by the experience of the church as witnessed to by the New Testament. The Bible in turn is best understood and interpreted in the light of a vital Christian experience.[31]

Thus, for Wesley, it was not a question of either Scripture or experience. Rather it was a fact of vital interaction between the two. Wesley, as we shall see, brought severe scriptural texts to bear upon alleged religious experiences, in an effort to avoid fanaticism. One must remember, however, that the Bible itself is a book of experience. According to Benjamin Garrison, "Any failure to recognize this truth implicit in all of Wesley's teachings will cause him to be misunderstood."[32] The Bible is pre-eminently and primarily a book which records the God-ward experience of men and the man-ward experience of God. Therefore, we must recognize the vital interaction between the two. The individual knows God through Scripture and experience. He can readily compare the two, but he also needs the testimony of others to test whether his own experience coheres with common experience and is not peculiar to himself and hence invalid.[33]

For Wesley no single, individual experience could stand alone. Harold Lindstrom in his book *Wesley and Sanctification* states that for Wesley, Christian experience is not simply that of the individual, but is also that of the fellowship. Wesley taught people who were individualists in their thinking to think beyond their own faith and fear to the one great witness of the universal church in all ages.[34] Again Isabel Rivers summarizes Wesley's view:

> The individual knows God through Scripture and experience. He can readily compare the two; but he also needs the testimony of others, partly in order to test whether his own experience coheres with common experience, and is not particular to himself, and is hence valid, and partly to encourage him to perseverance.[35]

Understanding the close connection between experience and Scripture, it is not surprising to find in reading Wesley's works this typical phrase, "All

---

[31] John Walvoord. *Inspiration and Interpretation.* (Grand Rapids, Mich.: Wm B. Eerdmanns Pub. Co., 1957) 310.

[32] Benjamin Garrison, "Vital Interaction: Scripture and Experience, John Wesley's Doctrine of Authority," *Religion in Life 25* (1956) 563.

[33] Isabel Rivers, "John Wesley and the Language of Scripture, Reason and Experience," *Prose Studies* (1981) 261.

[34] Benjamin Garrison, "Vital Interaction: Scripture and Experience, John Wesley's Doctrine of Authority," *Religion In Life 25* (1956) 569.

[35] Isabel Rivers, "John Wesley and the Language of Scripture, Reason and Tradition," *Prose Studies* (1981) 261.

experience as well as Scripture shows."[36] Here we consider several examples from Wesley's writings of his effort to combine Scripture, experience, and reason in dealing with doctrines and life.

In a letter to William Law in 1756 Wesley writes:

> But what do you mean by giving myself to God? You answer: 'Every sincere wish and desire after Christian virtues is giving up yourself to him and the very perfection of faith' (Spirit of Love, Part II. p. 217). Far, very far from it. I know from the experience of a thousand persons as well as from Scripture, and the very reason of the thing, that a man may have sincere desires after all these, long before he attains them.[37]

In a letter to his brother Charles in 1747, concerning the question of whether justifying faith was a sense of pardon, we find "But this is a supposition contrary to Scripture as well as to experience."[38]

Finally, in his work "A Plain Account of People Called Methodists" (1749) he writes the following concerning the band societies:

> But it was soon objected to the bands (as to the classes before) 'These were not at first. There is no Scripture for them. These are man's works, man's buildings, man's inventions.' I reply as before, these are also prudential helps, grounded on reason and experience, in order to apply the general rules given in Scripture according to particular circumstances.[39]

At this point it might be well to consider examples of Wesley using experience in a confirmatory way toward Scripture. Two good illustrations deal with the "Witness of the Holy Spirit" and the doctrine of "Christian Perfection."

To the subjective interpretation of Scripture emphasized by the Reformers, Wesley added the importance of the inward witness of the Spirit. Undoubtedly, this was the conviction that the direct work of the Spirit and the written testimony of the Spirit are in agreement.[40] Note the manner in which Wesley stresses the confirmatory value of experience in his sermon "The Witness of the Spirit I–II":

---

[36] .Albert Outler. *The Works of John Wesley. Vol. 3.* (Nashville, Tenn.: Abingdon Press, 1986) 204

[37] *Letters* 3:364.

[38] Frank Baker. *The Works of John Wesley. Vol. 26.* (Oxford, England: Oxford University Press, 1982) 255.

[39] Rupert Davies. *The Works of John Wesley. Vol. 9.* (Nashville, Tenn.: Abingdon Press, 1989) 268.

[40] John Walvoord. *Inspiration and Interpretation.* (Grand Rapids, Mich.: Wm B. Eerdmanns Pub. Co., 1957) 176.

"The Witness of the Spirit II" (1767):

> And here properly comes in, to confirm this scriptural doctrine, the experience of the children of God—the experience not of two or three, not of a few, but of a great multitude which no man can number. It has been confirmed both in this and in all ages, by 'a cloud of' living and dying 'witnesses.' It is confirmed by your experience and mine.[41]

Later in this same sermon, Wesley faced the objection that experience is not sufficient to prove a doctrine which is not founded in Scripture. He agreed:

> 1. It is objected, first 'Experience is not sufficient to prove a doctrine which is not found in Scripture.' This is undoubtedly true, and it is an important truth. But, it does not effect the present question, for it has been shown that the doctrine is founded on Scripture. Therefore, experience is properly alleged to confirm it.[42]

The issue of experience was very important to Wesley, especially concerning the doctrine of Christian perfection. He was convinced in the attainability of perfection, but it had to be shown to be consonant with Scripture and experience. If a particular interpretation of Scripture was not born out by the evidence of experience, then the interpretation was considered wrong. By comparing the doctrine again and again with the Word of God on the one hand, and the experience of the children of God on the other, the nature and property of Christian perfection should be made much more clear.[43] Wesley therefore tested the experiences of his converts who professed the experience of perfect love to support his exegesis of the passages believed to support the doctrine. The reason was simple and clear as he states in his *Plain Account of Christian Perfection:*

> If I were convinced that none in England had attained what has been so clearly and strongly preached by such a number of preachers, in so many places for so long a time, I should be clearly convinced that we had all mistaken the meaning of those Scriptures.[44]

---

[41] Albert Outler. *The Works of John Wesley. Vol. 1.* (Nashville, Tenn.: Abingdon Press, 1984) 290.

[42] Ibid., 293.

[43] Isabel Rivers, "John Wesley and the Language of Scripture, Reason and Experience," *Prose Studies 4* (1981) 271.

[44] John Wesley. *A Plain Account of Christian Perfection.* (Kansas City, Mo.: Beacon Hill Press, 1971) 67.

Thus we see, by surveying Wesley's writings, that in the use of experience in interpreting the Scriptures, experience was not to be an independent source of doctrine, but experience could confirm a biblical doctrine.[45] Wesley perhaps expresses this concept most clearly in a letter to the Countess Huntington in 1771, where he argues the experiential success of his scriptural interpretation proves its truth:

> ... the gospel, which I now preach, God does still confirm by new witnesses in every place ... Now, I argue from glaring, undeniable fact; God cannot bear witness to a lie. The gospel, therefore, which He confirms must be true in substance.[46]

While the correct use of experience was very valuable in biblical interpretations, Wesley also realized how easily the whole area of personal experience as a standard could be abused. He recognized the tremendous variety in religious experience, and that no one experience could be considered normative. Therefore, all experience had to be submitted to the final authority of Scripture. Wesley's fundamental precept was defined in a letter to Thomas Whitehead in 1748:

> The Scriptures are the touchstone whereby Christians examine all, real or supposed revelations. For though the Spirit is our principal leader, yet He is not our rule at all; the Scriptures are the rule whereby He leads us into all truth.[47]

In this quotation Wesley is responding to his concern about the Quakers making the Scriptures a "secondary rule subordinate to the Spirit." Wesley was convinced the Spirit of God would never lead in personal experience contrary to the Word of God. As such, his constant counsel as exhibited in *A Plain Account of Christian Perfection* is to:

> Try all things by the written Word, and let all bow down before it. You are in danger of enthusiasm every hour if you depart ever so little from the Scripture; yea, or from the plain, literal meaning of any text, taken in connexion with the context.[48]

There were a number of occasions when Wesley found it necessary to speak out against those who placed experience and impressions above the

---

[45] William Arnett, "John Wesley-Man of One Book," (Ph.D. diss., Drew University, 1954).
[46] *Letters* 5:259.
[47] Ibid., 2:117.
[48] John Wesley. *A Plain Account of Christian Perfection.* (Kansas City, Mo.: Beacon Hill Press, 1971) 97.

Scriptures. The Mystics, who had such a great impression early in Wesley's life, were viewed later as a danger because of this misplaced emphasis.

Though his own salvation was advanced by his contact with the Moravians, John Wesley later wrote to Charles in 1741 "As yet I dare in no wise join with the Moravians: (1) Because their general scheme is Mystical, not scriptural, refined in every point above what is written."[49]

On occasion Wesley spoke against individual Mystic writers such as Baron Swedenborg's "dreams and reveries, for experience was not to be an independent source of doctrine."[50] In his article "Thoughts on the Writings of Baron Swedenborg" (1782), after speaking of some of his dreams Wesley states, "31. Having now taken a sufficient view of the Baron's reveries, let us turn to the oracles of God. What saith the Scripture?"[51]

In another instance Wesley criticizes Madame Guyon for relying on her "inspiration" rather than the written Word in his "An Extract of the Life of Madam Guyon" (1776):

> 7. The grand source of all her mistakes was this, the not being guided by the written Word. She did not take the Scripture for the rule of her actions; at most it was but the secondary rule. Inward impressions, which she called inspirations, were her primary rule. The written Word was not a lantern unto her feet, a light in all her paths. No; she followed another light, the outward light of her confessors and the inward light of her own spirit.[52]

In his *Journal* of July 13, 1741, Wesley speaks of an incident of enthusiasm where some were treating impressions above the Word of God. He moved swiftly to disown that move:

> . . . for a spirit of enthusiasm was breaking in upon many, who charged their own impressions on the 'will of God' and that not written, but 'impressed on their hearts.' If these impressions be received as the rule of action instead of the written Word, I know nothing so wicked or absurd but we may fall into, and that without remedy.[53]

For Wesley enthusiasm, which might be defined as allowing one's religious experience to run contrary to the Written Word of God, was a dan-

---

[49] *Letters* 1:353.
[50] William Arnett, "John Wesley-A Man of One Book," (Ph.D. diss., Drew University, 1954).
[51] *Works* 13:447.
[52] Ibid., 14:277.
[53] Reginald Ward and Richard Heitzenrater. *The Works of John Wesley. Vol. 19.* (Nashville, Tenn.: Abingdon Press, 1990) 205.

gerous trend. His teaching upon experience was carefully balanced, so that its claims were not overemphasized, but were always subjected to the correction of the Scripture. For Wesley, to depart from the Word of God, even based on one's own religious experience, was to depart from God. Consider his comments in his *Journal* of 1778 concerning one Mr. Marsay:

> A remarkable piece was put into my hands, the Life of Mr. Marsay, and I saw no reason to alter the judgment which I had formed of him forty years ago. He was a man of uncommon understanding and greatly devoted to God. But he was a consummate enthusiast. Not the Word of God, but his own imaginations which he took for divine inspirations, were the sole rule both of his words and actions. Hence arose his marvelous instability, taking such huge strides backwards and forwards; hence his frequent darkness of soul for when he departed from God's Word, God departed from him.[54]

In closing, Wesley did more, as has been stated before, to include experience as a confirmatory factor in biblical interpretation than perhaps any other biblical scholar. At the same time, he would not allow experience to contradict Scriptures. As he states in a letter to John Glass in 1757:

> But will any lover of the Scriptures allow the possibility of this that the Spirit should ever speak a syllable to any man beside what He publicly speaks there? (the Bible)[55]

No, as important as experience was, Wesley shows in a letter to John Smith in 1745 that he would never allow:

> (2) An imagination that a doctrine not provable by Scripture might-nevertheless be proved by miracles. I believe not. I receive the written Word of God as the whole and sole rule of my faith.[56]

The Use of Tradition in Interpreting Scripture

In "Farther Thoughts on Separation From the Church" (1789) Wesley states:

> From a child I was taught to love and reverence the Scriptures, the oracles of God and next to these to esteem the primitive Fathers, the writers of the three first centuries. Next after the primitive Church,

---

[54] Ibid., 23:98.
[55] *Letters* 3:234.
[56] Frank Baker. *The Works of John Wesley. Vol. 26.* (Oxford, England: Oxford University Press, 1982) 155.

I esteemed our own, the Church of England, as the most scriptural national church in the world . . . 2. In this judgment and with this spirit I went to America, strongly attached to the Bible, the primitive Church, and the Church of England, from which I would not vary in one jot or tittle on any account whatever.[57]

The principle of "sola scriptura," did not necessitate the abandonment of the authority of the centuries of tradition of the church. For Wesley, Christian tradition was more than a curiosity or a source of illustrative materials. It was a living spring of Christian insight. Wesley, at one time, envisioned a uniformity of the Church Universal in the early Christian centuries which later study compelled him to discard in favor of a more fragmented development.[58] Still Wesley had a special appreciation for the positions of the early church. The Ante-Nicene Fathers Wesley believed to have particular value because of their proximity to Christ and the Apostles and because of the universal nature of the church in their time.[59] His views were a variation on the Anglican sense of the old Vincentian Canon, that the historical experience of the church, though fallible, is the better judge overall of Scripture meanings then later interpreters are likely to be.[60] Wesley remained quite committed throughout his life to the first principle from Deacon's book *Devotions:*

> The best method for all churches and Christians to follow, is to lay aside all modern hypotheses, customs and private opinions, and submit to all doctrines, practices, worship and discipline not of any particular, but of the ancient and universal church of Christ from the beginning to the end of the Fourth Century, which doctrine, practice, worship and discipline thus universally and constantly received could not possibly be derived from any other than the apostolic authority.[61]

Wesley introduced extracts from the Ante-Nicene Fathers in his Christian history and claimed these writings were to be valued just below the Scriptures themselves as "containing pure, uncorrupted doctrine

---

[57] Rupert Davies. *The Works of John Wesley. Vol. 9.* (Nashville, Tenn.: Abingdon Press, 1989) 538.

[58] Frank Baker. *John Wesley and the Church of England.* (London, England: Epworth Press, 1970) 33.

[59] Wayne McCowen and James Massey. *Interpreting God's Word for Today: An Inquiry Into Hermeneutics From a Biblical, Theological Perspective.* (Anderson, Ind.: Warner Press, Inc., 1982) 28.

[60] Albert Outler. *John Wesley.* (Oxford, England: Oxford University Press, 1964) 59.

[61] Frank Baker. *John Wesley and the Church of England.* (London, England: Epworth Press, 1970) 33.

of Christ, and so inspired as to be scarce capable of mistake."[62] Wesley, especially during his days at Oxford, earned the nickname, "Mr. Primitive Christianity."[63]

Wesley found the Fathers helpful in interpreting Scripture, and was quite unsympathetic to those who did not take them seriously in the history of biblical interpretation. This appreciation was not limited only to the Ante-Nicene Period. As has been shown, Wesley had great respect for later Church Fathers as well as leaders among the Reformers and biblical scholars of his time. He did not hesitate in difficult passages to compare his views with what others had written. When he was accused of setting aside all ancient and modern authorities he responded in a letter to William Dodd in 1756:

> 13. In your last paragraph you say, 'You set aside all authority, ancient and modern.' Sir, who told you so? I never did; it never entered my thoughts. Who it was who gave you that rule I know not; but my Father gave it to me thirty years ago, (I mean concerning reverence to the ancient Church and our own), and I have endeavored to walk by it to this day. But, I try every Church and every doctrine by the Bible. This is the Word by which we are judged in that day.[64]

Instead of ignoring the ancient traditions and authorities, Wesley makes it clear in the preface to his *Sermons* that:

> If any doubt still remains, I consult those who are experienced in the things of God, and then the writings whereby, being dead, they yet speak. And what I thus learn, that I teach.[65]

Wesley's respect for tradition was so great early in his ministry that there was a time when he placed the writings of the first four centuries almost on the same level as the authority of Scripture. Wesley apparently had been influenced by William Cave's *Primitive Christianity*. However, during his missionary stay in Georgia his view began to change.[66]

While in Georgia Wesley began to read William Beveridge's *Synodikon* and he became convinced that much of the early church tradition was not

---

[62] *Works* 14:223.

[63] Frank Baker. *John Wesley and the Church of England.* (London, England: Epworth Press, 1970) 34.

[64] *Letters* 3:172.

[65] Albert Outler. *The Works of John Wesley. Vol. 1.* (Nashville, Tenn.: Abingdon Press, 1984) 106.

[66] Allen Coppedge. *John Wesley and Theological Debate.* (Wilmore, Ky.: Wesley Heritage Press, 1987) 66.

of apostolic origin, and that he could not place church tradition, even that which was closest to the New Testament Church, on the same level of authority as Scripture. Note Wesley's change of thought in his *Journal* from September 13, 1736:

> We began reading Bishop Beveridge's *Pandectae Canonum Conciliorum*. Nothing could so effectively have convinced me that both Particular and General Councils may error and have erred; and of the infinite difference there is between the decisions of the wisest men and those of the Holy Ghost recorded in His Word.[67]

By the time Wesley returned from Georgia in 1738 he rejoiced that he had been delivered from error:

> 1. by making antiquity a co-ordinate (rather than a subordinate) rule with Scripture.
>
> 2. by admitting several doubtful writings as undoubted evidence of antiquity.
>
> 3. by extending antiquity too far, even to the middle or end of the fourth century.
>
> 4. by believing more practices to have been universal in the ancient church than were ever so.
>
> 5. by not considering that the decrees of one provincial synod could bind only that province and the decrees of a general synod only those provinces whose representatives met therein;
>
> 6. by not considering that most of these decrees were adopted to particular times and occasions, and consequently when those occasions ceased, must cease to bind those provinces.[68]

Thus it is clear that Wesley was willing to check his interpretations of Scripture with the great expositors of the church, but he was not willing to let them be the final authority. On a number of occasions Wesley warned against overemphasizing the teaching of the church against the authority of Scripture. In his essay "Roman Catholicism and Reply" he states:

> . . . as long as we have the Scripture, the Church is to be referred to the Scripture and not the Scripture to the Church; and that, as the Scripture is the best expounder of itself, so the best way to know

---

[67] Reginald Ward and Richard Heitzenrater. *The Works of John Wesley. Vol. 18.* (Nashville, Tenn.: Abingdon Press, 1988) 422.

[68] Ibid., 213.

whether anything be of divine authority, is to apply ourselves to the Scripture.[69]

Again he warns in his essay "The Advantages of the Members of the Church of England Over Those of the Church of Rome":

> I lay down this undoubted truth—The more the doctrine of any Church agrees with the Scripture, the more readily it ought to be received. And, on the other hand, the more the doctrine of any Church differs from the Scripture, the greater cause we have to doubt it.[70]

In closing, Wesley clearly recognized the value of church tradition in interpreting the Scripture, particularly the teachings of the Ante-Nicene Fathers. As Wesley advises Dr. Middleton in a letter in 1749:

> (2) The esteeming of the writings of the first three centuries not equally, but next to the Scriptures, never carried any man yet into dangerous errors, nor probably ever will. But it has brought many out of dangerous errors and particularly out of the errors of Popery.[71]

However, as we see in this quotation from "Popery Calmly Considered," the practice of placing the tradition of the church on an equal basis with the Scripture, must be excluded:

> The Scripture therefore, being delivered by men divinely inspired, is a rule sufficient of itself: So, it neither needs, nor is capable of, any farther addition.[72]

Concluding Thoughts on John Wesley and the Quadrilateral

In the Wesleyan Quadrilateral of Scripture, reason, experience and tradition, Wesley sought a balance when considering the issue of authority. While it is clear that for Wesley Scripture was the supreme, foundational authority, he had no wish that the other sources of authority be neglected. Instead, he wished to make Scripture the central focus, and use reason, tradition and experience as interpretive tools to understand the Bible better. In seeking a balance among these various forms of authority Wesley hoped to avoid the extremes of rationalism and empiricism on the one hand, and

---

[69] *Works* 10:94.
[70] Ibid., 133.
[71] *Letters* 2:325.
[72] *Works* 10:141.

mystical enthusiasm on the other. For Wesley, reason, tradition and experience were not to be considered equal to the authority of Scripture. However, to ignore them would be to sacrifice very important tools that could help one interpret the Bible more effectively. In any effort to interpret Scripture, who would not benefit greatly from an acquaintance with the wisdom of the early church, training in the use of reason and logical analysis, and a vital inward faith that makes the interpretation of Scripture a real personal study rather than merely a dry academic exercise? For accurate biblical interpretation, it is not the Bible "or" tradition, reason and experience. It must instead be the Bible better interpreted by the proper use of reason, tradition and experience.

Was Wesley a Critical Scholar?

After a careful analysis of Wesley's interpretive methods I believe it would be well to close this section by asking the question, "was Wesley a critical scholar?" E. H. Sugden, in the introduction to *The Standard Sermons of John Wesley*, makes the following comment, "Wesley was a critic, both higher and lower, before those much misunderstood terms were invented."[73] After studying Wesley's writings, I believe Sugden may have gone too far. I believe it would be safe to say that Wesley was a lower or textual critic, but not a higher critic.

John Wesley was a man of his time and his interpretive methods should be judged against an eighteenth century time frame rather than against the background of twentieth century higher criticism. It seems common, from my research, to dismiss Wesley's reliance on the authority of the Scripture, and his literalism, as mere indications that he lived in a pre-critical era. R. Benjamin Garrison in his study "Vital Interaction: Scripture and Experience" records that "Wesley lived in pre-critical times,"[74] and Wayne McCowen wrote in *Interpreting God's Word for Today*, "Wesley's biblical hermeneutic was essentially pre-critical."[75] It is true that Wesley lived at the beginning of the critical era, but I believe that it would be more accurate to describe Wesley as "pre-higher critical" rather than "pre-critical."

---

[73] *Sermons* 1:21.

[74] Benjamin Garrison, "Vital Interaction: Scripture and Experience, John Wesley's Doctrine of Authority," *Religion In Life 25.* (1956) 564.

[75] Wayne McCowen and James Massey. *Interpreting God's Word for Today: An Inquiry Into Hermeneutics From a Biblical, Theological Perspective.* (Anderson, Ind.: Warner Press, Inc., 1982) 128.

It should not be assumed that Wesley had no familiarity with the beginnings of modern higher criticism. Wesley was a voracious reader, and Richard Simon, identified as the Father of Biblical Criticism, was writing at the end of the seventeenth century. Jean Astruc in 1753 began the onset of Pentateuchal criticism.[76] His writings seemed to have little effect on Wesley's generation however. The storms had not yet broken, but the Bible was already under attack, and Wesley's belief in the reliability of Scripture was tested by the rationalistic climate of his age.

It should not be imagined that Wesley hid himself somewhere and was not aware of the movements in biblical studies. With the authority of Scripture as his standard, Wesley was ready to keep abreast of the most recent research. According to Dr. A. Skevington Wood, the Reformation had led to a renaissance of biblical studies and it has been claimed that it was pursued in the seventeenth century with an intensity unequalled before or since. Some of this carried over into the eighteenth century and manifested itself in the field of textual criticism and exegesis.[77]

In considering *The Explanatory Notes Upon the New Testament* we discovered Wesley's great debt to the Lutheran scholar Johannes Albrecht Bengel. Bengel was a brilliant pioneer in the realm of textual criticism. His text and critical apparatus of the New Testament published in 1734 marked the beginning of the modern scientific approach.[78] Wesley hailed Bengel as "the great light in the Christian world," and proceeded to draw freely from his resource.[79] Bengel was a purely textual or lower critic who avoided the questions of historical or higher criticism, particularly those of the genuineness of texts. He took the authenticity of a text for granted once he passed beyond the verbal variations.

Although Wesley might not be considered an expert in textual criticism, he was willing to make use of the critical tools available to him. He was a first rate Greek scholar, and was not adverse to correcting the text of the Authorized Version.[80] Wesley's method of interpretation also shows that he recognized Scripture as amenable to some kinds of analysis which one would apply to a merely human book. For instance, he recognized that

---

[76] A. Skevington Wood. *The Burning Heart*. (Grand Rapids, Mich.: Wm B. Eerdmanns Pub. Co., 1967) 217.

[77] Ibid., 216.

[78] Ibid., 217.

[79] John Wesley. *Explanatory Notes Upon the New Testament*. (London, England: Epworth Press, 1948) 7.

[80] Duncan Ferguson, "John Wesley on the Scripture: The Hermeneutics of Pietism," *Methodist History 22*. (1984) 243.

biblical studies were conditioned by time and culture, and that any correct interpretation, of any statement, demanded taking both of these into account. For example, in "An Answer to the Rev. Mr. Church's Remarks" (1745) he affirms:

> I apply no Scripture phrase either to myself or any other without carefully considering both the original meaning and the secondary sense, wherein (allowing for different times and circumstances), it may be applied to ordinary Christians.[81]

Also, Wesley recognized that following plain rules of grammar and syntax most often gave the meaning of biblical statements without recourse to esoteric spiritualizations. He also knew, as described in chapter eight, that to arrive at the plain meaning of a passage, one had to take into account not only the immediate context, but also the entire biblical context. Wesley had a feel for the wholeness of biblical theology, realizing that the Scriptures were not a group of unrelated statements.[82] William Pellowe described Wesley well when he said, "His method was biblical-expository, not text expository."[83]

A good example of Wesley's usage of this methodology would be his comments on predestination in his sermon "Free Grace" (1739). Wesley felt the Calvinists built this doctrine by isolating a few passages and building too much out of too little. He labeled this dogma "the horrible decree of predestination" and says in his sermon "Free Grace" (1739):

> 20. And as this doctrine manifestly and directly tends to overthrow the whole Christian revelation, so it does the same thing, by plain consequence in making that revelation contradict itself. For it is grounded on such an interpretation of some texts (more or few it matters not) as flatly contradicts all other texts and indeed the whole scope and tenor of Scripture.[84]

> But you say you will 'prove it by Scripture.' Hold! What will you prove by Scripture? That God is worse than the devil? It cannot be. Whatever that Scripture proves, it never can prove this. Whatever its true meaning be, this cannot be its true meaning. Do you ask, 'What is its true meaning then?' If I say, 'I know not,' you have gained nothing. For there are many Scriptures the true sense where-

---

[81] Rupert Davies. *The Works of John Wesley. Vol. 9.* (Nashville, Tenn.: Abingdon Press, 1989) 116.

[82] John Oswalt, "John Wesley's Use of the Old Testament in His Doctrinal Teachings," *Wesleyan Theological Journal 12* (1977) 40.

[83] Ibid., 41.

[84] Albert Outler. *The Works of John Wesley. Vol. 3.* (Nashville, Tenn.: Abingdon Press, 1986) 552.

of neither you nor I shall know till death is swallowed up in victory. But this I know, better it were to say it had no sense at all, than to say it had such a sense as this. It cannot mean, whatever it mean besides, that the God of truth is a liar. Let it mean what it will it cannot mean that the Judge of all the world is unjust. No Scripture can mean that God is not love, or that His mercy is not over all His works. That is, whatever it prove beside, no Scripture can prove predestination.[85]

A good example of Wesley's use of textual criticism would be his comments on I John 5:7 in his sermon "On the Trinity" (1775). Here Wesley comments:

> 5. 'As they lie in the text'-but here arises a question. Is that text genuine? Was it originally written by the Apostle or inserted in later ages? Many have doubted of this; and in particular that great light of the Christian church, lately removed to the church above, Bengelius- the most pious, most judicious, and the most laborious of all modern commentators on the New Testament. For some time he stood in doubt of its authenticity, because it is wanting in many of the ancient copies. But his doubts were removed by three considerations. (1). That though it is wanting in many copies yet it is found in more, abundantly more and those copies of the greatest authority. (2). That it is cited by a whole train of ancient writers from the time of St. John, to that of Constantine. This argument is conclusive; for they could not have cited it, had it not been then in the sacred canon. (3). That we can easily account for its being after that time wanting in many copies when we remember Constantine's successor was a zealous Arian who used every means to promote his bad cause, to spread Arianism throughout the empire: in particular the erasing of this text out of as many copies as fell into his hands.[86]

Thus, while one may not always agree with Wesley's conclusions, it is clear he was not uncritical. He carefully examined each text, exhorting preachers to know Greek and Hebrew and something of the historical context. Wesley used textual criticism in order that the meaning of the text might be made "better, stronger, clearer, or more consistent with the context" and that the wording might be, "better, or nearer the original."[87] However, Wesley was not ready to agree with those who believed that the

---

[85] Ibid., 556.
[86] Ibid., 2:378–79.
[87] John Wesley. *Explanatory Notes Upon the New Testament.* (London, England: Epworth Press, 1948) 6.

Bible writers were human, and therefore that they made mistakes. As quoted earlier for Wesley, one mistake was the same as a thousand.[88] Wesley was ready to recognize the possibility of error in the sources used by Matthew as he admits in his comments on Matthew 1:1 and 2:6 in his *Explanatory Notes Upon the New Testament*. Thus, we again have evidence that Wesley could be classified as a lower (textual) critic. As stated by Dr. George Turner, "He readily adjusted his beliefs to the evidence, but he instinctively reacted against any rationalistic bias inimical to the evangelical faith."[89]

In conclusion, Wesley was not uncritical. However, I agree with Luke Keefer in his unpublished dissertation *John Wesley, Disciple of Early Christianity*, that Wesley resisted the trend toward the 'higher criticism' of the Bible. He made a conscious choice to reject the critical views which gained attention in his century. Wesley simply could not believe that modern interpreters, separated from the New Testament era by sixteen centuries knew the meaning of Scripture better than those who immediately followed the apostolic age. He did not believe that sceptical men in a fallen age should charge the apostles, who lived in the purist age of the church, with making mistakes.[90]

But believing all Scripture to be divinely inspired, and uniformly authoritative, Wesley seemed at times to feel the freedom to move all over the Bible, pulling verses out of context for the purpose of homiletics or the support of a favorite doctrine, such as Christian perfection. He was unhindered by questions such as dates and authorship. He recognized a broad and important distinction between the years prior to the coming of Christ and those which succeeded it, but for the most part Ezekiel would serve as well Matthew, Zechariah as well as Paul.[91]

When Wesley used Scripture apologetically he was inclined to cite proof texts rather than surveying a general tenor of a particular book. This had been a universal practice for two centuries of Protestant thought. Scriptures were surveyed deductively or topically, that is a proposition was made and texts were cited in defense of it.[92]

---

[88] *Journals* 6:117.

[89] John Walvoord. *Inspiration and Interpretation*. (Grand Rapids, Mich.: Wm B. Eerdmanns Pub. Co., 1957) 162.

[90] Luke Keefer, "John Wesley, Disciple of Early Christianity," (Ph.D. diss., Temple University, 1982).

[91] W. E. Sangster. *The Path to Perfection*. (Nashville, Tenn.: Abingdon Press, 1943) 36.

[92] John Walvoord. *Inspiration and Interpretation*. (Grand Rapids, Mich.: Wm B Eerdmanns Pub. Co., 1957) 169.

Wesley could sometimes be accused of having a non-historical view of the Bible by failing to grasp the biblical writer's own thoughts. At times he failed to relate proof texts to context. According to George Turner, this is because Wesley was often inclined to look at Scripture theologically, rather than exegetically. He was inclined to interpret a disputed passage by the general tenor of Scripture without limiting himself to a literal historical interpretation. He was as apt to explain an Old Testament passage by an appeal to Paul as to consider it in the light of its own context.[93] A good example of his use of a text without regard to the context would be his sermon "Catholic Spirit" (1750). His text, II Kings 10:15, is used merely as a springboard. In fact, the Reverend Mr. Clark of Hollymount criticized Wesley's sermon saying "Your proposition and observations have no more foundation in the text than in the first chapter of Genesis."[94] Wesley used the text to support his theme, though this use of the text as a pretext was not his common practice.

In spite of these problems, a study of Wesley's use of the Bible does not give the impression that he is ignoring contrary evidence or bending ambiguous passages to his purpose. On the whole, the evidence is handled with a remarkable degree of honest mindedness. In most instances it is not apparent that a moral concern or a theological intent led Wesley astray or warped his judgment.[95] Seemingly his intuitive good sense, Christian character, knowledge of the traditional interpretation of the church, and a scholarly desire for truth gave him an interpretive balance. As stated, interpretive violations of the intent of Scripture were the exception not the rule in his work. As stated quite cogently by Duncan Ferguson, "A lesser person than Wesley using the same hermeneutical principles unchecked by the historical method might miss the meaning of Scripture."[96]

---

[93] Ibid., 170.

[94] William Arnett, "John Wesley-A Man of One Book," (Ph.D. diss., Drew University, 1954).

[95] John Walvoord. *Inspiration and Interpretation*. (Grand Rapids, Mich.: Wm B. Eerdmanns Pub. Co., 1957) 170.

[96] Duncan Ferguson, "John Wesley on the Scripture: The Hermeneutics of Pietism," *Methodist History 22* (1984) 245.

10

Closing Thoughts

As this consideration of John Wesley and his views of the Bible draws to a close, one point is abundantly clear. For Wesley, unless the Bible is studied and applied God's message to mankind will be wasted. Therefore, before I draw some conclusions about Wesley and the Scripture, I propose quoting Wesley concerning the relevance and the practice of effective Bible study.

Wesley's Advice for Bible Study

John Wesley outlines his approach to Bible study quite clearly in the preface of his *Explanatory Notes Upon the Old Testament:*

> This is the way to understand the things of God. Meditate thereon day and night 'so shall you attain the best knowledge' even to 'know the only true God and Jesus Christ whom he hath sent.' And this knowledge will lead you 'to love Him because he hath first loved us.' Yea, 'to love the Lord Your God with all your heart, and with all your soul, and with all your mind, and with all your strength.' Will there not then be all 'that mind in you which was also in Christ Jesus?' And in consequence of this while you joyfully experience all the holy tempers described in this book, you will likewise be outwardly 'holy as He that hath called you is holy in all manner of conversation.'
>
> 18. If you desire to read the Scripture in such a manner as may most effectively answer this end, would it not be advisable: (1) To set apart a little time if you can every morning and evening for that purpose. (2) At each time if you have leisure to read a chapter out of the Old and one out of the New Testament. If you cannot do this, take a single chapter or a part of one. (3) To read this with a

single eye, to know the whole will of God, and a fixed resolution to do it. In order to do his will, you should: (4) Have a constant eye to the analogy of faith, the connexion and harmony there is between those grand fundamental doctrines, original sin, justification by faith, the new birth, inward and outward holiness. (5) Serious and earnest prayer should be constantly used before we consult the oracles of God seeing 'Scripture can only be understood through the same Spirit whereby it is given.' Our reading should likewise be closed with prayer, that what we read may be written on our hearts. (6) It might also be of use if, while we read we were frequently to pause and examine ourselves by what we read both with regard to our heart's and lives. This would furnish us with matters of praise where we found God has enabled us to conform to His blessed will, and matter of humiliation and prayer, where we were conscious of having fallen short. And whatever light you then receive should be used to the uttermost and that immediately. Let there be no delay. Whatever you resolve begin to execute the first moment you can. So shall you find this word to be indeed the power of God unto present and eternal salvation.[1]

In considering this long quotation, it appears that Wesley's advice could actually be summed up in three basic principles; preparation, interpretation, and application. First, to study the Bible the reader needs to prepare himself. Wesley's advice is to set aside a period of time in the morning and evening for Bible study. In surveying Wesley's *Journal* this was clearly a daily discipline for him. He must have read through the Bible many times, and as I have mentioned, did much of his New Testament study in the original language. Careful, consistent study in the Scripture characterized the daily discipline of Wesley. The result was Wesley's thought and language being interwoven with Scripture.[2] It was Wesley's desire that not only he, but all his followers, would set aside time and dedicate themselves to direct, personal study of the Bible. This desire is made clear in his preface to *The Explanatory Notes Upon the Old Testament*:

> I design only like the hand of a dial to point everyman to this, not to take up his mind with something else, how excellent soever: but to keep his eye fixed upon the naked Bible, that he may read and hear it with understanding. I say again (and desire it may be well observed that none may expect what they will not find). It is not

---

[1] John Wesley. *Explanatory Notes upon the Old Testament*. (Salem, Ohio: Schmul Publishers, 1975) 9.

[2] Wayne McCowen and James Massey. *Interpreting God's Word for Today: An Inquiry Into Hermeneutics From a Biblical, Theological Perspective*. (Anderson, Ind.: Warmer Press, 1982) 3.

my design to write a book which a man may read separate from the Bible, but barely assist those who fear God, in hearing and reading the Bible itself by showing the natural sense of every part, in as few and plain words as I can.[3]

Another aspect of preparation for Bible study is that "serious and earnest prayer should be constantly used before we consult the Oracles of God." Both the reader and the Scripture should be bathed in prayer since "the Scripture can only be understood through the same Spirit in which it is given." Also prayer should be raised at the end of the study so what has been read "may be written on our hearts."[4]

Another interesting preparation for the study of Scripture that Wesley would probably have encouraged, that is a little different than the normal advice one might receive, would be the singing of hymns. There were hymns written and included in the Methodist Hymnal that were classified to be sung "before reading the Scripture." In the hymns, the emphasis once again is made, that the key to the Sacred Book is that the Holy Spirit Himself must take away the veil, so that literally it is re-revelation.[5] Remember, the reading of the Scripture was based on two-fold inspiration. As Wesley explained in his comments upon II Timothy 3:16 in his *Explanatory Notes Upon the New Testament*, "The Spirit of God not only once inspired those who wrote it, but continually inspires, supernaturally assists those who read it with earnest prayer."[6]

At this point allow me to share selected verses from a selection of these hymns to be sung "before reading Scripture":

HYMN 85
1. Come Holy Ghost our hearts inspire,
    Let us thine influence prove,
   Source of the old prophetic fire,
    Fountain of Life and Love.

---

[3] John Wesley. *Explanatory Notes Upon the Old Testament.* (Salem, Ohio: Schmul Publishers, 1975) viii.

[4] Ibid., 9.

[5] Franz Hildebrandt. *The Works of John Wesley. Vol. 7.* (Nashville, Tenn.: Abingdon Press, 1983) 178.

[6] John Wesley. *Explanatory Notes Upon the New Testament.* (London, England: Epworth Press, 1948) 794.

2. Come Holy Ghost (for moved by thee
      The prophet wrote and spoke)
   Unlock the truth, thyself the key,
      Unseal the Sacred Book.[7]

Hymn 86

2. While in Thy Word we search for Thee,
      (We search with trembling awe),
   Open our eyes, and let us see,
      The wonders of the law.

3. Now let our darkness comprehend,
      The light that shines so clear,
   Now the revealing Spirit send,
      And give us ears to hear.[8]

Hymn 87

1. Inspirer of the ancient seers,
      Who wrote from thee the sacred page,
   The same through all succeeding years,
      To us in our degenerate age,
   The Spirit of Thy Word impart,
      And breathe the life into our heart.

2. While now Thine Oracles we read,
      With earnest prayer and strong desire,
   O let Thy Spirit from Thee proceed,
      Our souls to awaken and inspire,
   Our weakness help, and darkness chase,
      And guide us by the light of grace.[9]

Hymn 247

1. Spirit of truth essential God,
      Who didst Thy ancient saint inspire,
   Shed in their hearts, Thy love abroad,
      And touch their hallowed lips with fire,
   Our God from all eternity,
      World without end, we worship Thee.

---

[7] Franz Hildebrandt. *The Works of John Wesley. Vol. 7.* (Nashville, Tenn.: Abingdon Press, 1983) 185.

[8] Ibid., 185–86.

[9] Ibid., 186–87.

2. Still we believe almighty Lord,
      Whose presence fills both earth and heaven,
   The meaning of the written Word,
      Is by Thy inspiration given,
   Thou only didst explain,
      The secret mind of God to man.

3. Come Thou divine interpreter,
      The Scriptures to our heart apply,
   And taught by Thee we God revere,
      Him in three persons magnify,
   In each the Triune God Adore,
      Who was and is forevermore.[10]

Wesley's second piece of advice for Bible study deals with interpretation. I do not wish to duplicate the information given in earlier chapters, but based upon this section from his *Explanatory Notes Upon the Old Testament,* we see a very sound method established. Wesley believed it was better to read longer (chapter length) passages of the Old and New Testaments. Read and interpret the text and then look to parallel passages with an eye always upon the analogy of faith. As was noted earlier, because of Wesley's understanding of revelation, he approached the Bible as a whole, interpreting it Scripture by Scripture with special attention to doctrinal teaching.

Wesley's final call is to make application an essential aspect of Bible study. As Wesley states:

> Read this with a single eye, to know the whole will of God, and a fixed resolution to do it . . . whatever light you then receive should be used to the uttermost and that immediately. Let there be no delay. Whatever you resolve begin to execute the first moment you can.[11]

For Wesley prompt and total obedience to the light was the immediate consequence of Bible Study. As stated by Dr. George Turner, "It was the characteristic of the early Methodists to proceed on the conviction that obedience to the will of God must precede and occupy mastery of the Bible.[12]

---

[10] Ibid., 388–89.

[11] John Wesley. *Explanatory Notes Upon the Old Testament.* (Salem, Ohio: Scmul Publishers, 1975) ix.

[12] John Walvoord. *Inspiration and Interpretation.* (Grand Rapids, Mich.: Wm B. Eerdmanns Pub. Co., 1957) 174.

Repeating an earlier quotation from Dr. Melvin Dieter, "Wesley would simply say that any pattern of biblical interpretation which does not have the practical results as its immediate goal is suspect."[13]

Final Thoughts on Wesley's Views of Scripture

In the introduction I outlined a number of purposes that I hoped to accomplish. Now, in the closing sections, I wish to consider whether I have accomplished these purposes. Finally, I will finish by offering some conclusions.

As my first area of consideration I proposed, in light of the current debate over the Bible in Christian scholarship, that it would be well, as stated by Daryl McCarthy, "to demonstrate in clear terms and with close reference to his own writings, what actually was Wesley's view of the Scriptures."[14] To accomplish this purpose it was necessary to study Wesley's own writings as a primary source, as well as secondary authorities in reference to Wesley's writings and views. A number of questions needed to be asked such as, what were the influences that shaped Wesley's view of Scripture? What were Wesley's views on authority, inspiration, and infallibility? How did he use the Scripture in his ministries? How did he interpret the Bible? I believe all of these questions have been carefully considered and to a large extent answered.

In my effort to answer the proposed questions, I discovered many books and articles that emphasized various aspects of the relationship between Wesley and Scripture. There were studies that considered one or more of the following areas, such as his family, the Mystics, the Church Fathers, and the Church of England and the influence they might have had upon his views. Other works spoke of Wesley's use of the Bible in his various ministries, or his views of subjects such as infallibility or inspiration. However, it was my desire to attempt an overview of John Wesley's view of Scripture. The result of this research has shown that Wesley was nurtured in a family and church background with a great love and reverence of Scripture. Without question Wesley's high view of Scripture was fostered by his home life, his devotion to the Church of England, his contact with the Mystics, his interest in the Primitive Church, and his own personal experiences in Georgia and at Aldersgate.

As a result of all these influences Wesley emerged in his own words as a "Man of One Book," a "Bible Bigot." As simplistic as it may sound, this

---

[13] Melvin Dieter, "Musings," *Wesleyan Theological Society 14* (1979) 1.

[14] Daryl McCarthy, "Early Wesleyan Views of Scripture," *Wesleyan Theological Society 16* (1981) 95.

Oxford Don, fluent and well read in many languages, publisher of over 400 books himself, depended upon, bowed down before, only one authority, the Word of God. The Scriptures alone were Wesley's only adequate and ultimate source of authority for doctrine, preaching, teaching and life. He based his convictions first on the Bible. All controversies, all judgments were to be tried at the scriptural court of inquiry. This did not eliminate the importance of reason, tradition, or experience, but they were certainly secondary to Scripture.

This total dependence was based upon his view that "all Scripture was given by inspiration of God, (consequently all Scripture is infallibly true)."[15] The Bible was God's message to man. Wesley always approached the Scriptures with humility, realizing his own fallibility, never with a stance of intellectual arrogance. Instead he wrote:

> Would to God that all the party names and unscriptural phrases and forms which have divided the Christian world were forgot, and that we might agree to sit down together, as humble, loving disciples, at the feet of our common Master, to hear His Word, to imbibe His Spirit, and to transcribe His life in our own.[16]

This is certainly a worthy sentiment. However, it might be viewed as rather unrealistic considering Wesley's debates over issues such as Mysticism, Catholicism, and predestination.

Perhaps even more than by what he said about the Bible we can see Wesley's faith in Scripture by the way the Bible "became the source of his spiritual life, guide of his conduct, authority of his ministry, sole standard of truth, ultimate judge of human destiny and instruction."[17] Actions speak louder than words. Wesley never left any doubt that the foundation of his ministry from beginning to end was the Word of God. He showed his faith in the Scriptures by giving his life to bring the light of the Word to men and women who sat in darkness. More than his words, it was this practical use of the Bible in every aspect of his teaching and preaching, in every element of his ministry that proved how totally Wesley relied upon the absolute authority and total reliability of the Word of God.

At the same time it should be recognized that Wesley had many gifts and graces. He had boundless energy and unusual discipline. From a Christian viewpoint one might suggest that God was with Wesley and

---

[15] Albert Outler. *The Works of John Wesley. Vol. 1.* (Nashville, Tenn.: Abingdon Press, 1984) 388.

[16] John Wesley. *Explanatory Notes Upon the Old Testament.* (London, England: Epworth Press, 1948) 8.

[17] John Hannah. *Inerrancy and the Church.* (Chicago, Ill.: Moody Press, 1984) 234.

blessed his work. However, one critical point must not be overlooked. Wesley had a tremendous confidence in the Word that he proclaimed. He had no question about his authority, mission or message. For Wesley, the infallible Word of God was the gospel of Jesus Christ. It was "the power of God unto salvation" (Romans 1:16), and "woe is me if I preach not the gospel" (I Corinthians 9:16).

The Wesleyan Revival was in many ways a restoration of emphasis on the plain Word of God which led to the founding of a movement and a zeal to evangelize the world. There was a difference between Wesley's approach and the approach of some other movements of his day, such as the Quakers. Andrew McGiffert explains this difference when he states that for the Methodists:

> The authority of the Bible was made more of by them than for a long time before. In opposition to the current recognition of the sufficiency of human reason, they delighted to belittle it, and to denounce its claims as presumptuous and irreligious. But they appealed in opposition to it, not to the Spirit in the hearts of all believers, as the Quakers did, but to the written and infallible Word . . . to venture to criticise its statements, to question its authority, to raise doubts as to the authenticity of any part, to set one's own judgment above it, to treat it as any way ill-adapted to present conditions, all this was intolerable to a genuine evangelical.[18]

When Wesley preached or taught he expected the Bible to speak to those willing to examine themselves and open themselves to its message. He expected the Word of God to influence men and women with regard to their piety, experientially and practically. He believed that the Bible gave practical precepts and specific guidelines for daily living and decision making. He felt the Bible spoke to men experientially in that a proper understanding would create peace and joy in the believer's heart. Finally, piety was created as the study of God's Word led Christians along the path toward holiness. Wesley had a firm confidence that God the Holy Spirit would use the pages of Scripture to speak directly to men's hearts.[19] According to Prof. James S. Stewart of Edinburgh, "The first axiom of effective evangelism is that the evangelist must be sure of his message. Any haziness or hesitation there is fatal."[20] No man could have been more certain about what he had to say, for

---

[18] Ibid., 33.

[19] Duncan Ferguson, "John Wesley on the Scripture: The Hermeneutics of Pietism," *Methodist History* 22 (1984) 238.

[20] A. Skevington Wood. *The Burning Heart*. (Grand Rapids: Wm B. Eerdmanns Pub. Co., 1967) 209.

it was burned into his mind and heart by his dramatic, personal experience. I do not believe that any of these statements, which characterize Wesley's total dependence upon the Bible in every aspect of his life and ministry, have been overstated. The research outlined in previous chapters clearly substantiates these claims. However, the point might be made that Wesley's views on the Scripture might be valuable as a historical curiosity, but that they have no real relevance for today. Some might say Wesley's eighteenth century views of the Bible have no place in the twentieth century. The times are too different and Wesley's ideas are not really tenable today.

I believe that suggestion ignores some interesting comparisons. In some ways the eighteenth century of John Wesley shows similarities to the twentieth century, in relation to the church and the Bible. For example, in the eighteenth century the Bible was being under used by many people who did not see its relevance to their everyday lives. As was shown in chapter seven, the authority of the Bible was under rationalistic attack. It was being dissected by those who overused rationalism, in deism, and it was being misused by those who overemphasized experience, in mysticism. Also, many in the established church found it more convenient to modify the parts of the Scripture that spoke against their lifestyles. Instead, the Bible was watered down and made more palatable. Preaching the Word of God had become less and less an integral part of the worship experience in many churches and movements. Preaching had lost its fire, its zeal, its sense of urgency and authority. Instead, quoting William Lecky from his book *A History of England in the Eighteenth Century*:

> the more doctrinal aspects of religion were softened down or suffered silently to recede; and before the 18th century had much advanced the sermon had generally become mere moral essays characterized chiefly by a cold, good sense and appealed almost exclusively to prudential nature.[21]

Henry Rack in his book *Reasonable Enthusiast*, commenting on preaching in the early eighteenth century states:

> Morality, effort, duty were the watchwords, and the fact that bishops as distant from evangelicalism as Gibson and Secker found it necessary to warn their clergy against preaching mere morality without reference to the atonement suggests that evangelical com-

---

[21] William Lecky. *A History of England In the Eighteenth Century I*. (London, England: 1892) 84.

plaints about a 'religion of works' and 'Pelagianism' were not simply the product of excessive prejudice.[22]

It is not difficult to see a number of similarities between Wesley's time and today. We still live in a very rationalistic and scientific age which questions the authority, inspiration, infallibility and interpretation of the Bible. These debates go on constantly inside and outside the church. As was mentioned in the introduction, the relevance of the Bible to every day life seems to be a mystery or an absent element to many people in twentieth century society. Even in the church, on many fronts there seems to be less confidence in and less use of the Bible as the central authority for doctrine, beliefs and the daily practices of life.

It would be naive and simplistic to ignore all the intellectual developments which have occurred over the last two centuries. It cannot even be assumed that Wesley would approach the Bible today in quite the same way that he did in the eighteenth century. However, that does not mean there is no value, for denominations which trace their roots to Wesley and the Methodistic movement, in examining current denominational views on Scripture in the light of historic views.

For those interested in a balanced approach to theology, the Wesleyan Quadrilateral may be the answer. This balanced approach with Scripture seen as primary, but emphasizing the co-joint use of tradition, reason and experience, would avoid the excesses sometimes seen as religious movements swing one direction or the other. The deists and mystics of John Wesley's day might be seen as examples of overemphasizing rationalism on the one hand, and experience on the other. A balanced approach to authority would desire a reasonable faith, but not neglect the warm heart of experience. It would appreciate and wish to learn from the history, liturgy and creeds of the early church, yet have no desire to stifle creativity of expression. Commitment to the Quadrilateral would provide a balance that takes into account a familiarity with Scripture, a confidence in the faith of our fathers, a belief in rational analysis, and a vital faith that energizes.

A study of Wesley's view of Scripture reveals his love and commitment to the Word of God. Just as evident is his desire that others benefit from God's message to man, as he had. I close with Wesley's own comments on Deuteronomy 11:18 in his *Explanatory Notes Upon the Old Testament*, as he expresses not only his own personal desire, but his admonition for all men:

---

[22] Henry Rack. *Reasonable Enthusiast*. (Nashville, Tenn.: Abingdon Press, 1993) 21.

Closing Thoughts

1. Let our hearts be filled with the Word of God. Lay up these words in your hearts as in a store-house, to be used upon all occasions.

2. Let our eyes be fixed upon the Word of God. Bind them for a sign upon your hand which is always in view and as frontlets between your eyes, which you cannot avoid the sight of.

3. Let your tongues be employed about the Word of God, especially with our children who must be taught this, as far more needful than the rules of decency, or the calling they are to live by.[23]

---

[23] John Wesley. *Explanatory Notes Upon the Old Testament.* (Salem, Ohio: Schumul Publishers, 1975) 620.

Bibliography

Primary Sources

IN ANY study of John Wesley, the primary sources must be Wesley's own writings. These include his sermons, *Journal*, letters, hymns and various other works. There have been many editions of Wesley's works over the last two centuries. A tremendous resource now becoming available is *The Works of John Wesley* published by Abingdon Press. This splendid collection was originally begun by Oxford Press, but Abingdon Press undertook publication in 1984. Unfortunately, this collection is not complete. In an effort to take advantage of this latest addition to Wesley studies, I quote from this set whenever possible. As each volume has a different date and different editors, I include them individually in the bibliography. If a volume of letters, his *Journal* or works is not available in the Abingdon publication, I quote from traditional and classic sets. Again to facilitate readers who wish to check notations against the bibliography, I list these sets of works by Wesley by their editors to make them easier to differentiate:

Curnock, Nehemiah. *The Journals of the Rev. John Wesley A.M 8 vols.* London, England: Charles Kelly, nd.
Jackson, Thomas. *The Works of the Rev. John Wesley A.M. 13 vols.* London, England: John Mason, 1829.
Sugden, E. H. *The Standard Sermons of John Wesley.* 2 vols. London, England: Epworth Press, 1961.
Telford, John. *The Letters of the Rev. John Wesley A.M. 8 vols.* London, England: Epworth Press, 1931
Wesley, John. *Explanatory Notes Upon the New Testament.* London, England: Epworth Press, 1948.
Wesley, John. *John Wesley's New Testament.* Philadelphia, Pa.: John C. Winston Company, 1953.
Wesley, John. *A Plain Account of Christian Perfection.* Kansas City, Mo.: Beacon Hill Press, 1971.
Wesley, John. *Explanatory Notes Upon the Old Testament.* Salem, Ohio.: Schmul Publishers, 1975.

Bibliography

Secondary Sources

Althaus, Paul. *The Theology of Martin Luther.* Philadelphia, Pa.: Fortress Press, 1966.
Arnett, William. "John Wesley-A Man of One Book." Ph.D. diss., Drew University, 1954.
———. "A Study in John Wesley's Explanatory Notes Upon the Old Testament." *Wesleyan Theological Journal 8* (1973) 14–32.
———. "Wesley and the Bible." *Wesleyan Theological Journal 3* (1968) 3–9
Ayling, Stanley. *John Wesley.* Nashville, Tenn.: Abingdon Press, 1979.
Baines-Griffith, David. *Wesley the Anglican.* London, England: MacMillan and Co. Ltd., 1919.
Baker, Frank. *The Works of John Wesley. Vol. 25.* Oxford, England: Oxford University Press, 1980.
———. *The Works of John Wesley. Vol. 26* Oxford, England: Oxford University Press, 1982.
———. *John Wesley and the Church of England.* London, England: Epworth Press,1970.
———. "Wesley's Puritan Ancestry." *London Quarterly and Holborn Press* (1962) 180–6.
———. "A Study of John Wesley's Readings." *London Quarterly and Holborn Review* (1943) 140–45, 234–42.
Barbour, Hugh. *The Quakers in Puritan England.* New Haven, Conn.: Yale University Press, 1964.
Bengel, John Albrecht. *New Testament Word Studies Vols. 1–2.* Philadelphia, Pa.: Kregel Publications, 1971.
Blankenship, Paul. "The Significance of John Wesley's Abridgement of the Thirty-Nine Articles As Seen From His Deletions." *Methodist History 2* (1964) 35–47.
Boshear, Onva. "John Wesley Bookman: A Study of His Reading Interests in the 18th Century." Ph.D. diss., University of Michigan, 1972.
Bowen, Marjorie. *Wrestling Jacob.* London, England: William Hennemann Ltd., 1937.
Burtner, Robert and Chiles, Robert. *A Compend of Wesley's Theology.* Nashville, Tenn.: Abingdon Press, 1954.
By a Methodist Preacher. *John Wesley the Methodist.* New York, N.Y.: Methodist Book Concern, 1903.
Calvin, John. *Calvin's Commentary Vol. XXI.* Grand Rapids, Mich.: Baker Book House, 1979.
———. *A Compend of the Institutes of the Christian Religion.* Philadelphia, Pa.: Presbyterian Board of Christian Education, 1939.
Campbell, Ted. *John Wesley and Christian Antiquity.* Nashville, Tenn.: Kingswood Books, 1991.
Cannon, William Ragsdale. *The Theology of John Wesley.* Nashville, Tenn.: Abingdon Press, 1946.
Carter, Charles. *A Contemporary Wesleyan Theology.* Grand Rapids, Mich.: Francis Asbury Press, 1983.
Cell, George. *The Rediscovery of John Wesley.* New York, N.Y.: University Press of America, 1935.
Chappell. E. B. *Studies in the Life of Wesley.* Nashville, Tenn.: The Publishing House of the ME Church South, 1916.
Chiles, Robert. *Scriptural Christianity: A Call to John Wesley's Disciples.* Grand Rapids, Mich.: Francis Asbury Press, 1984.
Church, Leslie. *Knight of the Burning Heart.* London, England: Epworth Press, 1938.
Clark, Adam. *Memoirs of the Wesley Family.* New York, N.Y.: Lane and Tempest, 1976.

Bibliography

Clark. Elmer. *What Happened at Aldersgate?* Nashville, Tenn.: Methodist Publishing House, 1938.
Clemons, James. "John Wesley-Biblical Literalist?" *Religion in Life 46* (1977) 332–42.
Climenhaga, Daryl. "Interpreting the Scripture." *Brethren In Christ History and Life* (1987) 198–209.
Coppedge, Allen. *John Wesley in Theological Debate.* Wilmore, Ky.: Wesley Heritage Press, 1987.
———. "John Wesley and the Issue of Authority." *Wesleyan Theological Journal 19* (1984) 62–76.
Cragg, Gerald. *The Works of John Wesley. Vol. 11.* Nashville, Tenn.: Abingdon Press, 1989.
Davies, Rupert. *The Works of John Wesley. Vol. 9.* Nashville, Tenn.: Abingdon Press, 1989.
Dayton, Wilder. "John Wesley and Infallibility." In *Inerrancy and the Church.* Chicago, Ill.: Moody Press, 1984.
———. "The Bible in the Wesleyan Tradition." *Asbury Theological Journal 40* (1983) 22–28.
Dieter, Melvin. "Musings." *Wesleyan Theological Journal 14* (1979) 1.
Dougherty, W. C. *John Wesley the Preacher.* London, England: Epworth Press, 1955
Downey, Edward. *The Knowledge of God in Calvin's Theology.* New York, N.Y.: Columbia Press, 1952.
Earle, Ralph. "John Wesley's New Testament." *The Asbury Seminarian 14* (1960) 61–67 .
English, John. "John Wesley and the Anglican Moderates of the 17th Century." *Anglican Theological Review 51* (1969) 203–220.
Ferguson, Duncan. "John Wesley on the Scripture: The Hermeneutics of Pietism." *Methodist History 22* 234–35.
Fitchett, W. H. *Wesley and His Century.* Nashville, Tenn.: Smith and Lamar, nd.
Frei, Hans. *The Eclipse of the Biblical Narrative.* New Haven, Conn.: Yale University Press, 1974.
Garrison, R. Benjamin. "Vital Interaction: Scripture and Experience, John Wesley's Doctrine of Authority." *Religion in Life 25* (1956) 563–73.
Green Richard. *John Wesley Evangelist.* London, England: The Religious Tract Society, 1905.
Green, V. H. H. *The Young Mr. Wesley.* New York, N.Y.: St. Martin's Press, 1961.
———. *Religion at Oxford.* London, England: SCM Press. Ltd., 1964.
Greenslade, S. L. *The Cambridge History of the Bible.* Cambridge, England: At the University Press, 1963.
Grider, J. Kenneth. "Wesleyanism and the Inerrancy Issue." *Wesleyan Theological Society 19* (1984) 52–61.
Gunter, Stephen. *The Limits of Divine Love.* Nashville, Tenn.: Abingdon Press, 1989.
Harmon, Noland and Bardsley, John. "John Wesley and the Articles of Religion." *Religion in Life 22* (1953) 280–91.
Harrison, Elsie. *Son of Susannah.* London, England: Ivor Nicholson and Watson Ltd., 1937.
Harrison, William. "Wesley the Anglican." *Methodist Review 102* (1927) 909–17.
Henry, Matthew. *Matthew Henry's Commentary on the Whole Bible.* New York, N.Y.: Fleming H. Revel Company, nd.
Heitzenrater, Richard. *Diary of an Oxford Methodist: Benjamin Ingham 1733–34.* Durham, N.C.: Duke University Press, 1985.
———. *The Elusive Mr. Wesley—John Wesley as His Own Biographer.* Nashville, Tenn.: Abingdon Press, 1984.

———. *The Elusive Mr. Wesley—John Wesley as Seen by Contemporaries.* Nashville, Tenn.: Abingdon Press, 1984.
———. *Wesley and the People Called Methodists.* Nashville, Tenn.: Abingdon Press, 1995.
Hildebrandt, Franz. *The Works of John Wesley. Vol. 7.* Nashville, Tenn.: Abingdon Press, 1983.
———. *From Luther to Wesley.* London, England: Lutterworth Press, 1951.
Hodge. Charles. *Systematic Theology I.* New York, N.Y., 1874.
Hutchins, Robert. *Great Books of the Western World Vol. XVIII-Augustine.* Encyclopedia Britannica.
Jarboe, Betty. *John and Charles Wesley—A Bibliography.* Metuchen, N.J.: The Scarecrow Press, 1987.
———. *Wesley Quotations: Excerpts From the Writings of John and Other Family Members.* Metuchen, N.J.: The Scarecrow Press, 1990.
Jones, Rufus. *George Fox-Seeker and Friend.* London, England: George Allen and University Press, 1930.
Joy, James. "Wesley-Man of a Thousand and One Books." *Religion In Life* 8 (1939) 71–84.
Keefer, Luke. "John Wesley—Disciple of Early Christianity." Ph.D. diss., Temple University, 1982.
Kerr, Hugh. *A Compend of Luther's Theology.* Philadelphia, Penn.: Westminster Press, 1943.
———. *Readings in Christian Thought.* Nashville, Tenn.: Abingdon Press, 1966.
Kik, J. Marcellus. *Ecumenism and the Evangelical.* Philadelphia, Pa.: Presbyterian and Reformed Publishing Co., 1958.
Kingdon, Harold. "John Wesley Bible Scholar Extraordinaire." *The Asbury Seminarian* 40 (1985) 39–54.
Langford, Thomas. *Practical Divinity—Theology in the Wesleyan Tradition.* Nashville, Tenn.: Abingdon Press, 1983.
Lake, Kirsop. *The Religion of Yesterday and Tomorrow.* Boston, Mass.: Houghton Press, 1926.
Lee, Umphrey. *John Wesley and Modern Religion.* Nashville, Tenn.: Cokesbury Press, 1936.
Lindsell, Harold. *The Battle for the Bible.* Grand Rapids, Mich.: Zondervan Publishers, 1976.
Luther, Martin. *Commentary on the Epistle to the Romans.* Grand Rapids, Mich.: Zondervan Publishing House, 1954.
———. *Martin Luther's Preface to the Epistle of St. Paul to the Romans.* Nashville, Tenn.: Methodist Evangelistic Materials, 1962.
McAdoo, Henry. *The Spirit of Anglicanism.* New York, N.Y.: Charles Scribner's Sons, 1965.
McCarthy. Daryl. "Early Wesleyan Views of Scripture. *Wesleyan Theological Society* 16 (1981) 95–105.
McConnel, Francis. *John Wesley.* Nashville, Tenn.: Abingdon-Cokesbury Press, 1939.
McCown, Wayne and Massey, James. *Interpreting God's Word for Today: An Inquiry Into Hermeneutics From a Biblical, Theological Perspective.* Anderson, Ind.: Warner Press, Inc., 1982.
McDonald, W. *John Wesley and His Doctrine.* Boston, Mass.: The McDonald and Gill Co., 1893.
McGiffert, Albert. *Protestant Thought Before Kant.* New York, N.Y.: Scribner's, 1915.
McKim, Donald. *Readings in Calvin's Theology.* Grand Rapids, Mich.: Baker Book House, 1984.
McNeil. John. *Calvin's Institutes of the Christian Religion.* Philadelphia, Pa.: Westminster Press, 1960.

———. "Luther at Aldersgate." *London Quarterly and Holburn Review 164 (1939) 200–17.*

Menzies, Allen. *The Ante-Nicene Fathers Vol. X.* The Christian Literature Publishing Co., 1886.

Mitchell, T. Crichton. *Great Holiness Classics Vol. 2.* Kansas City, Mo.: Beacon Hill Press, 1984.

Monk, Robert. *John Wesley: His Puritan Heritage.* Nashville, Tenn.: Abingdon Press, 1957.

Montgomery, John. *Crisis in Lutheran Theology.* Grand Rapids, Mich.: Baker Book House, 1967.

More, Paul and Cross, Frank. *Anglicanism.* London, England: SPCK Press, 1957.

Muller, Wilber. "John Wesley's Method of Biblical Interpretation." *Religion In Life 47.* (1978) 99–108.

New Catholic Encyclopedia Vol. 2. New York, N.Y.: McGraw Publishers, 1967.

Ockenga, Harold. "Resurgent Evangelical Leadership." *Christianity Today* (1960) 12.

Oden Thomas. *John Wesley's Scriptural Christianity.* Grand Rapids, Mich.: Zondervan Publishing House, 1994.

———. *Doctrinal Standards in the Wesleyan Tradition.* Grand Rapids, Mich.: Zondervan Publishing House, 1988.

Origen. *Origen on First Principle.* New York, N.Y.: Harper and Rowe, 1966.

Oswalt, John. "John Wesley's Use of the Old Testament in His Doctrinal Teachings." *Wesleyan Theological Journal 12*(1977) 39–53.

Outler, Albert. *John Wesley.* Oxford, England: Oxford University Press, 1964.

———. *The Works of John Wesley. Vol. 1.* Nashville, Tenn.: Abingdon Press, 1984.

———. *The Works of John Wesley. Vol. 2.* Nashville, Tenn.: Abingdon Press, 1985.

———. *The Works of John Wesley. Vol. 4.* Nashville, Tenn.: Abingdon Press 1987.

———. "The Wesleyan Quadrilateral." *Wesleyan Theological Journal 20* (1985) 7–18.

Pellowe, William. "John Wesley's use of the Bible." *Methodist Review 106* 353–374.

Pelikim, Jaraslov. *Luther's Works. Vol. 26.* Philadelphia, Penn.: Fortress Press, 1958.

———. *Luther's Works Vol. 30.* Philadelphia, Penn.: Fortress Press, 1958.

———. *Luther's Works Vol. 32.* Philadelphia, Penn.: Fortress Press, 1958.

———. *Luther's Works Vol. 34.* Philadelphia, Penn.: Fortress Press, 1960.

———. *Luther's Works Vol. 35.* Philadelphia, Penn.: Fortress Press, 1961.

———. *Luther's Works Vol. 36.* Philadelphia, Penn.: Fortress Press, 1959.

———. *Luther's Works Vol. 39.* Philadelphia, Penn.: Fortress Press, 1970.

Piette, Maximin. *John Wesley in the Evolution of Protestantism.* London, England: Sheed and Ward, 1937.

Pollock, John. *John Wesley.* USA.: Scripture Press, Inc., 1989.

Poole, Matthew. *Commentary on the Bible. 3 Vols.* London, England: The Banner of Truth Trust, 1962.

Portalie, Eugene. *A Guide to the Thought of St. Augustine.* London, England: Burns and Oates, 1962.

Rack, Henry. *Reasonable Enthusiast.* Nashville, Tenn.: Abingdon Press, 1993.

Reu, M. *Luther and the Scriptures.* Columbus, Ohio.: Wartburg Press, 1944.

Reventlow, Henning. *The Authority of the Bible and the Rise of the Modern World.* Philadelphia, Penn.: 1985.

Rivers, Isabel. "John Wesley and the Language of Scripture, Reason and Experience." *Prose Studies 4* (1981) 252–285.

Roberts, Alexander, and Donaldson, James. eds. *The Ante-Nicene Fathers. Vol. 1.* The Christian Literature Publishing, 1885.

———. *The Ante-Nicene Fathers. Vol. 2.* The Christian Literature Publishing, 1885.

———. *The Ante-Nicene Fathers. Vol. 3.* The Christian Literature Publishing, 1885.

Rogal, Samuel. "Scriptural Quotations in Wesley's Earnest Appeal." *Research Studies 47* (1979) 181–88.

Rowe, Kenneth. *The Place of Wesley in the Christian Tradition.* Metuchen, N.J.: The Scarecrow Press Inc, 1976.

Sandeen, Ernest. *The Roots of Fundamentalism.* Chicago, Ill.: University of Chicago Press, 1970.

Sanders, Paul. "The Puritans and Wesley." *Work/Worship 17* (1967) 13–19.

Sangster, W. E. *The Path to Perfection.* Nashville, Tenn.: Abingdon-Cokesbury Press, 1943.

Schaff, Phillip and Ware, Henry. *A Select Library of Nicene and Post-Nicene Fathers of the Christian Church. Vol. 1.* Grand Rapids, Mich.: Erdmann's Publishing House.

———. *A Select Library of Nicene and Post-Nicene Fathers of the Christian Church. Vol. 4.* Grand Rapids, Mich.: Erdmann's Publishing House.

———. *A Select Library of Nicene and Post-Nicene Fathers of the Christian Church. Vol. 5.* Grand Rapids, Mich.: Erdmann's Publishing House.

———. *A Select Library of Nicene and Post-Nicene Fathers of the Christian Church. Vol. 11.* Grand Rapids, Mich.: Erdmann's Publishing House.

Scroggins, Robin. "John Wesley Biblical Scholar." *Journal of Bible and Religion 28* (1960) 61–67.

———. *John Wesley a Theological Biography Vol. 2. Part 1.* Nashville, Tenn.: Abingdon Press, 1972.

Schmidt, Martin. *John Wesley a Theological Biography Vol. 2. Part 2.* Nashville, Tenn.: Abingdon Press, 1973

Shelton, Larry. "John Wesley's Approach to Scripture in Historical Perspective." *Wesleyan Theological Journal 16* (1981) 32–42.

Smith, Timothy. "John Wesley and the Wholeness of Scripture." *Interpretation: A Journal of Bible and Theology 39* (1985) 246–63.

———. "Notes on the Exegesis of John Wesley's Explanatory Notes Upon the New Testament." *Wesleyan Theological Journal 16* (1981) 107–13.

Spina, Frank. "More Criticism, More History, More Bible—Wesleyan Faith Seeking Biblical Understanding." *Wesleyan Theological Society* (1994)

Stacey, John. *John Wesley—Contemporary Perspectives.* London, England: Epworth Press, 1988.

Stokes, Mack. *The Bible in Wesleyan Heritage.* Nashville, Tenn.: Abingdon Press, 1979.

Swan, Norma. "John Wesley at Oxford." *Methodist Review 96* (1914) 408–14.

Telford, John. *The Life of John Wesley.* London, England: Robert Culley Publisher, 1910.

———. "John Wesley in Training." *Methodist Review 112* (1929) 9–19.

The Book of Common Prayer. New York, N.Y.: Seabury Press, 1977.

Trueblood, Elton. *The People Called Quakers.* New York, N.Y.: Harper and Rowe Publishers, 1966.

Turner, George. *The Vision Which Transforms.* Kansas City, Mo.: Beacon Hill Press, 1964.

Tuttle, Robert. *John Wesley and His Theology.* Grand Rapids, Mich.: Francis Asbury Press, 1978.

Tyerman, Luke. *The Life and Times of the Reverend John Wesley.* New York, N.Y.: Harper Bros. 1870.

———. *The Oxford Methodists.* London, England: Harper and Brothers, 1873.

Vuillamy C. E. *John Wesely.* Westover, N.J.: Barblur and Company Inc., 1985.

Bibliography

Ward, Reginald and Heitzenrater, Richard. eds. *The Works of John Wesley. Vol.18.* Nashville, Tenn.: Abingdon Press, 1988.

———. *The Works of John Wesley. Vol.19.* Nashville, Tenn.: Abingdon Press, 1990.

———. *The Works of John Wesley. Vol.20.* Nashville, Tenn.: Abingdon Press, 1991.

———. *The Works of John Wesley. Vol.21.* Nashville, Tenn.: Abingdon Press, 1992.

———. *The Works of John Wesley. Vol.22.* Nashville, Tenn.: Abingdon Press, 1993.

———. *The Works of John Wesley. Vol.23.* Nashville, Tenn.: Abingdon Press, 1995.

Walvoord, John. *Inspiration and Interpretation.* Grand Rapids, Mich.: Wm B. Eerdmanns Pub. Co., 1957.

Wartburg, Reu. *Luther and the Scriptures.* Columbus, Ohio.: Wartburg Press, 1944.

Watson, Richard. *The Life of the Rev. John Wesley A.M.* Nashville, Tenn.: Publishing House of the M.E. Church, 1918.

Welch, Herbert. *Selections From the Writings of the Rev. John Wesley, A.M.* New York, N.Y.: Methodist Book Concern, 1901.

Williams, Colin. *John Wesley's Theology Today.* Nashville, Tenn.: Abingdon Press, 1960.

Wood, A. Skevington. *The Burning Heart.* Grand Rapids, Mich.: Wm B. Eerdmanns Pub. Co., 1967.

Wood, Lawrence. "Presidential Address." *Wesleyan Theological Journal 16* (1981) 9.

Wynkoop, Mildred. "A Hermeneutical Approach to John Wesley." *Wesleyan Theological Journal 16* (1971) 13–22.

www.ingramcontent.com/pod-product-compliance
Lightning Source LLC
Chambersburg PA
CBHW062013220426
43662CB00010B/1306